Understanding Learning at Work

Work now invariably requires a continual focus on learning, to improve productivity, to enhance the flexibility of employees and to develop and transform organisations. This volume brings together leading experts from Australia, the USA, the UK and New Zealand to evaluate critically the current debates surrounding workplace learning and proposes directions for future developments in both research and practice, and includes:

- expectations about learning at work into the twenty-first century;
- learning theories, practice and performance implications;
- the relationship between workplace learning and other forms of life-long education;
- international developments in competency-based approaches to learning and assessment;
- the influence of language, power, culture and gender upon the 'construction' of learning.

Understanding Learning at Work will be an invaluable resource for students and practitioners interested in training, human resource development (HRD), continuing and adult education and provides a state-of-the-art summary of the issues and opportunities involved.

David Boud is Professor of Adult Education at the University of Technology, Sydney. His most recent publications include *Working With Experience: Animating Learning* (Routledge; 1996), *Learning Contracts: A Practical Guide* (Kogan Page; 1996) and *Using Experience for Learning* (Open University Press; 1995). **John Garrick** is a Senior Research Fellow at the Research Centre for Vocational Education and Training, University of Technology, Sydney. He is author of *Informal Learning in the Workplace* (also by Routledge), and has been widely published on the topics of workplace reform and industry training, informal learning, the politics of learning at work and HRD.

Understanding Learning at Work

Edited by David Boud
and John Garrick

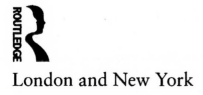

London and New York

First published 1999
by Routledge
11 New Fetter Lane, London EC4P 4EE

Transferred to Digital Printing 2003

Simultaneously published in the USA and Canada
by Routledge
29 West 35th Street, New York, NY 10001

In editorial matter and selection © 1999 David Boud and John
Garrick; in individual contributions © 1999 the contributors

Typeset in Sabon by Routledge

British Library Cataloguing in Publication Data
A catalogue record for this book is available from the
British Library

Library of Congress Cataloging-in-Publication Data
Boud, David.
Understanding learning at work / edited by David Boud and John
Garrick.
p. cm.
Includes bibliographical references and index.
1. Employees–Training of. 2. Learning. 3. Continuing education.
I. Garrick, John. II. Title.
HF5549.5. T7B593 1999
658.3' 124–dc21   98-45949
CIP

ISBN 0–415–18228–X (hbk)
ISBN 0–415–18229–8 (pbk)

Contents

Illustrations

Tables

Figure

Contributors

Ronald Barnett is Professor of Higher Education and Dean of Professional Development, Institute of Education, University of London, UK.

David Beckett is Senior Lecturer in the Department of Vocational Education and Training, University of Melbourne, Australia.

Stephen Billett is Director of the Centre for Learning and Work Research, Griffith University, Brisbane, Australia.

David Boud is Professor of Adult Education and Associate Dean (Research), Faculty of Education, University of Technology, Sydney, Australia.

Elaine Butler is in the Department of Social Inquiry and a member of the Centre for Labour Studies, University of Adelaide, Australia.

Philip C. Candy is Pro-Vice-Chancellor (Scholarship), University of Ballarat, Victoria, Australia.

Catherine Casey is Senior Lecturer in the Department of Management and Employment Relations, University of Auckland, New Zealand.

John Garrick is Senior Research Fellow in the Research Centre for Vocational Education and Training, University of Technology, Sydney, Australia.

Andrew Gonczi is Dean of the Faculty of Education, University of Technology, Sydney, Australia.

Paul Hager is Associate Professor in the Faculty of Education, University of Technology, Sydney, Australia.

Victoria J. Marsick is Professor of Education in the Department of Organization and Leadership, Teachers College, Columbia University, New York, USA.

Judith H. Matthews is Research Fellow in the Graduate School of Management, University of Queensland, Brisbane, Australia.

Belinda Probert is Professor of Sociology and Director of the Centre for Applied Social Research, Royal Melbourne Institute of Technology, Melbourne, Australia.

Nicky Solomon is Senior Lecturer in the Faculty of Education, University of Technology, Sydney, Australia.

Mark Tennant is Professor of Adult Education, University of Technology, Sydney, Australia.

Karen E. Watkins is Professor of Adult Education, University of Georgia, Athens, Georgia, USA.

1 Understandings of workplace learning

David Boud and John Garrick

Learning at work has become one of the most exciting areas of development in the dual fields of management and education. It has moved to become a central concern of corporations and universities; it is no longer the preoccupation of a small band of vocational training specialists. A new focus on learning is changing the way businesses see themselves. At the same time, educational institutions are realising that they need to engage with the world of work in a more sophisticated manner than ever before.

Modern organisations ignore learning at the cost of their present and future success. In the complex enterprises of the new millennium, learning has moved from the periphery – from something which prepared people for employment – to the lifeblood which sustains them. There are few places left for employees at any level who do not continue to learn and improve their effectiveness throughout their working lives. There is no place for managers who do not appreciate their own vital role in fostering learning. The future of enterprises and the agendas of educational institutions are becoming intimately linked within the present reconceptualisation of work and learning.

Today we see employees extending their *educational* capabilities in learning through their work. At the same time opportunities and problems within work are creating the need for new knowledge and understanding. Employees develop skills of expression and communication which spill over into their personal lives. They learn new ways of collaborating and planning which they apply in the families and community organisations to which they belong. They not only become more effective in their present responsibilities, but help transform the nature of the work in which they are engaged creating new work practices and forms of production. These are a part of the increasing pressures from work, with increased commitment demanded of employees. There are groups of workers who are marginalised and do not benefit from these trends. And, of course, there are those who find no place in the world of work. In all this, boundaries of education, learning and training begin to dissolve. Study and work are no longer polarised. Each feeds the other.

'Work' and 'learning' are concepts which used to belong in separate categories. Work was about producing or doing things to earn a living. Learning was about education; it occurred in life before work. Training might be necessary at first in the workplace, but everything else that was needed for a lifetime of employment could be picked up from experienced fellow workers. The world has changed dramatically since this was so.

In this changed world it is therefore surprising to find that dialogue between, on the one hand, those who have studied learning and, on the other, those who need to understand the learning implications of work has been almost absent. A gulf has existed between the two. Researchers interested in teaching and learning have overwhelmingly confined their explorations to educational institutions. They have looked to their academic peers for recognition. Human resource managers have had little interest in fostering research on learning. If they have thought about it they are likely to have assumed that the differences between their own organisations and those investigated by researchers are so great that there is, in all likelihood, nothing worth looking at. Researchers and managers have occupied such different cultures that there are substantial differences between the language they use and the views of the world which they hold. It is not surprising then that communication has been so limited.

This position is no longer sustainable. The imperatives of work mean that an understanding of learning issues is needed at all levels. Educators and managers have to find a way of communicating about this. This book aims to provide a starting point for such discussion. It brings ideas from the world of learning research to the challenges and demands of work. It provides an access point to the language and ideas of learning and research for those who want to pursue these ideas in organisations. It does so by presenting current work from researchers who have engaged with the challenges of the workplace and have developed ways of thinking which help us understand how learning occurs and can be fostered within them.

The main messages which the contributors give is that there is no single way of understanding learning at work, and that there probably should not be one. Many perspectives are needed not only because of the diversity of work and the differences which exist even within a single organisation, but because learning in work is, as we will show, so multifaceted. It has more dimensions which need to be considered than learning in educational institutions. Different perspectives are needed for different purposes. There is no universal model for learning at work.

The changing contexts of work and learning

Ideas about learning are now undergoing swift and dramatic transformation. In the context of rapidly changing markets, the development of 'knowledge workers' within high-tech 'knowledge societies' is occurring. This development is accompanied by a shift away from viewing educational institutions as the principal places of 'valid' learning towards recognition of the power and importance of workplaces as sites of learning. The nature of work is changing with 'knowledge' being regarded increasingly as *the* primary resource, thus giving rise to unprecedented demands for learning – delivered flexibly and in authentic work settings. Enterprises need integrated approaches to change. New notions of learning at work offer exciting ways of achieving this by challenging boundaries within and between organisations, and exploring new ways of being at work.

Along with the move towards 'knowledge workers' have been prescriptions for business and industry such as the creation of 'learning organisations' or 'learning companies' in which learning at work is seen as a pivotal concern. Regardless of the take-up of these particular ideas, the interrelationship between enterprise-based learning, work and employment remains a vital area for investigation and development. Interest in workplaces as learning environments is further reflected in new approaches to build award programmes from workplace experience. Practice-linked and cooperative education (sandwich courses) are a familiar part of post-secondary education; however, university award programmes in which the curriculum is based primarily in the workplace and driven by work are on the increase.

This book focuses on what we know about workplace learning and what we think it can encompass. It is about understanding the complex and multifaceted field of learning at work. It brings together what is currently known about workplace learning in ways which are helpful to practitioners, researchers and policy-makers. It focuses on the rich and varied research which has been undertaken on the important phenomenon of learning in work. It is our aim to generate discussion and critique directions for developing it.

We do not, however, want to offer prescriptions as to where workplace learning 'ought to go'. Unlike much of the literature in this field, we do not promote a how-to-do-it approach. We see workplace learning as an important activity both for contributing to organisations and for contributing to the broader learning and development of individual workers/participants. This dual purpose has always been the case, but what is now firmly on the agendas of business and government, as well as universities and colleges, is a new emphasis on the formalisation of what can be viewed as 'legitimate learning'. An understanding of workplace learning means recognising its complexities, its competing interests and the personal, political and institutional influences that affect it. We argue that it is imperative that learning at work be regarded as considerably more than techniques and strategies designed to improve performance or commercially exploit knowledge. It must always entail a consideration of the situated ethics of what is being learned and who is doing the learning.

This book acts as a starting point for those who want to engage with this newly emerging field of interest. It is directed towards practitioners who want to know about the implications of research on learning in enterprises. It is addressed to those who are assisting organisations to transform themselves with an emphasis on learning. It will also be of interest to researchers who wish to locate their own work in a broader perspective of economic and social change.

Workplace learning: why has it become so important?

Most countries with sophisticated economies are currently considering changes required to the organisation of work in order to be competitive beyond the year 2000. As society becomes more complex so too does professional labour. It becomes more fragmented and more subject to change. A significant aspect of the processes of unpredictable change is the breaking down and blurring of boundaries – 'de-differentiation'. Distinctions between life and work, learning and production, community and enterprise are becoming less firm. Shifting boundaries, changing values and purposes of work and learning affect the physical, emotional and cognitive demands on workers at all levels.

No longer are the pools of knowledge and expertise acquired in initial education sufficient for 'the new work order'. What is now required are abilities to put that knowledge and expertise to use in unfamiliar circumstances, and so we find demands for 'flexibility', 'communication skills', 'teamwork' and so on.

In part, these changes are tied to globalisation. As human capital becomes more internationalised and the globe more integrated into market mechanisms, new problems of advanced modern capitalism are emerging. Increased flexibility is now held by influential commentators such as Reich (1993) to be an essential labour form to match the requirements of capital accumulation. Indeed, flexibility of labour and of capital is intimately connected, but the trends for flexible labour are not experienced evenly across the globe.

OECD nations are actively supporting 'flexible' solutions to the requirements of capitalist enterprise. Many of these countries have initiated major change at a systems level in their vocational education and training sectors as a strategy for increasing international competitiveness. The OECD reforms include improving training opportunities for adults, and this involves improving the training of trainers, the integration of education and training and an emphasis on multiskilling and workplace assessment. This is reflected in developments such as the recognition of prior learning, competency-based standards for vocational and general education and the development of new models of formal education which link industry and education more closely.

It is not only employers who are urging a stronger relationship between industries and education but also unions and governments. The agendas of all these parties in the contemporary economic climate favour forms of knowledge which are 'useful' in which a key question about employees is not what do they know, or understand, but *what can they do*?

Alongside a market-driven emphasis on learning, there has been renewed interest in the 1990s in the idea of lifelong learning and its relationship to civil society. While much of the current rhetoric about lifelong learning is part of an economic agenda, there are quite distinct threads which see learning at work as a part of general education for citizenship and fuller participation in society as a whole. There have been notable initiatives, for example through new partnerships between employers and unions in the vehicle manufacturing industry in the UK, which explicitly promote *non*-vocational learning at work. Modern enterprise, in this view, has a responsibility to foster the development of the whole person, and foster civil society, not just simply invest in the skills and knowledge required for work.

While acknowledging the economic imperatives of our times, it is also necessary not to lose sight of some of the implications of such a focus. Even within the world of work, not everyone will be winners. A single-minded emphasis on learning *for* work can blind us to the unintended consequences for significant groups in the workforce and those not in work. This is not just an issue of social equity, important though that is, but it can rebound on the very goals of work itself. For example, assumptions about the aspirations of the work patterns and learning needs of full-time predominantly male workers cannot necessarily be transferred to other groups such as part-time staff, women and members of non-dominant cultural groups. Severe distortions to the well-being and development of individuals, families and communities can occur through the adoption of the dominant economic discourse.

What is workplace learning?

In this climate, learning has become too important to be left to educational institutions and in-house training departments. It cannot just be bought in or developed through initial training programmes; it is too intimately connected with productivity and the operation of contemporary enterprises. Understanding of workplace learning is required at all levels and in more diverse ways than ever before. Workplace learning is concerned not only with immediate work competencies, but about future competencies. It is about investment in the general capabilities of employees as well as the specific and technical. And it is about the utilisation of their knowledge and capabilities wherever they might be needed in place and time.

Universities, slow to respond to this at first, now have workplace learning firmly on their agendas. Faculty structures, teaching programmes and research activities are starting to place the needs of learning in organisations as a high priority. Learning through practice is no longer confined to courses for the traditional professions. Courses with a strong employment component are being renewed and work-based learning courses are being established. This of course has significant implications for what is regarded as 'legitimate' or valid knowledge so it is important to examine some of the major conceptions of workplace learning.

The workplace has become a site of learning associated with two quite different purposes, as we illustrated earlier. The first is the development of the enterprise through contributing to production, effectiveness and innovation; the second is the development of individuals through contributing to knowledge, skills and the capacity to further their own learning both as employees and citizens in wider society. This view of the workplace contains elements of the famous split between theory and practice, mind and body, and learning and work. The new relationships of theory/practice, mind/body, work/learning are, however, being actively explored and contested. While it has always been recognised that learning at work is required in order to do the jobs that are found there, in the world of education and training, workplace learning has, as mentioned before, been regarded as an adjunct to a period of formal study in an educational institution. In this conception, learning in the workplace is needed to translate theory into the practice of work. This system has exerted a powerful constraint on new approaches to learning as, in the division between 'hand' and 'brain', priority is invariably given to theory over practice even though most commentators now accept that this is a false dichotomy.

Nonetheless, the literature on workplace learning is confusing. There are many different accounts of what is encompassed by learning based in the workplace and there are also many different learning purposes. These purposes are not always immediately apparent. The most familiar of these can be summarised as follows:

- *Improving performance for the benefit of the organisation*
  - of self as worker
  - of the team or work community
  - of the enterprise

- *Improving learning for the benefit of the learner*
  - for self
  - for one's personal growth and lifelong learning

- *Improving learning as a social investment*
  - for citizenship (including the environment)
  - for team or work community (including 'learning organisations')
  - for future enterprises ('creating the future')

The emphasis varies across organisation, learner and society and the focus within each is directed to different parties or to different ends.

The divide between individualistic, enterprise-focused and socially focused conceptions has, however, created misunderstandings between industry bodies and employers on the one hand, and formal education institutions and academics on the other, about whether workplace learning should or should not be considered as 'valid' knowledge. Unfortunately this has given rise to a perception on the part of some educators that workplace learning is by definition somehow tainted, and by some in business that education outcomes are often 'too abstract' and not oriented to their interests. Many contemporary conceptions of workplace learning have thus been historically framed by a flawed logic based on polarities – what is and is not 'knowledge', what counts or does not count as 'learning' – as mentioned above. The breaking down of these binaries represents one of the principal challenges taken up here: to identify, clarify and question contemporary conceptions of workplace learning.

Scope of the book: crossing boundaries

The genesis of this book comes from the interests of a group of academics linked to the adult education area at the University of Technology, Sydney. Many projects there have been initiated on themes related to work, learning and professional practice. One major project examined current research on workplace learning and assessment. It proposed directions for future Australian research in this area (Boud 1998). Members of the project team found the exercise such an interesting one that it wanted to extend its work to incorporate an international dimension and prompt discussion on a much wider front.

David Boud, who led that project, saw work-related learning as an important vehicle for exploring his ongoing interests in innovative approaches to teaching and learning and how people learn from experience. All the challenges and dilemmas of adults learning find expression in new ways within the context of work. Theories of learning and innovations in practice which had placed the individual as central need to be rethought in the new environment. He joined with John Garrick, who had been working in complementary ways on workplace reform, approaches to industrial training and informal learning in work contexts (Garrick 1998), to identify a new group of contributors. Some were drawn from the original team, and others were invited to present broader and international perspectives.

Writing about learning in the workplace is dispersed over very many areas. Perhaps for this reason, it is not a well-mapped territory. Part of the explanation is that research into workplace learning does not comfortably sit within existing disciplinary areas or fields of enquiry. It necessarily crosses boundaries. There is a substantial literature on the topic within management and business, education and training, industrial relations, economics and politics, policy studies, information technologies, psychology and work sociology. But each discipline brings its own interests, characteristics, concerns and methodologies to discussion of the issues. It is too large a task to incorporate all of these perspectives within a single book. However, what we do here is recognise workplace learning as multidisciplinary in scope and nature. It is multilayered and can be viewed through many different lenses. The decision we have made is that rather than view the topic through all these different lenses, the book should use 'learning' as its organising theme. This means that the interests of those concerned with learning are foregrounded while other dimensions of the workplace are viewed as critical contextual influences. All the contributors are practising educators as well as researchers and this has influenced the approaches they have adopted. They draw on ideas beyond their immediate interests, but deploy their analyses to illuminate learning purposes, practices and outcomes.

Some decisions on the choice of material to include were easy. The present context of learning and work needed to be set, and key issues and important perspectives on research had to be included. In the end we opted for a strong focus on the *contexts* of learning, the location of learning in workplace cultures and the influences of management, difference and gender. Building on and celebrating difference is a vital concern for all organisations and individuals. There is consequentially less emphasis on traditional skills acquisition, assessment of workplace learning and structuring training and development, as the book is not about the technical aspects of learning and facilitation. Another major consideration was that we wanted to emphasise varied *learning perspectives* that centre on the workplace. Traditional management and organisational development research perspectives are well represented in human resource books and there is no need to cover that ground here. We saw the learning perspective as requiring further development beyond the idealisations and exhortations of 'management gurus'.

Even when viewed through the lens of learning, there are diverse views. The writers come from many traditions and backgrounds. While each draws on a considerable body of work from their own field or discipline, it is important to note that relatively little research and theorising has previously related directly to *workplace learning*. The current book is therefore one of the first attempts to map critically aspects of this growing field and to point to its implications.

The aim of the book is to bring together what is known about key aspects of workplace learning. Themes which appear throughout the book are the following:

- The rapidly growing recognition of the importance of workplace learning.
- The effects of work organisation on learning.
- Influences of power, culture, language and gender.
- The highly contextualised nature of learning.

- Rapidly changing contexts and changes in the nature of work.
- The inappropriateness of viewing research into workplace learning as a collection of predictive 'facts'.
- The need to engage with issues of practice and performance.
- The location of workplace learning in the context of lifelong learning.

Throughout, the authors provide accessible frameworks for and new ways of representing these complex issues. Simple prescriptions about 'how to enhance' workplace learning are avoided. We argue that such an approach would not reflect the diversity and richness that ought to accompany understandings of workplace learning.

The chapters which follow are grouped into four parts. Part I, Context, sets the scene, pointing to main features of learning *and* work in the current economic, social and political context and the directions in which this context has changed and is changing. Catherine Casey (Chapter 2) examines the changing nature of work in contemporary society, raising many implications for learning at work. This chapter provides readers with an orientation to the influences of workplace sociology on learning. Ronald Barnett (Chapter 3) comments incisively on the current context of learning in society and identifies a key feature of the present, what he refers to as 'supercomplexity', and the ways in which this challenges current notions of learning.

Part II, Perspectives, portrays some of the challenges which the present context and state of understanding of workplace learning throw up. The chapters within this part explore the dimensions of, and different ways of thinking about, learning and work. In addition it examines particular perspectives on management learning, gender issues and the types of learning opportunities obtained through work.

The notion of 'fusing' learning and work is explored by Judy Matthews and Phil Candy (Chapter 4). They identify five views of workplace learning ranging from the workplace as a site for formally accredited learning to the workplace as a part of the knowledge society and as an organic identity, capable of learning and adaptation in its own right. They consider the effects of management practices and organisational structures on learning in organisational settings. A range of perspectives from the wider educational literature is drawn on by Paul Hager (Chapter 5) and applied to workplace learning. He poses the question, 'what are the features of a good theory of workplace learning?' and discusses how we can select between the diverse theories which are available to us.

The learning needs of managers are considered by David Beckett in Chapter 6. He recognises that managers have new responsibilities for not only their own learning, but also that of others. He argues that under the umbrella of organisational learning, management learning needs to be shaped by pragmatic ('on-the-job') decision-making that is directed towards strategic priorities. He points out that research in this field has been driven by traditional management models, based on structures and applied theory, which no longer capture the dynamism, flexibility and inclusiveness of the contemporary workplace. This chapter argues a case for moving beyond formulae for learning towards conceptions which are contextually sensitive, pragmatic and strategic. This part concludes with Belinda Probert's examination of the ways that learning can be shaped by power, politics and gender relations at work (Chapter 7). A gendered reading of learning at work provides insights into how the construction of learning in the workplace is not 'simply' an individualistic event but deeply connected to underlying social forces that contribute to its shaping.

Part III, Issues in practice, continues the theme of examining particular dimensions of learning and work by focusing on key issues related to culture, difference and equity including the ways individuals construct knowledge as part of everyday work activities. In addition, discussions of the situated nature of workplace learning, the perennial problem of the transfer of learning and current views of the role of competency-based approaches are considered. The centrality of language, cultural under-standings and discourses of learning at work are teased out by Nicky Solomon (Chapter 8) and Elaine Butler (Chapter 9). In these chapters, equity and workplace learning are located within the broader social, economic and political fields of globalisation, work studies and labour relations, lifelong learning and the establishment of national systems of vocational education and training. Solomon focuses on the ways 'culture' tends to be used to enhance productivity, and Butler uses notions of equity to act as a framework for analysis to illustrate how advantage and disad-vantage are constructed within prevailing (and contradictory) discourses of workplace learning. While workplace learning is usually framed as non-problematic and a 'good thing', Chapters 8 and 9 argue powerfully that it is emerging as an integral component of the discourse of productive culture which can have destructive implications for many.

The starting point of Stephen Billett's contribution is the notion of learning as everyday thinking and acting (Chapter 10). He illustrates how these perspectives from cognitive and sociocultural literature can be used to inform us about goals for learning and where knowledge is required for expertise. He develops a model of organising learning in the workplace and includes practical examples of the potential and limitations of work-places as learning environments. Part III continues with a consideration of an important ongoing question in training: 'is knowledge transferable to situations other than those in which it was originally learned?' Mark Tennant (Chapter 11) begins by pointing out that the development of 'adaptable' and 'flexible' skills depends crucially on their transferability from one workplace context or situation to another. He argues that the issue of transfer goes to the heart of learning because it has to do with whether we can learn anything in a general way, and if so, how this is made possible. He traces a range of different perspectives on transfer, noting the tensions and differences between them. His concern throughout is to identify ways of enhancing transfer of learning in the workplace.

One of the major current influences in vocational learning is the competency agenda. It is this which Andrew Gonczi (Chapter 12) takes as his theme. He examines the current international position in competency-based training and education, including the role of competency-based assessment, in workplace learning. He highlights the tensions which exist between assessment for accreditation and the needs of productivity, and the vital importance of viewing 'competence' as an holistic notion – without which an impoverished conception of learning results.

Part IV, Futures, projects the debate forward to consider the emerging nature of links between learning and work, trends in organisational learning and the critical issues and research directions which have been highlighted throughout the book. Victoria Marsick and Karen Watkins (Chapter 13) review shifts of thinking which have occurred about learning in organisations over the last decade and highlight issues that hold particular significance for re-evaluating the ways in which we think about learning at work. They look at the learning organisation in light of metaphors which have been developed for it and examine implications for different stakeholders: managers, employees and human resource development professionals. They raise questions which go beyond the narrow economic agenda of corporations and set workplace learning in a wider context.

The book concludes with John Garrick (Chapter 14) returning to the main discourses on workplace learning discussed earlier in the book, noting the powerful influences of contemporary market economics in the production of new knowledge. He examines the state of our present understandings of learning at work and the prospects for future development. He points to important convergences between learning and the world of work as containing the potential to auger well for learning in work contexts including better connections between work and educational institutions.

References

Boud, D. (ed.) (1998) *Current Issues and New Agendas in Workplace Learning*, Adelaide: National Centre for Vocational Education Research.

Garrick, J. (1998) *Informal Learning in the Workplace: Unmasking Human Resource Development*, London: Routledge.

Reich, R. B. (1993) *The Work of Nations: Preparing Ourselves for 21st Century Capitalism*, London: Simon and Schuster.

Part I
Context

2 The changing contexts of work

Catherine Casey

Across much of the world in recent decades a proliferation and acceleration of economic, technological and organisational developments have occurred in the world of work. The contexts in which work is performed and socially positioned are undergoing considerable and enduring change. Every aspect of work, from its practical everyday organisation, its form and function in production and economy, to its meaning and value in individual and collective life, are affected by these changes. These are enormous, and highly contentious, developments. Both observers and workers debate and worry about their effects and implications. Amid the debates there is increasing, if reluctant, awareness that the changes in work are of sufficient magnitude to call into question our conventional modern industrial understanding of work, its central place in societal and economic organisation, and our expectations of our relationships to work in adult life.

This chapter explores the transformations that have occurred in work since the advent of what is popularly called the computer revolution, the Information Age, or more theoretically, post-industrial society. It examines the ways in which these post-industrial changes, that include advanced manufacturing and information technologies, organisational redesign and restructuring, and globalisation of production and control, now shape the contexts in which work is performed, located and valued. The effects of the altered contexts of work on people's experiences, and expectations, of work, and their conditions for learning at work are considerable.

People learn diversely and indelibly through their experiences of work and workplaces. In order to understand diverse human learning at work, and to encourage and discourage particular categories of learning, we need to understand the changing contexts in which work occurs across various domains. A greater appreciation of these contextual events and changes enables a more informed, adept and practical understanding of the contexts and processes of learning at work. Educators, managers, training and development practitioners, and workers generally may be better able to design, provide or seek workplace curricula most suitable to employees and to their organisation and industry.

The transformation of work

In pre-modern and early modern societies occupation in work provided a primary locus of identity, along with kinship and regional location. Many common English (and other European) surnames to this day indicate the occupation once held by forebears of those bearing names such as baker, weaver, goldsmith, carpenter, brewer, tailor and so forth. These occupations denoted not just skill and economic function but personal and social identity and location. The coming of modern industrial society encompassed vast social and economic changes, yet, as with all change, a degree of continuity endured. Ready recognition and identification of persons with occupation or village or kinship may have dramatically changed, but modern society, even more than previous societies, privileges the role of production and work in social organisation and in individual identity formation. People today continue significantly to define themselves, and are socially defined, by the type of work that they do.

In advanced industrial capitalist societies vast changes in production and work have occurred in the decades since the Second World War. In the first instance these changes are associated with the rapid development and expansion of electronic technology, particularly the development of automated production systems. Early, relatively simple, forms of automation in the 1950s and 1960s were rapidly surpassed by advanced electronic production and information systems. These include highly automated computer-integrated continuous-process technology, CAD/CAM (Computer-Aided Design, Computer-Aided Manufacturing), CIM (Computer-Integrated Manufacturing), flexible manufacturing systems and computer-integrated and informated offices. Sophisticated electronic data processing and financial transfer (e.g. EFTPOS: Electronic Funds Transfer at Point of Sale) and integrated telecommunications now include not just plant and office but banks, shops, hospitals and public organisations. Advanced production technologies, agri-technologies and artificial intelligence (that include 'smart' machines and 'seeing' and 'sensing' robots), and their derivatives, profoundly affect industry and commerce, and social life more broadly. These developments have consequential and accompanying influences on all domains of production, and are by no means specific to heavy industry or manufacturing.

The effects of technological change

Many of the accomplishments of industrial work organisation, such as Fordism, Taylorism, extensive bureaucracy and subjugated, disciplined workers, continue to provide the cultural contexts in which various new production technologies are implemented. Most salient among the implications of these new technologies are effects on the division of labour and specialisation, the patterning of skill, and the role of human labour in production. The effects on skill requirements directly affect a worker's experience and sense of value at work. Skills may be acquired, enhanced or discarded, and are among the most important of all learning that occurs at work.

Skill changes and decline in specialisation

Among the immediate implications, although by no means immediately recognised, of advanced automation and flexible manufacturing systems was the reversal of the typical trend of industrial society towards an increasing division of labour and specialisation of function (Casey 1995). This appeared initially as changes in skill levels. At first analysts observed changes in skill requirements as an effect of technological change in production and work organisation. Early attention focused most on the role of skill and the experience of skilled workers in heavy industry and manufacturing. Eventually attention was also drawn to similar trends of skill changes in office work (e.g. Dy 1990, Garson 1988, Hartmann 1987, Wright 1987). The discussion of changes in work and skill developed in this chapter includes both traditional domains of work including blue-, pink-[1] and white-collar work in manufacturing, offices and services (transport, hospitals, retail, etc.), by no means only so-called 'masculinist' blue-collar work, as well as the rise of new forms of work in services and information.

The decline in specialisation of function was first apparent in the change in the place of the worker's piecemeal labour as simply a unit in the elaborately specialised production process perfected under scientific management. The simplest, most reductionist of workers' mechanical or routine labour was immediately displaced by the automation of those tasks. The place of the worker in the overall process began to change. Consequently, the workers who had performed those simple repetitive tasks, now performed by automated machines, were rendered redundant from the production process and displaced from their jobs. For those workers still required in an automated or informated plant, a process of 'multiskilling' and 'up-skilling' tends to occur (Adler 1992, Davis 1988). But the debate among analysts and observers in the 1990s continues over the shift in skill requirements and the control of the labour process. Some argue that de-skilling, more apparent under typical industrial conditions, now occurs among workers formerly regarded as highly skilled. The low-skilled workers still retained by manufacturing companies are being retrained with a broader skills base than previously required (Adler 1992, Ayres and Miller 1983, Zuboff 1988). Yet traditionally highly skilled workers, such as those with a 'sense' for the quality of production (steel, oil, paper), are being rendered redundant or de-skilled, as computerised systems take over their skilled jobs.

The organisation of work, and its experience, is simultaneously changing with the restructuring enabled, and required, by the rapid implementation of technological developments, and the concurrent changes in organisational environments. Mechanised industrial work was divided up into its smallest parts, and organised by linear hierarchies of supervision and control. Advanced automation and flexible manufacturing technologies have integrated fragmented tasks and therefore no longer restrict the worker to one highly specialised, routine task. The worker is able both to perform a wider range of tasks and to take responsibility for the overall operation of a complex unit of production. At the very least, line workers know the tasks and procedures of other jobs on the line and can be readily redeployed as required.

In the new automated and computer-integrated workplace, 'multiactivity' jobs combine the tasks previously carried out by workers with different skills, and even occupational designations. In the office multiactivity teams, whose members all possess computer skills and can access data storage and processing networks, carry out the tasks previously performed by clerks, secretaries and lower-level office workers. Much of the unskilled, rote clerical work such as routine tasks in typing, filing, data processing, inventory, accounts, payroll and the like has been eliminated. As a result, fewer and multiskilled (yet not necessarily more highly paid) workers in both factory and office can perform the tasks of formerly more specialist workers with less supervision.

In the factory another significant change has accompanied the decline in specialisation. The fundamental requirements of industrial work, bodily exertion, manual dexterity and endurance, have been increasingly displaced by the requirements for rapid perception, attentiveness and the ability to analyse problems and make decisions (Hirschhorn 1984, Zuboff 1988). The rudiments of industrial work have visibly shifted from physical effort to the manipulation of electronic symbols through monitors, keyboards and press buttons. Furthermore, the capacity for 'flexibility' enabled by flexible manufacturing systems has been extended as a skill requirement of the worker. Workers must be willing and able to learn and perform new tasks, take on different roles and be easily redeployed in the flexible new workplace. This skill, along with other rudiments in service production, such as 'emotional work'[2] (Hochschild 1983), is now commonly required in office work.

By the 1980s a number of occupations and former job categories such as welder, riveter, switchboard operator, salaries clerk, bookkeeper, typesetter (among many others) had disappeared. In the 1990s, ledger machinists, typists and insurance underwriters are uncommon. These jobs have been automated, integrated or informated away. The tasks are performed by robotic systems; data processing packages or their remnant operations are undertaken by remaining multiskilled workers. Of course, other jobs, most especially in an expanded service sector, have emerged requiring different or entirely new skills. They present new opportunities for learning, and unlearning, to serve both workplace needs and personal development needs.

The expansion of the service sector

A significant aspect of the change in skill requirements in production following the deployment of advanced production and information technologies is the role of knowledge. Although there are wide industry variations and some national ones (e.g. Castells (1996) points to retention in Japan of a relatively high number of traditional craft-skilled workers), a decline in traditional and craft skills has been matched by a steady rise in formal and abstract skills exemplified, for instance, in the computer technologist, engineer or financial manager of contemporary firms. These new knowledge workers or 'symbolic analysts' (Reich 1991) comprise a significant new tier in the service sector. Evidence (Castells 1996, Reich 1991) points to an increasing proportion of skilled to unskilled workers, although this is geographically uneven, and does not suggest that low-skilled work will disappear. While knowledge has become a primary productive force, the demand for manual service work is also expected to increase. Knowledge work has generated considerable increases in productive output and quality levels (Drucker 1993).

The management processes of industrialised manufacturing generated the rise of a service class of white-collar office workers, from clerical to management, and a sector of scientists, technical and engineering workers to support industrial development. In more recent years, the 'old' service class (e.g. medicine, banking, law, etc.) has itself undergone post-industrial transformations, in composition, services provided and in work tasks. Significantly, a growing new division in the service sector has become established. Many of the middle-management workers comprising a large sector of the semi-professional services are no longer required by automated offices, the 'lean and mean' corporations and the downsized public sector of the 1990s. Not only are there fewer manual workers to supervise, but many of the responsibilities performed by skilled white-collar workers and middle-level managers are computer integrated and electronically centralised. Both banking and retail services are currently significant among the sectors being technologically transformed as various electronic funds transfer systems (e.g. EFTPOS) become widely practised (Sinden 1996). Some of these people are finding work in consulting businesses and contract services to multinational corporations. They designate themselves as, for example, information systems consultant, project manager, organisational development consultant and the like. This emergent development awaits empirical measurement and analysis. Furthermore, there is some evidence in the recent decade (in the UK but not in the USA) that there is an increase in the self-employed as many highly skilled new professionals contract themselves to various organisations for short-term projects and work from their own homes or cars (Brown 1997, Castells 1996). In the UK Brown (1997) argues that 'self-employment' in a range of sectors is a significant new trend in production and employment relations.

Most readily observable is the growth in the lower-paid tier of the service sector, particularly of fast-food workers, custodial, domestic and leisure industry workers. Such occupations as, for example, valet, beauty therapist, aerobics instructor, adventure tour guide, pizza delivery and so forth have recently emerged in western economies. Many of these new service workers do not hold full-time jobs with regular hours and once conventionally expected conditions of employment. Furthermore, although low paid and quickly trained, many are required to perform a range of responsibilities from dealing with customers to operating according to a company master plan of standardised procedures and principles (especially in fast-food services). Consequently, a process of multiskilling and lowering of wages is commonly practised in the low-paid end of the service sector. At the same time, as in the upper tier of new service workers, many service jobs are performed by contract, self-employed workers as cleaners, gardeners, caterers, etc. For the commissioning organisation these services are provided by workers 'casually' and variably required. Casualised out of a formerly regular and reliable employment relation these service providers (workers) are rarely protected by formal or collective employment contracts. The regulation of hours of work, rates of pay and other conditions of the employment relation elides under casualised arrangements and presents considerable implications for the workers involved.

Another trend in the transformation of the service sector is 'outsourcing', in which various services are contracted out of the organisation requiring the service (Drucker 1993). Outsourcing differs importantly from 'outworking', in which workers (typically women) assembled piece work in manufacturing such as clothing, packaging, mailings, and some telework was common in industrial conditions. Such workers were employed by a company and although off site were considered part of the organisation. The practice of 'outsourcing', however, does not involve the employment by the recipient organisation of the persons providing the service. Custodial, security, clerical, accounting, assembling, general labouring and many telecommunication operations may readily be outsourced, or contracted out, to individuals or service firms. High-skilled work in drafting, design, mathematical analysis, and some legal, financial or information systems work may be outsourced to 'consulting' individuals or small organisations.

Furthermore, another recent development is the 'virtual corporation' that employs a minimum of staff and that operates like the cast and support staff of a film set in which employees are contracted for specific productions for specific time periods. There is no 'downtime' or periods in which workers are retained during periods of low productivity or recession. Business analysts and management theorists (Drucker 1993, Handy

1995, 1996, McKinsey Global Institute 1992, Reich 1991) commonly regard the expansion of the service sector as the source of future employment opportunities as primary production and manufacturing require fewer workers. Yet its expansion associated with new flexibilities in employment relations, including that of casualisation and outsourcing, has important consequences for economic, as well as developmental, opportunities and the well-being of workers.

Organisation and management

Expectedly, concomitant changes in organisation and management present new challenges and opportunities for the organisation of production and of work in this, and the coming, decade. A rapid expansion of research in organisation and in management in recent decades adds to the long-standing research tradition in sociology of work, industry, organisation, labour relations and industrial psychology. This newer body of research and commentary presents variously an advocatory, practical and critical voice on the emergence and design of contemporary work organisations and their management. Almost in unison, however, these various voices speak the language of organisational change. The organisation of production, the rules and management of the employment relation, and the experiences and expectations of employees are currently undergoing significant changes in many western countries.

In the first instance, enthusiasts for the expansion of new production and information technologies in the workplace suggest that not only can production be increased, labour costs reduced, global markets established and financial operations electronically integrated, but also the experience of work can be enhanced and enriched. Technological advancements and organisational restructuring and workplace redesign give employees new opportunities for skill development and self-realisation through their work.

Much contemporary management and organisation literature (e.g. Hirschhorn 1984, Kanter 1992, Handy 1995, 1996, Peters 1991, Senge 1990) emphasises organisational restructuring that downsizes employee numbers, flattens hierarchies and encourages new approaches to organisational behaviour that are more collaborative and mutually responsible. It emphasises 'empowered' team-playing employees maximally performing in participatory organisational 'cultures'. And it encourages, too, the growing flexibility in employment relations as opportunities for workers and prospective workers to negotiate their own value and terms of contract.

Designing organisations around the capabilities enabled by new production and information technologies typically enables the organisation to downsize employee numbers yet increase production and competitiveness. Multiskilled, information-integrated workplaces require fewer levels of organisational hierarchy and lower formalisation to manage employees. In turn, flatter, more responsive organisational structures provide not only more rapid response capacities in the organisation to environmental change, but also employees with opportunities in which they can exercise new forms of skill, knowledge, responsibility and commitment. As work becomes more abstract, requiring flexibility, manipulability and analysis, employees experience new challenges and forms of mastery.

Organisational restructuring and participatory workplace management can allow managers and employees to move beyond their narrow functional perspectives and to create new roles and opportunities. A data-rich environment enables and requires new forms of work organisation and new management practices that recognise and positively exploit the blurring of boundaries and de-specialisation made possible by the new production technologies. As the range and quality of skills at each organisational level become similar, and as employees, ostensibly, become more responsible and organisationally integrated, hierarchical distinctions become both less necessary and less effective. Authority becomes based upon appropriate fit between knowledge and responsibility rather than upon traditional organisational rank and status structures. The new flows of information between multiple users create opportunities for innovative methods of information sharing and exchange. Teamwork among broadly skilled and knowledgeable employees, less fettered by the constraints of traditional hierarchies and spheres of responsibility, engenders a heightened sense of empowerment, commitment and collective responsibility. At the same time, the diminished bureaucratic structure enables the organisation to respond more rapidly to changing environmental conditions without the delay and inertia associated with vast, highly formalised, cumbersome bureaucracies.

These contemporary theories of organisation and management hold that advanced management information systems and attention to the generation of organisational cultures of team productivity and mutual care lead to a high degree of social integration within the organisation that surpass the need for bureaucratic control. The work conditions associated with more traditional technologies and industrial relations have been definitively altered by the de-differentiation capacities of advanced information technology. This has led, in some cases, to a reduction in the level of industrial conflict and to, the appearance at least, of closer relations between management and the workforce.

On the other hand, these popular organisation and management theories and contemporary organisational redesign programmes seldom recognise the persistence of traditional social relations of ownership and control notwithstanding the appearance of integrated, familial, workplaces. Critical analysts raise questions over the effects of increasing deployment of advanced technologies on jobs, wages and working conditions, skills training and labour markets, and also the effects of organisational restructuring and designed cultures on work experiences

(Casey 1995, Heckscher 1988, Jermier *et al.* 1994, Martin 1992, Willmott and Alveson 1994). Critical questions are raised about the efficacy of claims for transformed workplaces and 'empowered' workers.

Some analysts suggest that the new 'smart' technologies equipped with expansive artificial intelligence capacities not only surpass human physical capacities, but perform the functions of human brainwork as well. Notwithstanding the routine and de-skilled labour of early automated production there remained some capacity for human critical judgement and for localised modification of work practices and habits. Such capacity, it is feared, is now given over to the new intelligent machines, particularly in heavy industry, manufacturing and transport. Consequently, workers may become servants of the smart machines and become more docile and dependent in the workplace. Furthermore, while employees are not as bound by the rhythms of machines, they are now more subtly monitored and controlled by the electronic eye of management surveillance. This situation can cause workers to become more cynical, distrustful and distanced from one another. They perform their jobs routinely and perfunctorily and look for more ways to escape their jobs.

The new surveillance techniques that enable constant monitoring of workers' every activity may ensure a greater level of conformity to the new work practices, and elicit the manifestation of bonds of loyalty to the company. The ability to manage by remote control circumvents the traditional face-to-face encounter and the negotiating process with workers. New information technologies can displace interpersonal contacts, and the technologies themselves can become a new site of tension and sublimated confrontation. Increased productivity with fewer workers threatens the availability of jobs and the future of work. Employees can, once again, be controlled and disciplined under these conditions, despite 'empowering' policies, job enrichment and 'participatory management' programmes. Moreover, the drive towards outsourcing and contract work performed by self-employed entrepreneurial workers changes the context in which an employment relation is negotiated as well as the structure of labour markets.

These outcomes may be the result of unintended learnings at work, and contrary to espoused new management practices. But once employee and contractee have learned such attitudes and behaviours through experiences of the organisation's culture of work and everyday management practice, they are very difficult to unlearn and eradicate. New learning, encouraged, for instance, through establishing more genuinely participatory structures and processes, a much greater valuing of the role of workers in organisation success, and more fully accountable management practices, must be facilitated and maintained.

Globalisation and work

A further changing context of work is the process identified in the 1990s of 'globalisation'. Globalisation refers to a pattern of events facilitated by technological changes, economic shifts and organisational restructurings and networkings (Castells 1996, Robertson 1992, Reich 1991, Wallerstein 1991). The rise of the multinational and transnational corporation and the supranational organisation in recent years has been greatly facilitated by the capabilities of advanced information and telecommunication technologies. Differing from internationalism in an important sense – the diminished role of the nation-state – globalisation points to the rising importance of the multinational and transnational corporations that now control a large percentage of the world's economy and exert considerable influence on global policy agenda setting and legislation. The latest developments in the General Agreement on Tariffs and Trade (GATT) may have been signed by leaders of sovereign nation-states, but the influence of transnational business operations and supranational associations such as the European Union (EU) throughout the negotiations was considerable.

The social, economic, political and cultural implications of globalisation are immense and the debates over the future of the nation-states (or some of them), the emergence of regional blocs and 'global webs' (Castells 1996, Reich 1991) are likely to continue for many years. The transformations occurring in work are co-constitutive of these developments – they are at once facilitating some of the global reconfigurations as they are an outcome of the technological, political and social decisions made in this arena. There are many implications for work. There are implications for the structuring of occupations and labour markets, no longer on the scale of national economies, for the migrancy and mobility of high-skilled labour, for the marginalisation of low-skilled, low-wage labour, and for globally competitive markets for goods and services.

Most readily observable is the capacity to globalise an organisation through the electronic integration of geographically dispersed employees. Employees across geographic locations, with access to centralised databases, can access and coordinate many levels of data for a variety of purposes. Airlines, libraries, databanks and informated organisations have global computer access to their own and other contracted users' information twenty-four hours a day. These capabilities enable information processing work to be performed across the globe in a matter of minutes or seconds. Examples include translation services, copy-editing, multifarious document processing, even computer design and mathematical analysis, performed by contractors located in the South Pacific for global companies headquartered in North America, Europe or Asia. Other online co-workers include medical teams, research scientists, financial managers, designers and information technologists for transnational corporations. Geographic residence in the contracting or employing company's location is not necessary.

Another implication for, and changing context of, work is what I call an emerging 'decentred workplace' in which knowledge workers, or 'symbolic analysts' and 'outsourced' multiskilled entrepreneurial workers with their laptop computers and mobile phones, can work anywhere where they have access to a modem, fax or airport. Alongside global knowledge workers with diminished attachments to home nations, corporate 'families' and specialist occupations, are workers and non-workers experiencing dramatically altered conditions in existing workplaces and the effects of management practices designed to cope with the globally competitive marketplace.

The future of work

The course of the transition to post-industrial, informational society and work presents enduring and vital questions about work for workers, managers and organisations. Debates about future opportunities in work, or indeed to the role of work in our lives, are far from resolved. Castells' (1996) important book interprets extensive data to project a more highly skilled, employed workforce. He dismisses those who interpret data to suggest the 'end of work' (Rifkin 1996, Aronowitz and DiFazio 1994) or continuing high unemployment. His analysis and projections of work and employment in the twenty-first century predict, for the USA, that the bulk of increased employment opportunities will be in 'service activities' (Castells 1996: 221–7) including urban-oriented agricultural services – gardeners, groundskeepers, arborists – as well as those involved in food, cleaning, custodial services. Further increase in health services, business services, including temporary work and outsourcing, legal services, engineering, architectural and educational services is also expected. Growth in the retail division will also comprise a significant area for new jobs. In keeping with the trend towards the informational society, manufacturing jobs will continue to decline, agricultural jobs will even more dramatically decline (in the developed world) and service sector employment will increase. Occupationally, there will be considerable growth for skilled professionals, technicians and semi-skilled service occupations. Sales and clerical workers will remain relatively stable, and craft workers may actually increase their share of total occupational employment. This represents a tendency to stabilise a central core of skilled technical or manual workers around craft skills (Castells 1996: 224).

The situation in Europe, however, does not present the same optimism of increased employment opportunities. Recent reports from the Commission of the European Union (1994) and the OECD (1994, 1995) indicate that Europe continues to experience high unemployment even in high-tech countries such as Finland and Germany. Brown (1997) also notes that in the UK the number of part-time jobs has grown while the number of full-time jobs continues to decline. Increase in jobs in the newly developing countries may be accounted for by both the globalisation of manufacturing operations and the increase in part-time and women's employment.

In the developed countries of Asia and Oceania, including Australia and New Zealand, unemployment levels remain problematically high, notwithstanding the increase in the number of jobs. Increase in absolute job numbers may indicate growing rates of part-time and short-term employment that do not equate with the living wage of full-time work expected until the 1990s. Furthermore, in contrast with the expectations of earlier generations of workers in many sectors of industry in which employer initiatives in staff training and skill development were typical, the current and coming generations of workers are increasingly expected to advance their own education and skills training independently of employing organisations. This controversial and uneven trend does not imply that learning opportunities do not, or should not, be encouraged and enhanced in the workplace.

Conclusion

At the very least, there is little doubt that the contexts and organisation of production and work are changing dramatically as the twenty-first century begins. Notwithstanding Castells' optimistic projections, millions of workers, managers and political and government leaders express concern over the effects of production, organisation and economic change on work and employment. Work remains significant in shaping the lives of individuals, in the character of the self and in societal organisation. The productive bases of social life, and the institution of work, that became deeply entwined with the cultural sphere throughout modernity, remain fundamental in determining the structures and processes of social solidarity and cohesion – at least transitionally – in the emerging new era.

In this period of considerable industrial change much attention is being placed on the practical tasks of designing new ways of organising, managing and educating workers for both the tasks of production and the pressing requirements in some sectors for more 'meaningful', more developmental and more satisfying experiences of work. Opportunity for enhanced self-development through participation in some fields of work is another new development emerging in contemporary organisations. Finding ways in which diverse learning experiences, effective for both employee and organisation, are provided is a challenging task for organisations and their training and development specialists. Yet it is one that holds considerable potential for serious and immensely worthwhile returns in both material and affective domains for workers and organisations in the coming decades.

Notes

1 Pink-collar work refers to traditional women's work in office, retail and services, for example typist, shop assistant, nurse. Traditional women's work has often been omitted from discussions of technological changes in industrial work, and post-industrial developments of knowledge and new professional work.
2 Emotional work refers to the work, typically performed by women, of nurturing, supporting, understanding and attuning to the emotional needs of others: workers, managers and customers or clients. Such labours are typically 'invisible' in terms of their recognition and reward yet explicit in terms of their effects on others and the generation of workplace harmony, congeniality and productivity.

References

Adler, P. (ed.) (1992) *Technology and the Future of Work*, New York: Oxford University Press.

Aronowitz, S. and DiFazio, W. (1994) *The Jobless Future*, Minneapolis: University of Minnesota Press.

Ayres, R. and Miller, S. (1983) *Robotics: Applications and Social Implications*, Cambridge, MA: Ballinger.

Brown, R. K. (ed.) (1997) *The Changing Shape of Work*, London: Macmillan.

Casey, C. (1995) *Work, Self and Society: After Industrialism*, London: Routledge.

Castells, M. (1996) *The Rise of the Network Society, Vol.1*, Oxford: Blackwell.

Commission of the European Union (1994) *Growth, Competitiveness, Employment: The Challenges and Ways Forward in the 21st Century*, Luxembourg: Office of the European Communities.

Davis, D. (1988) 'Technology and de-skilling: the case of five principal trade areas in New South Wales', *New Technology, Work and Employment* 3(1): 47–55.

Drucker, P. (1993) *Post-Capitalist Society*, New York: Harper Collins.

Dy, J. (ed.) (1990) *Advanced Technology in Commerce, Offices, and Health Service*, Aldershot: Avebury.

Garson, B. (1988) *The Electronic Sweatshop*, New York: Simon and Schuster.

Handy, C. (1995) *Gods of Management: The Changing Work of Organisations*, New York: Oxford University Press.

Handy, C. (1996) *Beyond Certainty: The Changing World of Organisations*, Boston: Harvard Business School.

Hartmann, H. (ed.) (1987) *Computer Chips and Paper Clips: Technology and Women's Employment*, Washington, DC: National Academy Press.

Heckscher, C. (1988) *The New Unionism: Employee Involvement in the Changing Corporation*, New York: Basic Books.

Hirschhorn, L. (1984) *Beyond Mechanization: Work and Technology in a Postindustrial Age*, Cambridge, MA: MIT Press.

Hochschild, A. (1983) *The Managed Heart*, Berkeley, CA: University of California Press.

Jermier, J., Knights, D. and Nord, W. (eds) (1994) *Resistance and Power in Organisations*, London: Routledge.

Kanter, R. M. (1992) *The Challenge of Organizational Change*, New York: Free Press.

Martin, J. (1992) *Cultures in Organisations: Three Perspectives*, New York: Oxford University Press.

McKinsey Global Institute (1992) *Service Sector Productivity*, Washington, DC: McKinsey Global Institute.

OECD (Organization for Economic Cooperation and Development) (1994) *Employment/Unemployment Study: Policy Report*, Paris: OECD.

OECD (Organization for Economic Cooperation and Development) (1995) *Economic Outlook*, June, Paris: OECD.

Peters, T. (1991) *Beyond Organizational Hierarchy in the 1990s*, New York: Knopf.

Reich, R. (1991) *The Work of Nations: Preparing Ourselves for 21st Century Capitalism*, New York: Knopf.

Rifkin, J. (1996) *The End of Work*, New York: Putnam.

Robertson, R. (1992) *Globalization: Social Theory and Global Culture*, London: Sage.

Senge, P. (1990) *The Fifth Discipline*, New York: Doubleday.

Sinden, A. (1996) 'The decline, flexibility and geographic restructuring of employment in British retail banks', *The Geographical Journal* 162(1): 25–40.

Wallerstein, I. M. (1991) *Geopolitics and Geoculture*, Cambridge: Cambridge University Press.

Willmott, H. and Alveson, M. (eds) (1994) *Critical Management Studies*, London: Sage.

Wright, B. D. (ed.) (1987) *Women, Work, and Technology*, Ann Arbor, MI: The University of Michigan Press.

Zuboff, S. (1988) *In the Age of the Smart Machine: The Future of Work and Power*, New York: Basic Books.

3 Learning to work and working to learn

Ronald Barnett

In this chapter, I shall suggest that, in understanding their relationships in the contemporary era, work and learning can profitably be placed against the background of wider societal and even global shifts. I shall suggest that we live in an age of supercomplexity. That is to say, we live in an age in which our very frameworks for comprehending the world, for acting in it and for relating to each other are entirely problematic. We live in a world characterised by contestability, challengeability, uncertainty and unpredictability.

My argument is that, under conditions of supercomplexity, work has to become learning and learning has to become work. These imperatives – as they have now become – arise out of the fragility of the supercomplex environment in which we are all placed. We cannot escape the conditions of supercomplexity which face us in 'the global age' (Albrow 1996). As a result, learning in work takes on a new urgency. Equally, learning has itself to be seen as work, as a set of activities which stand, to some extent, outside of individuals and which yields value beyond that of the individuals' efforts. Only through taking work and learning seriously in these ways can we begin to address the age of supercomplexity in which we find ourselves.

Learning and work

What are the relationships between learning and work? Do we learn in order to work more effectively? In other words, is learning prior to effective work? Or do we learn through our work? Does learning occur simultaneously with work? It must be both. But is the learning in the two kinds of situation the same form of learning? The answer that I want to offer in this chapter is twofold: they can be understood as separate activities but they are rapidly converging.

Learning acquired independently of the work situation could be propositional in form; learning acquired within the work situation could be a matter of knowing how to get by in similar circumstances. Effective work seems to require both kinds of learning: knowing that certain things are the case; and coming to intuit the particular 'form of life' (Wittgenstein 1978). For example, an accountant simply has to know a great deal of business law, codes of practice and regulations; but he or she has also to acquire much in the way of experiential understanding of what is appropriate professional conduct in engaging with clients in different business milieux.

There is no problem here, then. Each profession has its own mix of factual knowledge, theoretical principles, action understanding, process knowledge, tacit knowledge and communicative competence.[1] The precise mix will be intuited through engagement over time within each profession. The differences will be subtle. Multinational, medium- and small-sized enterprises in different sectors of the economy will have their own styles of communication and interaction, their own attitude to formal knowledge and their own views on the value of research and evaluation. What counts as being effective in particular environments within the world of work may not be spelt out but it will be picked up; the mysteries are revealed even if they are not made explicit.

This is a philosophy of 'it will be all right on the day' and it is increasingly being recognised as being inadequate in the modern age. Three strategies are being developed to address the matter.

Firstly, training and development are taking on a more systematic character through the provision of in-house training schemes (Becher 1996). Secondly, professionals are developing their own forms of peer development; often ranging across companies (Gear *et al.* 1994). For example, in the UK, tax advisers of the major international firms have their own professional association transcending company loyalties. Thirdly, institutions of education, through both face-to-face learning and distance learning, are finding markets in the corporate sector for their services for mid-career training and development.

These three forms of continuing learning, while analytically distinct, spawn hybrid forms of employee development combining formal and informal learning in different degrees. For example, employers are increasingly opening opportunities for personal development, which have no immediate connection with their staff's working environment. As a further example, informal mutual activities which professionals initiate – often in a regional locality – are reinforced by the relevant professional bodies as the latter seek to institute forms of continuing professional development, even, on occasions, requiring evidence of such development in order for individuals to retain their professional status. A yet further example of such hybrid forms of professional development lies in the action learning programmes being promoted by institutions of higher education, which call for professionals in different fields to pool and reflect on their experiences over time and engage in mutual learning circles.

Does all this amount to an incoherent mess or does it represent a proper range of responses to a complex situation? Clearly, the relationships between work and learning are complex; and there is a complexity quite apart from the particular and manifold interests of different kinds of company, of the private and public sectors, of professional bodies and associations, and of state agencies and policies. So a mix of strategies to foster continuing learning through work and beyond would appear to be a proper response. Is that it, then? Complexity of situation requires complexity of response – end of story. Not quite. The complexity facing us in this situation is more problematic than this characterisation.

A supercomplex world

That the world is changing, is even facing exponential rates of change, is part of our modern commonplace understanding. Technologies, economic arrangements, systems, institutions, roles, patterns of work and patterns of consumption are changing with increasing rapidity. The causes of these increasing rates of change are also, to a marked degree, understood. The development of a global economy, with flexible labour markets, networked systems and infrastructures, and international corporations aided now by the information technology revolution, making possible virtually instantaneous flows of information, decisions and capital around the world: these are the main features of the causes of increasing rates of social change.

What, however, is less understood is the deep-seated character of these changes. When we are faced with changes in our technologies, systems and patterns of work, we are also faced with challenges to our basic concepts. Work, communication, identity, self, knowing and even life: the meaning of fundamental concepts such as these is no longer clear in a world of change. As a consequence, the very frameworks that we deploy for making sense of the world in us, between us and around us are dissolving. There is no security available to us; this is an unstable world.[2]

It is a world not just of complexity but of supercomplexity. Complexity is a situation in which a multitude of facts or ideas or possibilities present themselves within a particular domain of activity or understanding. The physicist, the doctor and the company manager are each continually faced with complexity. One of its manifestations is informational overload, whether overload – respectively – of research papers unread, of new drugs to assimilate or data streams on economic performance of the company's activities. With increasing media – fax, e-mail, Internet, mobile phones – such informational overload increases. Increasing information expands one's range of options, so making decision-making more complex. Accordingly, being a professional becomes as much a matter of handling complexity as it is about having first-order expertise as such.

By contrast, supercomplexity is a situation in which different frameworks present themselves, frameworks through which we understand the world and ourselves and our actions within it. In the contemporary era, again such frameworks multiply and are often in conflict with each other. The physicist may start to consider whether he or she is encouraging the use of the Earth's non-replenishable resources. The doctor may reflect as to whether his or her role is increasingly one of counsellor and health adviser, and that the perspectives offered by a background in medical science are insufficient for the widening role. The director of a multinational company may find that local value systems are presenting challenges in communication and that, as a result, both values and communication have to be given attention in themselves rather than treated as taken-for-granted means of action.

Instances such as these are instances of supercomplexity. They present not just additional facts or ideas which can be accommodated within one's basic framework of assumptions and values. Rather, they run against one's basic framework itself. They cannot be accommodated straightforwardly. If situations such as these are to be negotiated with a positive outcome, if presented challenges are seriously to be worked through, then one's basic framework – or part of it, at any rate – has itself to be changed. To say this, of course, is to say that the person concerned, faced with such challenges, has him- or herself to change, for one's basic framework is not entirely separable from the kind of person one is.[3]

To put it another way, through disjunction between the presenting conceptual frameworks (Jarvis 1992), one is faced with a learning experience, or, at least, the potential for a learning experience. Through such experiences, if met in a positive spirit, one can come to see both the world and oneself in a different way. One can move on effectively, in the light of one's new understanding. Supercomplexity, accordingly, can be not just challenging but disturbing. Having one's dominant presuppositions of the world and oneself challenged – whether beliefs, values or understandings – can be unsettling. But it can also present opportunities for development and learning.[4]

Learning in work

This idea of supercomplexity compels us to take a particular view of the relationship between learning and work. In an age of supercomplexity, work and learning cannot be two distinct sets of activity.

Learning is embedded in work: that much is clear from what I have just said. But even that idea – that learning is embedded in work – has to be re-understood. It is often said that work itself presents opportunities for growth and learning. It does, but by no means always. Much work is built upon a set of routines. This is not just a characteristic of low-skill work. Professionals and others in senior positions in major organisations with near-monopoly situations may feel tacitly that their way of seeing the world, their forms of practising in the world, are secure, and do not require much adjustment. Their work, accordingly, becomes largely a matter of a set of routines that are, in turn, set within the context of frameworks held with some firmness, even dogmatic firmness. Doubtless, this is to be regretted. But it happens. Work is not necessarily a site of learning at the individual level.

On the other hand, learning is necessarily embedded in work at a more general or, as we might put it, a sociological level. Work is increasingly coming under the influence of forces external to itself, which are bound to bring at least change and adaptation, if not learning, in their wake. There are at least three dominant factors at play. Firstly, the spread of markets worldwide: globalisation is the name of this shift and it affects the public sector as much as it affects the private sector. The resultant interconnectedness of economies – now the global economy – means that events and actions have effects, even at a distance. Crashes in the stock market in the Pacific Rim affect small investors, as well as large companies, around the world; international ecological agreements could have unforeseen consequences not just for economies but also for rural communities in tropical rainforests. But such global markets are also seen in the public sectors. Their labour markets – the movement of health workers and academics, for example – are increasingly global in character.

The second dominant force for unforeseen change at work is the state. Governments of whatever hue across the world are wishing to limit public spending and to ensure value for money in the services that they do fund. As a consequence, we have seen the rise of the evaluative state (or the audit state) as it is variously called (Neave 1990, Power 1997). The health and education sectors come under ever-proliferating forms of intrusive evaluation which, in turn, spawn more and more complicated internal quality assurance systems.

In the public sector, markets and standards coincide: for example, professions are increasingly having to be sensitive to international standards of work in their own domains, firstly, because there is greater international movement of clients, and, secondly, because standards of professional credentialism are becoming increasingly international in character. Democratic governments also find themselves – sometimes on an international basis – being drawn into themselves developing regulations or standards governing the conduct of affairs in the private sector. (These two factors – markets and audit – often cut across each other, producing tensions in public policies.)

The third major force causing learning to be embedded in work is the information technology revolution. It could be said to be an outcome of the global economy but it has become such a significant feature of the modern world that it deserves to be understood as a major factor in its own right. The significant learning that the information technology revolution is generating lies not in the mastering of the hundreds of techniques for manipulating data that the computer requires, whether numerical, visual, linguistic or aural in character. Rather, the significant learning which the information technology revolution generates lies in the forms of communication which the computer makes possible. The issue is whether, in some respects and in some of its uses, the computer is actually changing our forms of human understanding both of the material world and of the human world.

'Netiquette' is an example of just how we may be dimly aware that such profound changes are occurring. Human communication on a two-dimensional screen affects the character of the information passing between human beings: the result is that the meaning of messages is changed and even, we might say, distorted. Hence 'netiquette' arises in which protocols are developed to lessen the corruption of the information via the computer. It may be said that the computer is in a relatively embryonic form and that the arrival of sound and pictures will restore human communication to its non-digital form. The response misses the point that computers – for example, in three-dimensional design, in the manipulation of chemical compounds, and in the production of mega-databases – are both changing the forms of knowledge production itself and generating opportunities for new forms of intersubjectivity to develop.[5]

These three forces – globalisation, the rise of the audit state and the information technology revolution – are inserting themselves inescapably into work. Individuals may, for a time, ignore them; even companies may do so. But, sooner or later, the press of each of these individually, and all of them collectively, catches up with the recalcitrant. There is no hiding place.

The result is that learning is necessarily embedded in work but, as we might put it, structurally so. Individuals may find themselves in positions where work is relatively routine or they may simply not be inclined to seize every learning opportunity that comes their way. Equally, corporations may be unwilling to learn and to change. But, sooner or later, the world will catch up with them. Whether at the individual or the corporate level, they are likely to find themselves out of kilter: they will be redundant but it will be largely – although not always – a self-imposed redundancy.

The key point is that since change is structural and is an inescapable feature of the world in which we live, so too learning is structural. We might be tempted to say that learning is a necessary feature of work, but, as I have just indicated, this is not the case. Some will avoid it, for a time at least. Rather, we should say that there is an impetus to learn now built into work, and that this impetus is pervasive. Ultimately, the call to learn now embedded in work cannot be ducked.

Work in learning

If learning is structurally embedded in work, work is also embedded in learning. At one level, this is a trivial statement. Learning calls for work –

often, indeed, hard work! But the sense in which learning constitutes work deserves explication.

In the first place, the sense of learning being work arises because learning presents personal challenges as well as presenting intellectual challenges. Learning is unsettling in personal terms: in it, we are dislodged. Our sense of ourselves as individuals with a certain authority, rooted in what we know and understand, is easily shaken if we have to disclose to our peers that we still have much to learn. Learning, we might say, is existentially discomforting, and especially so in a work setting. Learning is typically associated with being young, and being in a state of personal development (or even immaturity). Having publicly, as an adult, to disclose that one is in a state of learning is likely, therefore, to generate mixed messages in relation to one's organizational persona. Self-images of maturity, self-reliance and authority suddenly contrast with those of dependency and of lack of understanding.

In those circumstances, it is not quite clear to whom one is, organizationally, speaking. One is having to admit that work is no longer something over which one has control and command, including one's relationships with other work colleagues. To admit to being a learner is to admit to being uncertain, and in that admission, all too frequently, one is in danger of losing one's authority – or one feels that that is the case. This is particularly so if, in that disclosure, one opens oneself up to a learning situation in which one has to learn a technique or grasp a set of ideas imparted by a more junior colleague. Learning about the Internet from a much more junior colleague and in the company of other more junior colleagues can, for many, be unnerving.

The unnerving is the natural result of roles, work identities and work relationships being built on preconceptions of an equivalence of knowledge and status. In the learning organization, everyone is a learner, but such a mantra requires a particular kind of organizational culture, one in which its implications are fully understood by everyone. If everyone is a learner, then – potentially, at least – we can all learn from each other all the time. It is this latter step that is rarely made: that we can all learn from each other all the time. At best, the recognition that we are lifelong learners leads merely to the acknowledgement that learning opportunities need to be opened up to individuals. The more radical step in collective understanding – that we can all learn from each other all the time – is much more rarely taken on board. And it is partly the existential challenges to one's personal authority, status and legitimacy that that further step would usher in that prevents it from being seriously tackled.

Learning, then, is work. It is challenging in personal terms, and not just through its adding to one's workload. Extending the point, the earlier distinction between formal and informal learning may appear to be helpful. Formal learning undertaken in the company of others brings elements of self-disclosure and status uncertainty, which less often accompany informal learning. It can appear more as work than as informal learning, where one simply accommodates to new experiences and challenges. But the distinction cannot be completely sustained. Both formal and informal learning constitute work. Both often add to one's workload, and they add to one's existential load. Formal learning can be undertaken privately and allows personal adjustments in one's own time and space; informal learning is often experienced in a group setting, where one's felt clumsiness is all too apparent, particularly to those who 'know' each other.

It follows that learning of any kind can be felt as somewhat alien, having an externality to which one has to accommodate. The degree to which learning is alien is a feature of its load on the individual concerned. And load can be cognitive (having to master new concepts) or operational (having to master new skills) or experiential (having to accommodate to a new set of relationships with the world and with those around one in the work environment).

What, then, does it mean to say that learning is work? Precisely this: that the learning, in a sense, stands outside of oneself. It is a kind of object, an entity in its own right which, in some way, has to be confronted. It contains its own challenges, and perhaps has even come to be configured by 'standards' which have to be attained. In that sense, in its externality, learning takes on characteristics of work. Whatever the opportunities that may be developing for negotiating one's pattern of work in the environment of so-called post-Fordist organizations, work characteristically presents a givenness to which one has to yield.

The challenge that learning presents is not just a matter of willingness or unwillingness. After all, the work that learning represents can be undertaken willingly: witness the professional pianist who practises several hours each day. We sometimes hear people say that 'my work is not really work: I do it happily'. Actually, their happiness is immaterial. People can be happy in their work. The point such a comment is really bringing out is that, where work does not feel like work, it has become part of one's self-identity such that work no longer stands over one, apart from one. The concert pianist may, indeed, say that the practising did not constitute work. The practising incorporates a learning dimension, so it is not being implied that no learning is taking place. What is rather being said is that the practice–is so part of one's self-identity as a concert pianist that the demands that it represents come from within the pianist rather than being imposed externally.

Learning is work, then, in the sense that one has to yield to the new experiences that come with learning. The new experiences, if they are worthwhile and if they offer opportunities for learning of any significance, will be complex and will be challenging. They will be challenging because they present demands of understanding, of a capacity to act or of self-reflection. Through the new experience,[6] one is challenged to understand the world in a new way (a new idea or even perspective is presented to one), or to act in the world in a new way (one engages with others around one differently), or one comes to understand oneself in a new light.

Often, learning – especially in a work setting – incorporates a mix of these forms of learning and is, therefore, challenging in multiple ways. That is why it can feel like work: it is challenging in terms of one's knowing, acting and reflecting simultaneously. External features of the world exert their claims on oneself, on one's organizing frames for experiencing and for engaging with the world. At the same time, one is being asked to comprehend a new process or product or set of ideas, a new way of dealing with those ideas (e.g. through information technology) and a new way of interacting with others and handling oneself. In the more open networking environment of modern work, ideas may be coming at one from other domains of professional life. Equally, in the global economy, one may have to interrelate to others around the world whose culture one does not know and with whom communication is inevitably problematic. Not surprisingly, learning opportunities may be formally acknowledged as just that, as opportunities, but, inwardly, may be felt as threats. Accordingly, a challenge to those concerned to develop learning organizations is to turn the inward sense of learning as threat into a more publicly visible sense of learning as opportunity.

Work, then, is inherent in learning. Work increasingly – but not universally – provides opportunities for personal change and development; learning opportunities, in other words. But learning of any seriousness and challenge is a form of work: it calls on individuals to yield to the demands of an experience or set of experiences. (These experiences may be more or less organized, or they may arise organically – 'informally' – in work situations.)

Some will feel that the argument has unhelpfully run together the experience of learning with the facticity of work and has produced an equivocation that turns on the notion of work itself. It may be said that, while learning may sometimes be felt to be 'work', inner experience should not be confused with the external institutionalisation of work. The matter is crucial for my argument. Under conditions of supercomplexity, the phenomenology of work and learning, as it were, are merging. Work is becoming learning; that is perhaps relatively uncontentious. But learning is also becoming work through the expanded challenges that supercomplexity presents. Learning is no longer just a matter of inward experience and challenge but is a matter of confronting multiplying expectations, standards and evaluations which stand outside of oneself and which – as with work itself – cannot, to a significant degree, be anticipated in advance.

This intertwining of work and learning itself presents opportunities and challenges, as we have seen. Just as work can be demotivating, overburdensome and even threatening, so too can learning, especially if 'learning' is imposed on individuals and if they are poorly supported – in personal as much as in resource terms – as they are struggling to learn. Learning, therefore, whether it arises intentionally or unintentionally, requires support if it is to be undertaken successfully. This is not to say that all learning requires support; learning is likely to be all the more rapid and meaningful where it is undertaken through an individual's own motivations. But even then, and more generally, learning can often benefit from the presence of a supporting framework, a framework which is designed (e.g. through a system of mentorship) to address the existential anxiety of learning as much as it is designed (e.g. through designated time allowances and, where necessary, financial support) to address the more material aspects of effective learning.

Engaged responsiveness

For all its possible conceptual gain, it might be thought that the past discussion has yielded rather little. Of course, it might be accepted, effective learning requires a supportive framework. Yes, it has to include attention to the more personal and emotional aspects of learning, aspects which are not easily calculable and do not easily lend themselves to a profit-and-loss assessment. But once all that has been put in place, what more is there to be said?

Here, we need to return to the idea of supercomplexity. Supercomplexity, it will be recalled, is that form of complexity in which frameworks for understanding the world are themselves challenged. Whether it is an international oil company being obliged seriously – and not just cosmetically – to take on board ecological features of its activities, or doctors beginning to take seriously the prospect that their main purpose is not to treat disease but to prevent it, or university academics beginning to take seriously the idea that teaching is only occurring if effective learning is taking place: all of these are challenges to frameworks of self-understanding, of one's understanding of the world and of one's relationships to others. Such challenges to fundamental frameworks call for the abandonment of one's primary way of looking at the world, or, at least, to take seriously that there can be other, quite different and legitimate ways of viewing the world. The learning challenges that we all face in and through work are increasingly of this supercomplex kind. They require of us not simply that we learn new techniques, or new ideas or new practices. They call upon us to change or at least to widen the very frameworks through which we interpret the world. They demand of us, in effect, that we become different kinds of human being.

Sometimes, perhaps often, we refuse those demands. The challenges to our ways of looking at the world are so considerable that we find it difficult to embrace them. We feel that we cannot become other than we are.

We see, in this idea of supercomplexity, just why learning in work and why work in learning are so pervasive and so problematic, if not to say often threatening. Change becomes daunting because it often calls for fundamental changes in self-conception.

But, as we have just implied, such challenges, and the learning that is caught up in them, are often organisational in character. 'The learning organization' is a well-worn phrase, but what is perhaps not always understood is that organizational learning has itself to take on a supercomplex dimension. In fact, there are two levels of responsiveness to supercomplexity at work. The first is, indeed, simply that of reactive responsiveness, of trying to cope with supercomplexity. Challenges to a company's frame of reference, its self-understanding and the framework of its structuring operations, are met belatedly, only when they cannot be ducked. Responses are, as a result, *ad hoc* and ill-thought through. Here, organizational learning is a matter of *force majeure*: it occurs when, and only when, it has to do so. The second level of responsiveness is more anticipatory in character. We might be tempted to call such responsiveness either 'strategic' or 'proactive' in character. Both terms have a point but each is somewhat misleading. If the environment within which institutions are having to operate and survive is not only changing but liable to change unpredictably, and in ways which challenge fundamental frames of self-understanding, of an organization's place in its own market and its relationships with its clients or customers (and, therefore, of its 'mission'), both the ideas of strategy and even of being proactive become problematic. For both rest on the assumption that the future can be in some measure like the past or, at least, where the future can be foretold to some degree. One can develop strategies where the opposed forces are known and can be measured; one can be proactive where it is clear what actions might be fostered. In an age of radical uncertainty, neither of these sets of conditions can be assumed to hold. Accordingly, a different form of responsiveness is required.

Earlier, I suggested the idea of 'anticipatory responsiveness', but even that overplays the matter. For the idea of anticipation is itself problematic under conditions of discontinuous change. But if the future is liable not to be like the past, then we can perhaps develop an organizational responsiveness in which at least that state of affairs is collectively understood. Accordingly, anticipatory responsiveness points us towards not just a readiness to respond to change (for that hardly escapes the position of reactive responsiveness) but, rather, to an engaged responsiveness. This is a form of responsiveness in which the organization is continually engaging with its environment and in a critical way. For that, it will have multiple frames of reference up its corporate sleeve, or, at the drop of a hat, will be able to generate them.

Organizational learning, then, under conditions of supercomplexity, becomes a matter of generating the capacities for continuing creative insertions into an organization's environment. It is not suddenly obliged to review its mission, its values, its assumptions, its sense of itself, or its view of its relationships with its clients because these are continually kept under review and new conceptions of each are continually being generated. The organization becomes literally an organization which knows how to learn.

Learning and supercomplexity

Learning is inherent in work, and work is inherent in learning. That is a double story, worth understanding, even under conditions of relative stability. But under conditions of supercomplexity, this double story becomes doubly more forceful. Under conditions of supercomplexity, work demands learning; it does not just promote it or encourage it. Correspondingly, under conditions of supercomplexity, learning becomes ever more challenging, fraught and unsettling. It takes on the features of work: it becomes as work.

As we have seen, this story of the interrelationships between learning and work has to be worked out at different levels and in different modes: personal and organisational; formal and informal. The following grid may, accordingly, be a helpful *aide-mémoire* but only if it is interpreted under conditions of supercomplexity.

	Formal	*Informal*
Organisational		
Personal		

Misinterpreted, the grid could simply stamp in forms of learning which are *inappropriate* to conditions of supercomplexity. The static character of such a grid and its demarcation of different modes (formal and informal) and different levels (organisational and personal) of learning retain and are liable to freeze outmoded conceptions of learning. Rather than being understood as dynamic and interrelating systems of learning, such a grid could reinforce conceptions of separateness which will be inadequate in facing up to conditions of supercomplexity. Supercomplexity – the challenge of multiple, conflicting and ever-emerging frames of understanding and action – requires continual critical reflection and development not in segregated compartments but in ways that are interacting. Supercomplexity repudiates boundaries of learning.

The grid, however, may take on a heuristic value provided that the forms of learning to which it points are not held entirely separate from each other. Total responsiveness is called for: individuals are part of their organizations, and organizations live through the individuals who are attached to them; informal learning is often made effective by formal learning goals or through formal learning situations, while formal learning can only be effective if backed up by informal learning. But, as we have seen, under conditions of supercomplexity, even total responsiveness is insufficient! It is insufficient because the responsive stance is itself insufficient. The responsive stance condemns the learner (individual or organization) to being always behind the game. What is called for is an engaged responsiveness, in which one is learning through bringing alternative frames of reference to bear on the frames of reference with which one is presented.

We can only live effectively under conditions of supercomplexity if we are engaging with the total environment with which we are presented. In turn, that means that we learn not by responding to supercomplexity but by contributing further to it. We can never get on top of supercomplexity, as it were. Instead, we cope with it by intervening in the world, learning as we are doing so.

We could say that learning under these conditions is necessarily action learning. So it is, but we still have a responsibility to bring to our interventions and to our learning frameworks of interpretation and evaluation. We contest the frames that are presented to us not by resisting them in any facile way but by presenting to them alternative frames. We learn not just by acting and evaluating but additionally by bringing to the party and inserting into the world – through our thinking and our acting – multiple frames of understanding. As for Gorky (1979), life itself remains our best university but only through our best critical, active and creative efforts that we bring to bear in the process.

Conclusion

Work and learning are not synonymous. They are different concepts. Some kinds of work offer little in the way of learning opportunities; some learning would not be called work. But the two concepts overlap. Work can and should offer learning opportunities; much learning is demanding, calling upon the learner to yield to certain standards, and contains the character of work. Whether the overlap between work and learning is slight or extensive, therefore, is a key issue in modern life: in many ways, the challenge here is that of bringing about the greatest overlap between work and learning.

This challenge – of bringing about a greater confluence between work and learning – takes on a particular urgency in a situation in which none of our frames of reference (of thought, action and self-understanding) are reliable. This is the contemporary situation, a situation of supercomplexity, in which all of our frameworks of knowledge and action are unstable. We have to live effectively in a world which is radically uncertain.

In such conditions, conditions of uncertainty, we will survive and prosper only by engaging in a critical way with the world. We combat multiple and conflicting frameworks not by resisting them or by giving into them in any facile way. Instead, we live dangerously with them by bringing to bear yet further possibilities of thought and action, which in turn we subject to critical scrutiny. Under conditions of supercomplexity, therefore, work has to become learning; that much is clear. Work has to be understood as presenting infinite learning opportunities. There is no resting place. All of our frameworks of action, interpretation and self-understanding – whether on an individual or an organizational level – have to be available for perpetual scrutiny. This in itself means that our contemporary situation cannot be a place, or places, of comfort.

But, at the same time, and perhaps less obviously, learning has to become work. It has to become work in the sense of becoming serious. Learning cannot be undertaken lightly. The stakes are too high for that. Not just organizational and personal survival are in question, but so, too, is the fate of whole societies if not of the planet itself. Learning, accordingly, has to become work such that it is undertaken to the most exacting standards. Learning cannot be a matter of self-indulgence. It takes on collective responsibilities, and has to yield a value added far beyond itself. In a situation of supercomplexity, therefore, work has to become learning, and learning has to become work. This is not necessarily an enjoyable state of affairs, but it is the state of affairs in which we find ourselves.

Notes

1 On process knowledge, see Eraut (1994); on tacit knowledge, see Polanyi (1966); on communicative competence, see Habermas (1996: 17–19). Alternatively, it can be said that work involves a combination of Mode 1 knowledge, that is formal knowledge created systematically, and Mode 2 knowledge, knowledge created in action for solving pragmatic problems (Gibbons *et al.* 1994).

2 The 'manufactured risk' (Giddens 1994) characteristic of 'risk society' (Beck 1992) is implicated in this instability but they should be distinguished. The risks that Beck is pointing to are essentially risks in our technological and biological environment, whereas the insecurity to which I am pointing is essentially one that arises out of a contestability of our conceptual frameworks. Giddens' notion of manufactured risk goes somewhat wider, allowing for challenges in our self-identity and self-understanding, but the distinction between my sense of instability here and his may still be drawn. Of course, there is significant overlap in that both their conceptions of instability and the one to which I am alluding involve a cognitive and experiential sense of dislocation.

3 Examining the differences between 'expert' and 'novice' approaches to work, Laufer and Glick (1996) conclude that 'to be an expert one must participate in a particular work activity and transform it *and in the process be transformed*

oneself (my emphasis). 'Therefore, expertness and noviceness cannot be isolated from the individual who is the expert or novice.'

4 Supercomplexity, accordingly, calls ultimately for 'double-loop' learning (Argyris and Schön 1974), in which one attends to one's frameworks themselves rather than, as in 'single-loop learning', attempting simply to maintain 'constancy' through adjustments within one's frames.

5 For example, Kenway (1997) argues that 'Netiquette' is gendered, typically supporting 'male communication patterns'.

6 The concept of experience is crucial. Jarvis (1997) somewhat overstates the matter in saying that 'experience is both subjective and internal' since it also contains external components: 'experiencing cannot be severed from what is experienced' (Boud *et al.* 1993: 6). But Jarvis's main point is key: that is, that only through reorderings of one's inward understandings can learning take place. In other words, in itself, external change does not cause fundamental change in one's experience: for that, 'reflection-in-action' (Schön 1987) and – we might add – a willingness to change one's internal schemas is required.

References

Albrow, M. (1996) *The Global Age*, Cambridge: Polity.

Argyris, C. and Schön, D. (1974) *Theory in Practice: Increasing Professional Effectiveness*, San Francisco: Jossey-Bass.

Becher, T. (1996) 'The learning professions', *Studies in Higher Education* 21(1): 43–56.

Beck, U. (1992) *Risk Society*, London: Sage.

Boud, D., Cohen, R. and Walker, D. (eds) (1993) *Using Experience for Learning*, Buckingham: Open University Press.

Eraut, M. (1994) *Developing Professional Knowledge and Competence*, London: Falmer.

Gear, J., McIntosh, A. and Squires, G. (1994) *Informal Learning in the Professions*, Hull: University of Hull, Department of Adult Education.

Gibbons, M., Limoges, C., Nowotny, H., Schwartzman, S., Scott, P. and Trow, M. (1994) *The New Production of Knowledge: The Dynamics of Science and Research in Contemporary Societies*, London: Sage.

Giddens, A. (1994) *Beyond Left and Right: The Future of Radical Politics*, Cambridge: Polity.

Gorky, M. (1979) *My Universities*, London: Penguin.

Habermas, J. (1996) *Theory and Practice*, Cambridge, Polity.

Jarvis, P. (1992) *Paradoxes of Learning: On Becoming an Individual in Society*, San Francisco: Jossey-Bass.

Jarvis, P. (1997) 'Learning and reflective practice in an organisation', *Staff and Educational Development International* 1(1): 12–17.

Kenway, J. (1997) 'Backlash in cyberspace: why "girls need modems"', in L. G. Roman and L. Eyre (eds) *Dangerous Territories: Struggles for Difference and Equality in Education*, London: Routledge.

Laufer, E. and Glick, J. (1996) 'Expert and novice differences in cognition and activity: a practical work activity', in Y. Engestrom and D. Middleton (eds) *Cognition and Communication at Work*, Cambridge: Cambridge University Press.

Neave, G. (1990) 'On preparing for markets: trends in higher education in Western Europe 1988–1990', *European Journal of Education* 25(2): 105–23.

Polanyi, M. (1966) *The Tacit Dimension*, New York: Doubleday.

Power, M. (1997) *The Audit Society: rituals of verification*, Oxford: Oxford University Press.

Schön, D. (1987) *Educating the Reflective Practitioner*, London: Jossey-Bass.

Wittgenstein, L. (1978) *Philosophical Investigations*, Oxford: Blackwell.

Part II

Perspectives

4 New dimensions in the dynamics of learning and knowledge

Judith H. Matthews and Philip C. Candy

It is generally accepted that individuals learn throughout their lives and that much of that learning takes place in workplace settings. Learning as a concept has been well researched and documented, with literature that focuses on individual learning, learning in groups and learning in organisations or enterprises. The coming of the knowledge era has created opportunities and demands for learning to move to centre-stage in the context of globalisation of markets and production, increased competitiveness and technological advancement.

This chapter aims to summarise some of the myriad ways in which learning as a dynamic process occurs in organisations and discuss important links between learning and knowledge creation and distribution. Learning processes which are emerging in today's knowledge economy both influence and are influenced by the dynamic changes in organisational structures and practices. The chapter focuses on the centrality of learning and the importance of a context in which learning is encouraged. The ability and potential to go on learning is important not only for individuals but for teams and entire organisations as well.

The knowledge era and the nature of work

The recent history of civilisation has been reflected in shifts from the agricultural age to the industrial age, and, more recently, from the industrial to the post-industrial (or post-capitalist) age. Whereas, in the past, land, labour, capital and machinery were the sources of wealth and of wealth creation, as Catherine Casey discussed in Chapter 2, the new era depends on knowledge, which has become the new organisational wealth (Sveiby 1997). This new focus has also been referred to as the 'knowledge revolution' (Cannon 1996), where knowledge is the principal asset of corporations and, indeed, of countries (Drucker 1993).

The transition from the industrial era to the knowledge era has been accompanied by other transitions:

1 from routine to complexity;

2   from sequential activities to parallel iterative activities;
3   from industrial era principles and modes of production to those of the knowledge era; and
4   within organisations, in structure, control, authority and communication (Savage 1996: 243–4).

The nature of work in the knowledge era, or 'knowledge work', is fundamentally different from what we have traditionally known, and hence requires a different order of thinking. It also requires new structures and processes as well as changes in many areas and types of work, with implications for employee loyalty and careers. Despres and Hiltrop (1995) spell out some of these differences between traditional work and knowledge work, in Table 4.1.

One outcome of this shift from traditional to knowledge work has been the growing recognition that an organisation's wealth exists principally in the heads of its employees, and, moreover, that it effectively 'walks out the gates' every day. This understanding fundamentally changes priorities,

Table 4.1 A comparison of knowledge work and traditional work

	Traditional work	*Knowledge work*
Skill/knowledge sets	Narrow and often functional	Specialised and deep, but often with diffuse peripheral focuses
Locus of work	Around individuals	In groups and projects
Focus of work	Tasks, objectives, performance	Customers, problems, issues
Skill obsolescence	Gradual	Rapid
Activity/feedback cycles	Primary and of an immediate nature	Lengthy from a business perspective
Performance measures	Task deliverables	Process effectiveness
	Little (as planned), but regular and dependable	Potentially great, but often erratic
Career formation	Internal to the organisation through training, development, rules and prescriptive career schemes	External to the organisation, through years of education and socialisation
Employee's loyalty	To organisation and his or her career systems	To professions, networks and peers
Impact on company success	Many small contributions that support the master plan	A few major contributions of strategic and long-term importance

Source: Despres and Hiltrop (1995: 13)

work processes and employee relations. As de Geus puts it: 'Within companies, our success depends on our skill with human beings: building and developing the consistent knowledge base of our enterprise' (de Geus 1997: 28).

In line with this realisation, the move to the knowledge era has brought about significant changes in organisational structures, strategies, culture and patterns of interaction. More flexible organisational forms designed to maximise knowledge development have replaced bureaucratic structures and relationships, and there has been a move from command and control to more participative or collaborative management, often through teams.

At the heart of these changed practices is the increased valuing of the organisation's intangible assets – its people – along with the recognition that the important factor is not so much the static 'stock' of knowledge which employees and others have, as the dynamic process through which that knowledge is enhanced and renewed. In fact, the rapid rate of change in most occupational areas, the explosion of knowledge in many fields, the increasingly widespread impact of technology, and the issue of both geographic and occupational mobility, mean that few if any can escape the need for continuing work-based learning. In her book entitled *In the Age of the Smart Machine*, Zuboff puts it this way:

> The [truly successful] organization is a learning institution, and one of its principal purposes is the expansion of knowledge...that comes to reside at the core of what it means to be productive. Learning is no longer a separate activity that occurs either before one enters the workplace or in remote classroom settings. Nor is it an activity preserved for a managerial group. The behaviors that define learning and the activities that define being productive are one and the same. Learning is not something that requires time out from productive activity; learning is the heart of productive activity. To put it simply, *learning is the new form of labor*.
>
> (Zuboff 1988: 395, emphasis added)

Because some of this learning is achieved through deliberate, planned programmes of staff training and development, in recent years there has been renewed and enhanced attention to issues of 'human resource development'. Furthermore, because much of it occurs through the self-directed or group-based learning activities of the employees or practitioners themselves, a good deal of scholarly attention has been devoted to studies of self-directed learning by one name or another (Candy 1991). However, rather than being consciously planned, it is now recognised that by far the greatest proportion – perhaps as much as 90 per cent – of organisational learning actually occurs incidentally or adventitiously, including through exposure to the opinions and practices of others also working in the same context. The consequence of this realisation, not unexpectedly, has been sharply increased attention to incidental workplace-based learning (see, for instance, Marsick and Watkins 1990).

Irrespective of the form of the learning, or of its location, there is now considerable evidence to suggest, as Barnett does in Chapter 3, that the effective practitioner today is one who actively seeks out opportunities for new learning and who is constantly scanning the environment in an attempt to predict what the major new directions will be. This type of learning is referred to as 'generative' or 'anticipatory', to distinguish it from the more common concept of 'reactive' or 'maintenance' learning (Botkin *et al.* 1979).

In view of this new-found (or, more correctly, rediscovered) emphasis on anticipatory learning and continuous improvement, the ability to learn is itself being regarded as a principal competency, one which distinguishes the successful from the less successful practitioner, and hence the successful from the less successful organisation. This ability to learn is made up of a complex of personal attributes and abilities, many of which may then be enhanced through educational interventions. Thus, the development of learning competence is one feature of the effective workplace (Cheren 1990), as is the opportunity (rather than simply the imperative) to go on learning.

In fact, the opportunity to learn has long been recognised as a major element in effective work practices. As long ago as 1969, the importance of the opportunity to learn and go on learning in the workplace was identified, in research carried out in workplaces in Scandinavia, the UK and Australia, as one of the six psychological requirements of productive activity (Emery and Thorsrud 1969). The other five psychological requirements for productive activity were: autonomy, or some areas of responsibility within jobs; an optimal level of variety in work; mutual respect and support; doing meaningful work; and working towards a desirable future.

In acknowledging the central place of learning in worklife, therefore, modern theorists are doing little more than affirming a long-standing belief in the dignity of work and the place of knowledge in it. At the same time, however, they are devoting much more careful attention to what is meant by both 'learning' and 'knowledge'. Accordingly, before considering the types of work-based learning and the sorts of managerial practices which facilitate such learning in the knowledge era, it is necessary to consider what the terms 'learning' and 'knowledge' mean.

Notions of learning and knowledge

Learning

Until relatively recently, psychological investigations of learning focused largely on the individual as the unit of analysis, rather than the individual within his or her social context. However, recent research into learning has placed greater emphasis on learning-in-context (Lave and Wenger 1991, Moll 1990, Sternberg 1994, Vygotsky 1978), as well as extending definitions of learning to include change at a group or even an organisational level.

Vygotsky, a Russian psychologist, was among the first to describe a dynamic process of learning within the individual's immediate context or environment. He postulated what he called a 'Zone of Proximal Development' (Vygotsky 1978: 86), where the context in which an individual lives is the arena which provides challenge and development. He claims that the individual's consciousness is the product of learning, as the previously internalised learning becomes a set of tools for new thinking and learning. Vygotsky's contribution is twofold: firstly in focusing on the learner's context as an important variable, and secondly in shifting the focus from what has been learned to the learning capability which has been produced through the learning process itself. He states that the immediate product of learning is the potential to learn more (Moll 1990).

Learning in context has become increasingly a matter for research and scholarly enquiry. In formal education settings, including the higher education sector, researchers have come to recognise the importance of the context in which the learning takes place. Two distinguished researchers into learning in universities – from Sweden and Australia – argue that it is not productive to try to derive general principles of learning independent of context and content of learning, because the way individuals learn is a function of the way they perceive the learning task and the learning environment (Marton and Ramsden 1988). 'Learning', they write, 'should be seen as a qualitative change in a person's way of seeing, experiencing, understanding, conceptualising something in the real world' (Marton and Ramsden 1988: 271).

Others have concentrated on learning in everyday settings such as the home, the marketplace or the racetrack. Within this tradition of studying 'situated learning' (Lave and Wenger 1991), the notion that learning is a process of participation in a community of practice has important implications for learning in the workplace.

For reasons already mentioned, organisational learning has emerged as a major preoccupation, both of organisational theorists and of learning researchers in the past five to ten years. It has been described in many shapes and forms (Cohen and Sproull 1996, Moingeon and Edmondson 1996, Starkey 1996), although as Marsick (1997) suggests, early writing on organisational learning was aimed primarily at describing the phenomenon. The result of this is that there was no common definition or integrated study from which to draw conclusions.

In the past decade, however, researchers and theorists have directed their attention to changes in organisations. Some have approached the issue from the point of view that knowledge is a major organisational asset, with a consequent focus on intellectual capital (Quinn 1992, Sveiby 1997, Stewart 1997), and leveraging intellectual capital (Quinn *et al.* 1996). Others, on the other hand, have been more interested in learning as a process; keeping up to date with changes in technology involved in both the production and the service sectors, or in markets and marketing processes.

In both cases, there has been a growing tendency to view organisations themselves as capable of learning, and to speak and write about them as more or less organic entities, comparable in some ways with the human beings who make them up. This is a theme to which we will return later.

Personal knowledge, social knowledge and knowledge management

At the same time that the boundaries and definitions of learning have been extended by researchers, the concept of 'knowledge', formerly thought of and treated by many as a relatively simple and straightforward concept, has also been refined. In fact, there are many different aspects or facets to knowledge. Some is declarative ('knowing what') and some is procedural ('knowing how'). Some knowledge is explicit and publicly shared, whereas some is tacit or implicit. Sternberg notes that the knowledge we need in order to adapt to an environment (such as the unspoken rules which govern any workplace) is not explicitly taught and indeed is often not even verbalised. As he puts it, knowledge here is not disembodied facts, or even information, rather it is the 'veil through which we see and interpret the world, and interact with the world' (Sternberg 1994: 223).

Knowledge has also been classified according to whether it is personal or social. Kolb (1984), for instance, describes personal knowledge as a combination of the direct apprehensions of experience and socially acquired comprehensions used to explain experience and guide actions. He describes social knowledge as the culturally transmitted network of words, symbols and images based solely on comprehension (Kolb 1984). Other researchers also differentiate between personal and social knowledge: 'Knowledge construction is...simultaneously personal and social as it entails the interdependence of the active person and the socially organized world' (Valsiner and Leung 1994: 215).

Clearly there is a resonance here with recent thinking about learning, and the notion of learning for competitive advantage has been an impetus to focus on the development and distribution of knowledge (de Geus 1988, 1997, Moingeon and Edmondson 1996, Stata 1996). A large proportion, although not all, of an organisation's knowledge resides in three human reservoirs, namely (1) the cognitive understandings, (2) the learned skills and (3) the deeply held beliefs of individuals. According to Quinn, 'Bringing the three together has been the success formula for most outstanding teachers, entrepreneurs and coaches whether in education, sports, the professions or general business' (Quinn 1992: 254).

Drawing together new insights into learning and more sophisticated concepts of knowledge has given rise to new ways of thinking about management; in particular, viewing it as a complex and subtle process of developing learning opportunities and facilitating flows of information. In their paper 'Building and diffusing learning capability', Ulrich *et al.* (1993) report on the experience of the chief executive officer of a global communications company who wanted both to extend learning across organisational boundaries and to develop his staff's learning capability – the ability to generate and generalise ideas with significance – for the organisation. The key principles used were: generating a large number of learning opportunities; generalising the learning beyond the individual; and building in the desire and opportunity to work and learn from others (Ulrich *et al.* 1993: 53).

Work-based learning

Over time, conceptions of work-based learning have changed and evolved, reflecting changes in the environment and changes within companies and other organisations. The roles of workplaces in learning can be summarised as follows:

- The workplace as a site for formally accredited learning.
- The workplace as a site for complex technical interactions and problem-solving.
- The workplace as a site for sharing and creating knowledge.
- The workplace as a part of the knowledge society.
- The workplace as an organic entity, capable of learning and adaptation in its own right (Candy and Matthews 1998).

Each of these conceptions is discussed more fully in Candy and Matthews (1998). The first two conceptions, although they recognise the importance of the workplace as a site for learning, deal with the notion of individual knowledge. The first builds on a view of knowledge primarily as an artefact to be conveyed to learners by 'experts'. The second recognises the nature of complex processes and the non-recurrent nature of some forms of work. In both of these conceptions, however, learning is viewed as an individual activity, and knowledge is seen as existing outside the learner. The last three conceptions are of particular interest in the knowledge era, and will accordingly be dealt with in greater depth here.

The workplace as a site for sharing and creating knowledge

As previously mentioned, it has been customary to think about knowledge essentially in the context of the individual knower, and, as Spender (1994) points out, a useful distinction can be made between individual knowledge which is consciously held, and that which is tacit or implicit. However, of particular relevance to the study of organisations is the fact that there is also social knowledge, which likewise might be either explicit or tacit. A simple taxonomy of knowledge appears in Table 4.2.

Table 4.2 Taxonomy of types of knowledge

	Social	Individual
Explicit	Scientific	Conscious
Taken for granted	Collective	Non-conscious

Source: Constructed from Spender (1994)

Much workplace knowledge is collective; that is, it is taken for granted, yet, at the same time, socially shared. Indeed, collective knowledge is embedded in social activity in ways that are relatively hidden from, or invisible to, the social actors involved (Spender 1994: 396). This 'invisibility' often makes it difficult for individuals to talk about and to share consciously what they know. Spender notes that dynamic concepts are not only held collectively but also generated and applied collectively within a pattern of social relationships (Spender 1994: 397).

These social relationships are sometimes referred to as 'communities of practice'. Orr's work on the knowledge required by photocopier repairers in practice, for instance, disproves any notion either that repairers operate as isolated individuals, or that they do so on the basis of the knowledge supplied through the company's 'directive documentation' (Brown and Duguid 1991). The process of generating, distributing and applying new knowledge turns out to be both social and dynamic.

In workplace settings, much of the process of generating, distributing and applying knowledge actually occurs in team settings, wherein a group creates knowledge for its members, for itself as a system, and for others, using processes of framing, reframing, experimenting, crossing boundaries and integrating perspectives. In their research, Kasl *et al.* undertook case studies of two companies in order to investigate 'how the team-learning processes and conditions change qualitatively to create distinct modes of learning' (Kasl *et al.* 1997: 244). From this study, they identified three conditions which influence teamwork.

The first condition is an *appreciation of teamwork*: openness to hearing and considering other's ideas. The second is *individual expression*, or the extent to which people have the opportunity to make an input into forming the team's mission and goals and influencing the operation on an ongoing basis as well as feeling comfortable in expressing their objections and misgivings in team meetings. The third condition is the *operating principle*, or the extent to which the team has organized itself for effective and efficient operation. This operating principle includes how well the team has established a set of commonly held beliefs, values, purposes and structures, and how effectively it has balanced working on tasks with building relationships within the group (Kasl *et al.* 1997: 230). Clearly, this sort of balance rarely if ever occurs spontaneously, and hence it is apparent that team learning, if it is to occur, must be carefully and deliberately managed.

When this principle of managing the creation and sharing of knowledge is scaled up to the level of an entire enterprise, it may be referred to as a 'knowledge-creating company'. Using concepts very similar to those identified by Spender (above), Nonaka and Takeuchi (1995) have expertly described how, in a knowledge-creating company, the processes move from the personal to the social, building on tacit as well as explicit knowledge in what they term a 'knowledge-creating spiral'.

Another name for the knowledge-creating company is the 'learning laboratory', which is defined as

> an organization dedicated to knowledge creation, collection and control. Contribution to knowledge is a key criterion for all activities. In a learning laboratory, tremendous amounts of knowledge and skill are embedded in physical equipment and processes and embodied in people.
>
> (Leonard-Barton 1992: 23)

An example is the Chaparral Steel mini-mill in Texas which, since its inception in 1975, has been setting records in steel production, and much of this productivity is attributed to its being managed as a learning laboratory. The four distinguishing characteristics critical to a learning laboratory are: (1) problem-solving (in current operations); (2) internal knowledge integration (across functions and projects); (3) innovation and experimentation (to build for the future); and (4) integration of external information flows (Leonard-Barton 1992: 24). Together these characteristics comprise the knowledge assets of the firm (Leonard-Barton 1992) which, as discussed earlier, must be consciously and continuously managed.

One organisation which, perhaps more than any other, had taken seriously the imperative to manage learning and to create a 'learning laboratory' environment was Rover, the largest car manufacturer in the UK. In 1990, Rover set up a parallel corporation – Rover Learning Business (RLB) – to establish corporation-wide learning as the cornerstone for the company's survival and its return to success (Marquardt 1996). At Rover, the concept that every employee was responsible for his or her immediate learning as well as for long-term employability within the firm had been intensively promoted. RLB had developed a 'Success through People' philosophy, which required Rover associates in their learning activities to seek to accomplish three goals: 'enhance job skills; acquire knowledge of new technologies; expand both personal and corporate vision thus creating the environment as well as opportunities for innovation' (Marquardt 1996: 205).

The commitment to learning extended well beyond corporate philosophies, however. Rover had also developed learning resources to help people learn. These learning resources included a pamphlet entitled *Learning as an Essential Way of Life*, which addressed the benefits of learning to the individual and the company, and strategies for learning; the annual *Learning Diary* with suggestions for organisational and individual learning strategies; and the *Personal Learning Pays* audiotape, which helped learners to identify the learning style best suited to them. The response to this initiative was outstanding, with over 6,000 employees (referred to as 'associates') taking advantage of this package in the first year (Marquardt 1996: 207–8).

The workplace as a part of the knowledge society

As an enterprise committed to learning, Rover was extraordinary by any standard. But the company went further, by extending the learning enterprise philosophy to its customers, dealers and suppliers, all of whom were able to participate in learning programmes with the company. Special programmes for Rover dealers, for example, included skill-improvement videos, industry-leading literature and videotapes covering sales, product knowledge and servicing techniques, and service correspondence courses attracting more than 500 participants each year (Marquardt 1996: 204).

Although very few organisations have gone as far as Rover, the recognition that organisations are not merely production functions, but instead are nodes in a complex network of economic relationships, dependencies and mutual obligations (Spender 1994) seems to have gained greater prominence and impetus in recent years. Increasingly, the workplace is viewed as essentially boundary-less, and learning occurs, at least in part, because of the organisation's fuzzy and porous perimeters. This perspective is well conveyed in the following quote from a paper by Wachtman and Lane entitled 'Principles of global competition':

> In an increasingly competitive global economy, business leaders need to think *and* behave differently. They have to manage a diverse work force often scattered across the entire expanse of the globe. Managing across all twenty-four time zones means there is literally no end to the workday. Vital information is constantly flowing into the organisation; it has to be digested, deployed and acted on almost immediately. Decisions have to be made quickly, taking into consideration a multi-

tude of factors: diverse markets, cultural differences, and geographical distances, changing economic and political circumstances, to name but a few. Managers in successful global organisations are able to master the inter-relationships between these factors. The competitive advantage of the next century will be determined less by the exploitation of key raw materials and the investment of capital, and more by the ability of managers to rapidly absorb and act upon this extensive array of information.

(1995: 1)

With information passing seamlessly across national, disciplinary and time boundaries, the organisation is inextricably woven into its environment by the impact of modern technology. In his paper on technology and innovation, Dodgson writes:

Analysis of the innovation process has...progressed from seeing innovation as an activity which occurs within the boundaries of individual firms to understanding that numerous organisations acting in concert contribute to the generation and success of new products, processes and services....Analyses of the contemporary innovation process show that the major transformations occurring *within* firms as they move towards becoming creative, process-based 'learning' firms need to be complemented with close *external* alliances with suppliers, customers and joint venture partners, and directed by increasingly effective and well articulated technology strategies.

(1996: 216–17)

Indeed, many people working within organisations and in the professions are in a situation analogous to that of academics, who have traditionally enjoyed dual relationships: on the one hand with the institution as an employer and a locus of their work, and, on the other hand, with a commitment to the discipline or community beyond the employing organisation or workplace (Harman 1989). Such a view of work means that practitioners who may be competitors in some contexts are collaborators in others, which is changing significantly the potential multilateral flow of information, and the learning opportunities and demands on them.

It is apparent that as the emphasis moves from a traditional focus on land, labour, capital and machinery to intellectual resources and knowledge as primary factors of production (Despres and Hiltrop 1995: 9), and as organisations engage more directly with their environments in focusing on the knowledge of their workers and their enterprises, just about every aspect of corporate life is affected. Some of the essential differences in design, structure and authority between conventional companies and so-called 'knowledge-intensive firms' are made explicit in Table 4.3.

Table 4.3 Changing from conventional to knowledge-intensive firms

	From	To
Environment	Variable but knowable	Complex and changing
Strategic corporate design	An assembly of individuals who execute instructions through structures and functions	Knowledge community that draws on the strength of the collective mind
Organisational structure	Hierarchical, mechanistic, atomic	Holographic, organic, overlapping
Boundaries	Fixed: the organisation has an identity relationship with itself	Fluid: organisation is networked with various others at different times, for different purposes
Managerial focus	Functions	Processes
Authority/power	Hierarchical position, command and control	Professional influence, communication, collegiality
Control of work	Vested in supervisory process	Vested in individuals
Control of work outcomes	Remains with central management	Negotiated between supervisors and groups of knowledge workers

Source: Despres and Hiltrop (1995: 21)

If, as Drucker (1992) argues, knowledge is the only meaningful resource, and as Savage (1996) puts it, 'knowledge is not a commodity but rather a capability to see new patterns among the old', all organisations will find in future that they have to embrace some of the characteristics outlined by Despres and Hiltrop.

In 1992, Drucker's classic book *Managing for the Future* appeared. In that book, he offered a number of views which have been vindicated by the passage of time: organisations are fast becoming knowledge communities, where knowledge is created, shared and stored; the practices of the past are no longer suitable for the commercialised, corporatised present and future, and organisations have to build continuous learning into the system; and organisations are having to take account of the new technology and changing conditions, and recognise their implications as a driver for learning (Drucker, 1992: 280).

Drucker (1992) did not stop at identifying these issues, however. He painted a picture of multidimensional workplaces – with novel networked, or even cellular, organisational structures and with fewer defined boundaries between workplaces and suppliers and distributors. His vision of the future has already arrived: Dr David Wyatt, Managing Director of Panbio, an innovative biotechnical company in Brisbane, stated recently that one of his customers is simultaneously a supplier and competitor. Here the old boundaries between customers and suppliers no longer exist, creating not only new visions of organisational relationships, but indeed of organisations themselves.

The workplace as an organic entity, capable of learning and adaptation

In each of the previous conceptions, learning – although increasingly complex and sophisticated – is viewed as an activity of people within organisations. However, some authors (including Choo 1995, de Geus 1997, Dixon 1992, Hedberg 1981, Huber 1996) have come to the view that organisations themselves – including teams or groups within the organisation – are capable of learning. To embrace such terminology is to some extent an affront to common sense; in the final analysis only *people* can actually learn. However, there is no denying that groups of people (including organisations) can change, indeed if they are to survive and flourish, they must change, and accordingly it is appropriate to use the term 'learning organisation' or 'learning enterprise' to refer to such entities. An excellent summary of the characteristics of the workplace as a learning entity is found in Ford's work:

> A learning enterprise is one where individuals, teams *and the enterprise itself* are continually learning....In a world characterised by multi-dimensional and often multi-directional changes, the long-term survival of enterprises is increasingly dependent on their ability to learn how to continually meet old and new customer demands; to learn how to effectively use new technologies; to learn to develop new work organisations; and to learn how to change their balance of skills and knowledge. An important conceptual shift is from the traditional and false dichotomy of education and training to the more integrating concept of continual skill formation. That is, from a front-end model of classroom instruction to a lifelong model of learning. At the enterprise, this means a more systematic interlacing of theory and practice, through the development of learning-based work organisations.
>
> (1991: 60–1, emphasis added)

Clearly, this 'systematic interlacing of theory and practice' is a delicate and complex process which, as Watkins and Marsick (1993: 44) put it, depends on 'the creation of a learning environment [which] goes far beyond the design of learning itself. It involves the design of work, work environments, technology, rewards systems, structures and policies'. Steps to create such a learning organisation include:

- creating continuous learning opportunities;

- promoting enquiry and dialogue;
- encouraging collaboration and team learning;
- establishing systems to capture and share learning;
- empowering people towards a collective vision; and
- connecting the organisation with its environment (Watkins and Marsick, 1993).

An interesting example of such an organisation is the Centre for Army Lessons Learned (CALL), whose goal is to generate learning in support of future strategic initiatives. The purpose of this process is 'to interpret historical data and present observation in order to create versatile, expert-enhanced learning tools for use in coping with and managing strategic events yet to happen' (Watts *et al.* 1997). This organisation identifies strategically beneficial events; gathers information through direct observation, interview and discussion of the findings by outside experts and local participants; and generates new knowledge from the consensus of understanding. This new knowledge then has implications for preparation, planning and performance of the staff in later circumstances. CALL exemplifies the four components of what de Geus calls a 'Living Company': adaptiveness to the outside world (learning), its character and identity (persona), its relationships with people and institutions (ecology), and the way it developed over time (evolution) (de Geus 1997). De Geus's much-quoted dictum that 'the ability to learn faster than your competitors may be the only sustainable advantage' (de Geus 1988) is now a battle cry, not only for companies, but even for armies in the knowledge era!

Principles for action

From this brief review, it is apparent that learning in the knowledge era offers new challenges and opportunities for managers. It is also apparent that conventional views of learning and of the nature of knowledge, especially those which consider learners as isolated individuals without a social context, are inconsistent with recent advances in the development and management of 'learning organisations'. Accordingly, the following insights and principles may be derived from this brief study of workplace-based learning.

Firstly, individuals must be thought of and treated as purposeful beings who flourish under the requirements for work, and workplaces must be developed which not only meet the requirements for productive activity, but build on the foundation of Emery and Thorsrud's prerequisites for working life. Environments must be created which develop opportunities for continuing learning, and which provide for autonomy, for optimum variety, for meaningful work, for mutual respect and support and for creating desirable futures (Emery and Thorsrud 1969). Expressed in a different way: 'every worker is a knowledge worker. Everyone benefits from being treated as an intelligent, knowledgeable human being' (Allee 1997: 216).

Secondly, it is important to see individuals within their social contexts. It is vital to recognise that individuals both shape and are shaped by their work (and other) contexts, and that they are capable of bringing to their workplaces a great deal of knowledge, experience and insights which help to accommodate to and capitalise on a rapidly changing world.

Thirdly, and related to the above point, it is important to acknowledge and accept that learning takes place in communities of practice, through sharing knowledge, and through conversations. Workplaces must be structured and managed in such a way that individuals and groups can act as research and development alliances, and can generate knowledge as well as apply it.

Fourthly, there is merit in viewing organisations almost as living entities, which are more than the sum of their parts, and in investigating the possibilities that this frame of reference offers. When organisations exist for long periods, they tend to transcend the individuals who make them up, and this longevity inevitably influences both the staff they employ and their environments. The approaches of these companies to ongoing learning and knowledge development are often exemplary (Collins and Porras 1994).

Fifthly, it is vital to see our knowledge society as needing to be grounded in democratic principles which value and invite the contributions and influence of all citizens for the common good (Saul 1997). Organisations are part of the mechanism through which society advances and reproduces itself.

These insights lead to a sixth and final point of view, which is the inextricable interconnectedness and reciprocal relationships between and among different levels of learning. It is increasingly apparent that individuals, teams, entire workplaces and even society at large are bound together by a common concern for and commitment to learning. Moreover, insights gained into learning within one context are increasingly relevant to other settings, either by direct transfer or by analogy. It is perhaps apposite to consider learning in organisations, as Leonard-Barton does, as a fractal:

> Just as the piece of fern mirrors the whole frond, as the twig mirrors the tree branch and the tree, so does the behavior of individuals and small groups reflect the attitudes toward knowledge-creating and controlling activities of the organization. In this sense, the individual is responsible for the organization and vice versa.
>
> (Leonard-Barton 1995: 261)

As the paradigm of the knowledge era becomes more dominant, it seems safe to predict that workplaces will become even more critical sites, sources and contexts for individual and collective learning and knowledge development. Indeed, as organisations face new situations, structures and challenges, it is evident that our constructs of learning and knowledge development will continue to take new forms. Moreover, and perhaps more importantly, it becomes evident that, because of the dynamic nature of organisations and their relationships with their employees, customers, suppliers and distributors, the task of managing learning for individuals, for teams and for entire organisations will blend imperceptibly until it becomes indistinguishable from the task of managing more generally.

References

Allee, V. (1997) *The Knowledge Evolution: Expanding Organisational Intelligence*, Boston: Butterworth–Heinemann.

Botkin, J., Elmandjra, M. and Malitza, M. (1979) *No Limits to Learning: Bridging the Human Gap*, Oxford: Pergamon.

Brown, J. S. and Duguid, P. (1991) 'Organizational learning and communities of practice: toward a unified view of working, learning and innovation', *Organization Science* 2(1): 40–57.

Candy, P. C. (1991) *Self-direction for Lifelong Learning: A Comprehensive Guide to Theory and Practice*, San Francisco: Jossey-Bass.

Candy, P. C. and Matthews, J. H. (1998) 'Fusing learning and work: changing conceptions of learning in the workplace', in D. Boud (ed.) *Current Issues and New Agendas in Workplace Learning*, Adelaide: National Centre for Vocational Educational Research.

Cannon, T. (1996) *Welcome to the Revolution: Managing Paradox in the 21st Century*, London: Pitman.

Cheren, M. E. (1990) 'Promoting active learning in the workplace', in R. M. Smith and Associates, *Learning to Learn Across the Life-span*, San Francisco: Jossey-Bass.

Choo, C. W. (1995) *Information Management for the Intelligent Organization: The Art of Scanning the Environment*, Medford, NJ: Information Today for the American Society for Information Science.

Cohen, M. D. and Sproull, L. S. (eds) (1996) *Organisational Learning*, London: Sage.

Collins, J. C. and Porras, J. I. (1994) *Built to Last: Successful Habits of Visionary Companies*, New York: Harper Collins.

de Geus, A. (1988) 'Planning as learning', *Harvard Business Review* 66(2): 70–4.

de Geus, A. (1997) *The Living Company: Growth, Learning and Longevity in Business*, London: Nicholas Brealey.

Despres, C. and Hiltrop, J. M. (1995) 'Human resource management in the knowledge age: current practice and perspectives on the future', *Employee Relations* 17(1): 9–23.

Dixon, N. M. (1992) 'Organisational learning: a review of the literature with implications for HRD professional', *Human Resource Development Quarterly* 3(1): 29–49.

Dodgson, M. (1996) 'Technology and innovation: strategy, learning and trust', in P. J. Sheehan, B. S. Grewal and M. Kumnick (eds) *Dialogues on Australia's Future:*

In honour of the late Professor Ronald Henderson, Melbourne: Centre for Strategic Economic Studies, Victoria University.

Drucker, P .F. (1992) *Managing for the Future*, Oxford: Butterworth–Heinemann.

Drucker, P. F. (1993) *Post-capitalist Society*, London: Butterworth–Heinemann.

Emery, F. E. and Thorsrud, E. (1969) *Form and Content in Industrial Democracy*, London: Tavistock.

Ford, G. W. (1991) 'The learning enterprise: integrating total quality management and workplace reform and renewal', *Proceedings of the Total Quality Management Institute Second National Conference, 21–23 August 1991*, World Congress Centre, Melbourne, 59–63.

Harman, K. M. (1989) 'Professional loyalties of university academics: four ideal types', *Australian Educational Researcher* 16(2): 1–11.

Hedberg, B. (1981) 'How organisations learn and unlearn', in P. C. Nystrom and W. H. Starbuck (eds) *Handbook of Organisational Design. Vol. 1: Adapting Organisations to their Environments*, Oxford: Oxford University Press.

Huber, G. P. (1996) 'Organisational learning: a guide for executives in technology-critical organisations', *International Journal of Technology Management, Special Issue on Unlearning and Learning for Technological Innovation* 11(7/8): 821–32.

Kasl, E., Marsick, V. J. and Dechant, K. (1997) 'Teams as learners: a research-based model of team learning', *Journal of Applied Behavioural Science* 33(2): 227–46.

Kolb, D. A. (1984) *Experiential Learning: Experience as the Source of Learning and Development*, Englewood Cliffs, NJ: Prentice Hall.

Lave, J. and Wenger, E. (1991) *Situated Learning: Legitimate Peripheral Participation*, Cambridge: Cambridge University Press.

Leonard-Barton, D. (1992) 'The factory as a learning laboratory', *Sloan Management Review* Fall: 23–38.

Leonard-Barton, D. (1995) *Wellsprings of Knowledge: Building and Sustaining the Sources of Innovation*, Cambridge, MA: Harvard Business School.

Marquardt, M. J. (1996) *Building the Learning Organisation: A Systems Approach to Quantum Improvement and Global Success*, New York: McGraw-Hill with the American Society for Training and Development.

Marsick, V. J. (1997) 'Current thinking on the learning organization', *Keynote Address. 'Good Thinking, Good Practice: Research Perspectives on Learning and Work': Fifth Annual International Conference on Post-Compulsory Education and Training*, Centre for Learning and Work Research, Griffith University, Australia.

Marsick, V. J. and Watkins, K. (1990) *Informal and Incidental Learning in the Workplace*, New York: Routledge.

Marton, F. and Ramsden, P. (1988) 'What does it take to improve learning?', in P. Ramsden (ed.) *Improving Learning: New Perspectives*, London: Kogan Page.

Moingeon, B. and Edmondson, A. (eds) (1996) *Organisational Learning and Competitive Advantage*, London: Sage.

Moll, L. C. (ed.) (1990) *Vygotsky and Education: Instructional Implications and Applications of Sociohistorical Psychology*, New York: Cambridge University Press.

Nonaka, I. and Takeuchi, H. (1995) *The Knowledge-Creating Company: How Japanese Companies Create the Dynamic of Innovation*, New York: Oxford University Press.

Quinn, J. B. (1992) *Intelligent Enterprise*, New York: Free Press.

Quinn, J. B., Anderson, P. and Finkelstein, S. (1996) 'Leveraging intellect', *Academy of Management Executive* 10(3): 7–27.

Saul, J. R. (1997) *The Unconscious Civilisation*, Melbourne: Penguin.

Savage, C. M. (1996) *Fifth Generation Management: Co-creating through Virtual Enterprising, Dynamic Teaming and Knowledge Networking*, rev. edn, Newton, MA: Butterworth–Heinemann.

Spender, J.-C. (1994) 'Knowing, managing, learning: a dynamic managerial epistemology', *Management Learning* 25(3): 387–412.

Starkey, K. (ed.) (1996) *How Organisations Learn*, London: International Thomson Business Press.

Stata, R. (1996) 'Organisational learning: the key to management innovation', in K. Starkey (ed.) *How Organisations Learn*, London: International Thomson Business Press.

Sternberg, R. J. (1994) 'PRSVL: an integrative framework for understanding mind in context', in R. J. Sternberg and R. K. Wagner (eds) *Mind in Context: Interactionist perspectives on human intelligence*, Cambridge: Cambridge University Press, 218–32.

Stewart, T. A. (1997) *The New Intellectual Capital: The New Wealth of Organizations*, London: Nicholas Brealey.

Sveiby, K.-E. (1997) *The New Organisational Wealth: Managing and Measuring Organisational Wealth*, San Francisco: Berrett-Koehler.

Ulrich, D., Jick, T. and von Glinow, M. A. (1993) 'High-impact learning: building and diffusing learning capability', *Organizational Dynamics* 22(2): 52–66.

Valsiner, J. and Leung, M. (1994) 'From intelligence to knowledge construction: a sociogenetic process approach', in R. J. Sternberg and R. K. Wagner (eds) *Mind in Context: Interactionist Perspectives on Human Intelligence*, Cambridge: Cambridge University Press, 202–17.

Vygotsky, L. S. (1978) *Mind in Society: The Development of Higher Psychological Processes*, Cambridge, MA: Harvard University Press.

Wachtman, E. L. and Lane, L. (1995) 'Principles of global competition', Unpublished paper, LLA Pacific Limited, Hong Kong.

Watkins, K. E. and Marsick, V. J. (1993) *Sculpting the Learning Organisation: Lessons in the Art and Science of Systemic Change*, San Francisco: Jossey-Bass.

Watts, S. A., Thomas, J. B. and Henderson, J. C. (1997) 'Understanding "Strategic learning": linking organisational learning, sensemaking and knowledge management', Paper presented at the Conference of the Academy of Management, Boston, 10–14 August.

Zuboff, S. (1988) *In the Age of the Smart Machine*, New York: Basic Books.

5 Finding a good theory of workplace learning

Paul Hager

In recent years workplace learning has gone from being largely unnoticed to attracting unprecedented interest. One aspect of this expanded attention is a concern to ensure that formal workplace training is effective. However, the growing interest in workplace learning also includes a focus on the role and significance of the informal learning that results from actual work experience. This new interest in workplace learning has led to a search for suitable theories that can deepen our understanding of this phenomenon. The belief is that better description and explanation of workplace learning will offer guidance on how to do it well.

However, one difficulty is the sheer number of available theories that are arguably relevant to workplace learning. This situation of abundance is due to workplace learning being a typical interdisciplinary topic in that it can be viewed, and has been viewed, from the perspective of a variety of disciplines and fields, such as sociology, cognitive psychology, policy studies, management theory, adult education, economics, learning theory and industrial psychology. As well, there are various literatures which can be seen as relevant to an understanding of workplace learning, even though their main focus is somewhat different. These include research on the nature of expertise, on professional practice and on situated learning. Finally there is an abundant literature that is concerned with the broader sociopolitical aspects of the workplace. Hence, research on workplace learning represents a convergence of an unusually diverse range of literatures.

One response readers might make to this bewildering array of theories is to give up on theory as being too abstract and elusive, and simply get on with their immediate concerns. However, apart from the fact that there is nothing so practical as a good theory, such readers cannot entirely opt out of theory since it will be natural for them to try to explain and understand their own experiences of workplace learning. They will do this if only to avoid repeating in future their obvious failures and to be able to consolidate those aspects of their practice that seem to be successful. Basic sorts of questions that many readers inevitably will want to answer, which will involve some recourse to theory, include:

- Why, in this instance, did this training session not work, whereas previously its success has been reliable?
- How can we best help staff to reflect more on their performance in non-routine situations?
- What would be a simpler way to achieve this outcome?
- Who should be trained? Why, when and where?

In asking and seeking answers to questions like these, readers will draw inevitably on theory at some level, even if it is only their own partial and informal theories that they have developed, perhaps unconsciously, from their own practice. If so, the issue becomes whether such informal theories can become even more useful by some conscious refinement and extension.

The central questions which this chapter aims to address are:

- What are the features of a useful theory of workplace learning?
- What different aspects of workplace learning do the available theories seek to explain?
- What are the scope and limits of the various kinds of theories about workplace learning?
- What different assumptions are made by different theories about the nature of workplace learning?

To answer these questions this chapter will:

- Say something about what theories do.
- Explain why the topics of training and learning in general are ones which attract a diverse and bewildering range of theories, a situation that represents both strengths and weaknesses.
- Offer guidance on how to select from the range of available theories.

What theories do

A good starting point for considering the nature of theories is Foley's account in a popular introductory book on adult education. According to Foley (1995: 8), a theory is a 'supposition explaining something, based on evidence'. Foley contrasts a theory with a concept as a 'general notion' or a 'class of objects'. He adds that to 'theorise is to attempt to make connections between variables, to explain outcomes and to predict what will happen if particular courses of action are taken in the future' (Foley 1995: 7). Foley then goes on to distinguish formal and informal theory drawing on the work of Usher (1987, 1989a) and Usher and Bryant (1989). Formal theory is 'organised (and) codified bodies of knowledge – embodied in disciplines and expressed in academic discourse', whereas informal theory is 'the understanding that emerges from and guides practice' (Foley 1995:

9). The latter includes contextual and situational understanding that is largely a product of workplace experience and learning. Both of these kinds of theories are the concern of this chapter.

As Foley's comments suggest, theories should not be thought of as rules that direct our practice. Rather, theories are analytical tools which enable us to reflect on and understand aspects of our experience and thereby to improve our practice. What sorts of understandings are provided by theories? They enable us to explain events that have occurred in our practice and they enable us to predict likely outcomes of other events that we or others might put into place. Because particular theories are applicable to all events that have the relevant features, they bring an element of generality or system to our understanding. Thus we can say that a theory is an attempt to consolidate in a systematic way our knowledge of some particular aspects of our experience. The worth of the understanding that is thereby achieved is judged by our enhanced capacity to explain selected features of our experience and/or to predict successfully trends in future experiences.

There is a further feature of theories that is important for work discussed later in this chapter. This is that theories typically employ concepts different from ones that refer to what is more or less directly observed. According to Miller (quoted in Phillips 1992: 136): 'A theory is whatever explains empirical facts (often, regularities or patterns) of relatively observational kinds, through the description of less directly observable phenomena'. For example, Argyris and Schön (1974, 1978) propose the phenomenon of double-loop learning to explain certain changes in the beliefs, values and assumptions of workers who have overcome significant non-routine challenges during the course of their work. The notion of double-loop learning (something less directly observable) is used to explain the changes in the beliefs, values and assumptions of workers (these changes being relatively more available to observation).

Making sense of the proliferation of theories relevant to workplace learning

Naturally, readers will want some means to select from the proliferation of theories those ones that offer to meet their needs to understand, explain and predict. Such guidance is a main aim of this chapter. However, I want to suggest that the great diversity of theories relevant to understanding workplace learning is both to be expected and provides some definite advantages. The basis of this theoretical pluralism is argued to be threefold as follows:

1   Different theories often have very different scope, that is they are addressing very different kinds of questions.
2   Even where different theories have the same scope, it is a common situation that there is little agreement on which is the best theory. This

situation of different, equally adequate theories being available is typical of interdisciplinary fields such as management or nursing.

3　The history of thought suggests that theoretical pluralism is a strength rather than a limitation. Not only does pluralism encourage fresh approaches to understanding perennial issues, but also it reminds us that the likely fate of our current favoured theory is to be displaced sooner rather than later by a successor theory.

Each of these will be discussed now in turn. The first in some detail, as it is the most important, the others somewhat more briefly. In the process a picture will steadily emerge as to why the current plurality of theorising about workplace learning is actually a healthy situation.

Different theories have very different scope

An important aspect of theories is that they differ in scope: that is, theories can be thought of as coming in all different sizes that often address very different aspects of the same broad topic. The largest theories cover entire subjects or disciplines, for example the theory of evolution. Somewhat less large theories cover parts of subjects or disciplines, for example the theory of relativity in physics. Smaller-sized theories might focus on a few key problems in a field, for example the nature of workplace learning, or even on one single important idea, for example Schön's theory of reflection-in-action. Thus, the size of the field or topic covered is one important aspect of the scope of a theory. But it is also typical of theories that they deal with only selected aspects of the topic that they purport to cover. This is important in the case of workplace learning, where we will find that different writers are interested in quite different aspects of the topic, thereby leading them to support theories with quite different foci. This situation is not unusual since each different theory takes certain problems to be central and consigns others to secondary status. Thus the main focus of one theory of workplace learning will be of marginal concern for another. Though theories aim to be comprehensive about their main focus, they are inevitably selective about what they cover. So this provides another way in which theories can differ in scope. If there is controversy about what are the central issues in a topic, as is the case for workplace learning, then rival and opposing theories are only to be expected, since they will be seeking answers to different questions. Thus there will be alternative ways of theorising about the one topic which have little or nothing in common with each another.

There is a further reason why there might be a number of different theories each with some claim to cover the same topic. Theories are sometimes proposed as hypotheses before their grounds are well established or their consequences can be tested. They are, simply, tentative theories that might work. The relatively new field of workplace learning is one where such a situation is not unlikely. Given these considerations it will be no surprise to find that workplace learning is a field that features alternative theories offering to explain various topics, with no strong grounds available to tell us that any one of these theories is the correct one for doing so.

A very helpful way to illustrate the variety of scope of different theories is to consider a model due to Frankena (1970). This model, which Frankena originally developed as a way of analysing any philosophy of education, is, in fact, equally applicable to theories about any broad area of education and training, such as workplace learning. This model serves to identify the different types of principles and assumptions contained in such theories. Frankena's model also has some similarities to Foley's 'framework for analysing adult education and training' (Foley 1995: 8–9). My preference for the former in this instance is due to its greater capacity to elucidate the nature of theories.

The following aims to summarise and make sense of the main points of Frankena's model. This model as applied to the analysis of any broad theory is based on the idea that such a theory would typically include up to five different kinds of statements. These statements represent claims that the theory being examined makes about different aspects of the area being theorised. That there are five kinds of statement stems partly from the different natures of some of the statements and partly from the fact that some kinds of statement serve as premises for others, that is they are presupposed by others. Hence the five kinds of statement can be arranged in levels, with the various levels also having different degrees of generality or abstraction from the level of practice. As represented in Figure 5.1, Frankena assigns the five different kinds of statements to 'boxes' as follows: A, basic values or aims; B, basic factual or theoretical premises; C, knowledge, skills and attitudes to be fostered; D, methodological premises; and E, recommendations for practice. The differences between the boxes and levels will be clarified in the following discussion.

So the model distinguishes between five different kinds of statements that it is claimed might appear in a prescriptive theory about workplace learning; that is, one which describes how workplace learning should be carried out. Three of these kinds of statements are themselves prescriptive, namely those about fundamental values or aims for workplace learning (box A), those about the knowledge, skills and attitudes that ought to fostered in workplace learning (box C), and those about the practical methods and procedures that ought to followed to achieve workplace learning (box E). As well there are factual and/or theoretical statements either about what knowledge, skills and attitudes are conducive to achieving the fundamental values or aims of workplace learning (box B), or about methods that are useful/effective for the acquisition of particular knowledge, skills and attitudes (box D). Frankena argues that some such factual and/or theoretical statements, including possibly hypotheses that explain factual statements, psychological theories,

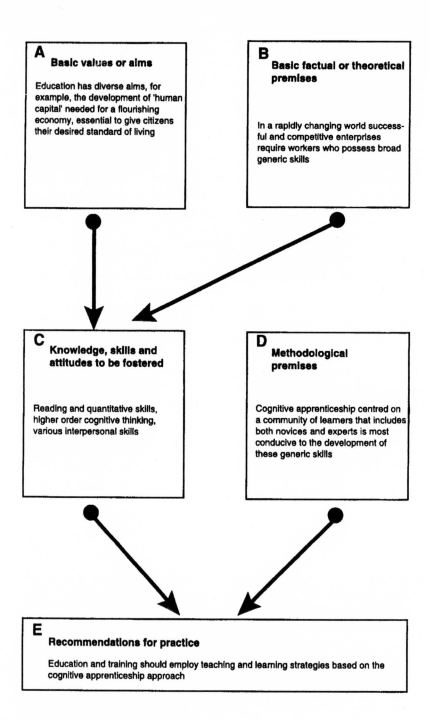

A Basic values or aims

Education has diverse aims, for example, the development of 'human capital' needed for a flourishing economy, essential to give citizens their desired standard of living

B Basic factual or theoretical premises

In a rapidly changing world successful and competitive enterprises require workers who possess broad generic skills

C Knowledge, skills and attitudes to be fostered

Reading and quantitative skills, higher order cognitive thinking, various interpersonal skills

D Methodological premises

Cognitive apprenticeship centred on a community of learners that includes both novices and experts is most conducive to the development of these generic skills

E Recommendations for practice

Education and training should employ teaching and learning strategies based on the cognitive apprenticeship approach

Figure 5.1 Analysis of Berryman's theory

experimental findings, predictions and the like, are necessary for a complete prescriptive theory. In addition, Frankena allows that any of the boxes, where appropriate, will include some bits of analysis, for example definitions of concepts etc.

The second noteworthy feature of Frankena's model is that it comprises two parts: arguments with A and B as premises for C as conclusion (ABC pattern), and arguments with C and D as premises for E as conclusion (CDE pattern). Of these two parts, Frankena (1970: 21) points out that the ABC pattern is the more general or theoretical, while the CDE pattern is the more practical. He suggests that his model distinguishes three kinds of theories: (1) one that is complete in that it incorporates both the ABC and CDE patterns; (2) one that is more theoretical (the ABC pattern), which leaves the details of implementation to practitioners; and (3) one that is more practical (the CDE pattern), whose author might take the list of knowledge, skills and attitudes from some more theoretical work, or eclectically derive them from a range of sources, or simply accept what is valued by industry, the state, society, etc. Sometimes, arguments, which initially appear to be of the CDE pattern, will turn out to include statements from boxes A and B as assumed premises. Figure 5.1 shows my use of the model to analyse the major features of Berryman's (1993) generic skills version of 'human capital theory'. Berryman's theory is 'complete' in the sense that it encompasses both parts of the Frankena model.

The Frankena model shows clearly that theories of different kinds and scope are employed in theorising. While all boxes in the model might incorporate theoretical material, boxes A, B and D have theories as their main occupants with these theories being of different kinds and levels in each case. Box A is characterised by theories about fundamental values for workplace learning. In previous work (Hager 1998) five major accounts of workplace learning were analysed in terms of the Frankena model. The theories analysed were:

1   Experience-based learning.
2   Dewey's theory of learning.
3   Argyris and Schön's work on professional practice.
4   Marsick and Watkins' theory of informal and incidental learning.
5   The 'generic skills and economics' perspective of Carnevale and Berryman.

This analysis identified two main types of theories about the values that should underpin workplace learning. They were:

1   Theories that refer to the overall flourishing of human beings, for example 'personal growth and development is an ultimate good'.
2   Theories that refer to the needs of the economy, for example 'the development of human capital is needed for a flourishing economy'.

These reflect a basic dilemma. Is learning for work or work for learning? What should be the central focus? This illustrates the point made earlier that the field of workplace learning is one in which different theories take certain issues to be central and consign others to secondary status.

In the Frankena model the contents of box B can range from relatively uncontroversial factual claims (e.g. that post-industrial society is marked by an historically unprecedented rate of change) to highly theoretical general theories (e.g. Foucault's power–knowledge theory). The analysis of five major accounts of workplace learning referred to above (Hager 1998) found that two main theoretical statements occurred here:

1   Learning from experience is fundamental to individual personal growth and development.
2   In a rapidly changing world successful and competitive enterprises require workers who have certain broad generic skills.

While these two basic theoretical statements can be seen as being in conflict, I have argued elsewhere (Hager 1998) that they can be viewed as supporting and reinforcing one another.

Box D of the Frankena model contains theories that are much closer to practice, including the informal theory that 'emerges from and guides practice'. Not surprisingly, much less commonality was found here in the accounts of workplace learning that were analysed. The methods proposed as useful/effective for workplace learning covered much of the range of strategies found in the education and training literature; however, a common theme was that they were not the strategies that drive the learning in traditional classrooms. Rather, they were strategies that focus on kinds of learning that are often not given any formal credit, such as prior experiential learning. Also common to these strategies was an emphasis on active approaches to learning, approaches centred on learners rather than on teachers. Thus workplace learning was thought of as very different from formal classroom learning as it has traditionally operated.

Thus the Frankena model applied to accounts of workplace learning shows clearly that various theories of different kinds, level and scope are typically employed. However, theorising about workplace learning is even more complex in that, as well as the theories of different kinds, level and scope already identified, it involves still other kinds of theories that are not captured by the Frankena model. An example is provided by Edwards and Usher (1994). The main focus of their paper is competency-based training, a topic of some importance to workplace learning. However, as Edwards and Usher themselves stress, their paper is not about the workings of competency-based training, an approach which would lend itself to analysis in terms of the Frankena model. Rather, they are interested in 'the work' that a theory (or ideology) of competency-based training 'does' (Edwards and Usher 1994: 1). That is, they are offering a theory about the function of a particular theory. In this sense, their proposed theory is a meta-theory – a theory about a theory. The scope of this theory is therefore very different from others considered so far in this chapter.

Overall then, the claim that theories about workplace learning differ both in size and scope has been well illustrated by reference to the Frankena model. Such theories range from those (both formal and informal) that focus relatively directly on practice (e.g. box D of the Frankena model) to those that propose fundamental values for workplace learning (box A of the Frankena model) and those that offer very general theories that are relevant to learning and its requirements (box B of the Frankena model). As well there are meta-theories, such as the Edwards and Usher one, which have a very different focus, namely the function of theories of workplace learning.

The availability of alternative theories is a feature of an interdisciplinary field

One reason why there is usually no general accord about which theories to support is that education, which includes adult and vocational education and training, is a field rather than a discipline. This is usually taken to mean that educational theorising is an interdisciplinary endeavour that brings together thought from disciplines such as psychology, philosophy, sociology and history. The diversity of perspectives and frameworks within each of these disciplines is enough in itself to suggest that theorising about workplace learning will feature many diverse and mutually incompatible theories. The Frankena model also shows this. In the model there is room for differences of opinion about what goes in box A, in box B and in box D. This provides for much diversity, although, of course, the contents of the respective boxes for any given theory of workplace learning have to form an overall coherent account.

The history of thought supports theoretical pluralism

The history of thought, as well as of the social sciences and humanities generally, points very clearly to the failure of past 'grand theories' to provide satisfactory understandings for very long. This history is littered with once popular 'monotheories' that have since lost their appeal. By 'monotheories' I mean theories that sought to reduce the explanation of social phenomena, including workplace learning and training, to a single principle or factor. Examples of monotheories are scientism, Marxism, Freudianism, behaviourism. Despite the failure of past monotheories, new ones continue to appear. Foucault's power–knowledge is a recent candidate. Likewise, with the decline of the fortunes of the scientific approach in the late twentieth century, scientism seems to have been replaced by 'discursivism' as its mirror image. Whereas scientism is the extreme view that all genuine understanding is scientific, discursivism is the equally disputable view that language is the key to all understanding. Warnings about human susceptibility to the attractions of monotheories have been around for a long time:

> It is the nature of an hypothesis, when once ... conceived ... that it assimilates every thing to itself as proper nourishment, and, from the first moment of your begetting it, it generally grows the stronger by every thing you see, hear, read, or understand.
>
> (Laurence Sterne, *Tristram Shandy*, 1760)

Despite this, monotheories retain their seductive appeal. It needs to be stressed that I am not claiming that past and present monotheories have *no* explanatory value. My point is simply that history teaches us that we need to be wary of their claims to have *all* of the important answers. Pluralism with respect to theorising is important, because if everyone subscribes to the current fashionable monotheories, the effect is actually to close off enquiry whilst at the same time giving the impression that critical investigation is being encouraged. The Frankena model serves to point out the limitations of monotheories. Typically, when such theories figure in an account of some aspect of education or training, they appear in box B of the model. Notoriously, even if we accept their recommendations in box C, they are very vague about what should go into boxes D and E. For example, Marxist theories of education were very popular during the 1970s, but they achieved surprisingly little consensus about their implications for actual teaching practice. Thus the Frankena model highlights the importance of pluralism in theorising. Some further difficulties with monotheories will be discussed in the final part of this chapter.

A final point in favour of pluralism with respect to theorising about workplace learning is that it encourages the creation of new views and approaches. An acceptance that none of the current or future theories is likely, by itself, to provide a complete understanding of workplace learning is itself a stimulant to further creativity in theory development. Overall, it can be concluded with confidence that the situation in which there is no general accord about theories of workplace learning is likely to persist.

Judging the worth of theories

The complex variety of theories of workplace learning means inevitably that people will be comparing the merits of different theories and judging which ones they prefer to work with. Far from being an objective exercise, this process will reflect the particular current needs and interests of the people making the comparisons and judgements. Main points about theories from the earlier discussion that are important for judging the worth of particular theories include the following:

- Theories provide understanding via explanation and/or prediction.
- Theories are very diverse in terms of their scope.
- Alternative theories are common, though they often focus on different aspects of the problem, thereby reflecting their very different basic presuppositions.

Each of these points will be discussed further in turn as they relate to judging the worth of theories.

The degree of understanding offered by a theory

Given the complexity of theories of workplace learning and the way that many of them operate at different levels, it is only to be expected that different people will be looking for different kinds of understanding. For example, a trainer or HRD manager looking for better understanding of the training activities in their workplace will very likely prefer a theory that impacts more directly on their practice. So they will probably prefer theories that pay major attention to the more practical levels of the Frankena model, such as those of Marsick and Watkins (1990) or Berryman (1993), rather than theories whose focus is less directly on actual practice, such as that of Edwards and Usher (1994) which, as pointed out earlier, is a theory about the function of a particular theory, namely competency-based training. On the other hand, a trainer or HRD manager who is fed up with increasing work demands, and is starting to question the value of what they do, will likely find Edwards and Usher much more suggestive than Marsick and Watkins or Berryman.

From this it would be easy to conclude that a theory/practice divide is inevitable. However, while the immediate focus of people such as trainers and HRD managers will be boxes C, D and E of the Frankena model, they will also want boxes A and B to contain theories and principles that provide a sound and coherent rationale for the workplace learning that takes place in their organisations. Current workplace learning theories that are complete, in the sense that they cover all of the boxes of the Frankena model, tend to propose some variant of human capital theory (i.e. the view that the proper development of an organisation's human resources is the key to economic success) in box A, for example those of Marsick and Watkins, and Berryman (see Hager (1998) for details). On the other hand, theories that reject human capital theory as an underpinning for workplace learning tend to be short on details relating to the more practical aspects (boxes C, D and E of the Frankena model). Garrick and Solomon (1997: 79) refer to this as a 'lack' that needs urgent attention and offer some suggestions on what is needed. Until critics of human capital theory can come up with viable practical alternatives, it seems likely that many will perceive their work as 'good in theory only but not in practice'.

This section can be summarised as being about the *usefulness* of theories of workplace learning. Because people are seeking to use theories in a variety of ways, they look for different strengths in the theories that they select.

The scope of the theory

An important question in judging the worth of a theory is 'what can it cover?' The traditional view is that the more a theory can explain the more powerful it is. Hence, proponents are usually keen to claim maximum scope of explanation for their favoured theories. Caution in accepting such claims is advisable as the following discussion will show.

For a start, the Frankena model shows vividly some important points about the notion of scope. Firstly, it makes it clear why no one theory will provide an adequate account of workplace learning. As the structure of the model suggests, a *set* of theories of very different kinds, levels and scope, that also fit together in the required way, is a prerequisite for any satisfactory 'complete theory' of workplace learning. As discussed earlier, the set of theories that constitute the model include theories that propose fundamental values for workplace learning, general theories that are relevant to learning and its requirements, and theories that focus relatively directly on practice. So the scope of a 'complete theory' of workplace learning would be the product of the satisfactory integration of its diverse sub-theories.

Secondly, the model draws our attention to the different kinds, levels and scope of the sub-theories that comprise it. The most limited in scope tend to be the theories at the lower levels of the model that focus relatively directly on practice. They seek to provide understanding of a rather limited domain of phenomena and are judged in terms of their observed capacity to explain and predict. An experiential rule of thumb is that as the domain covered by theories in the social sciences expands, their explanatory and predictive power correspondingly tends to decline. This is likely to be the case for the broader theories at the higher levels of the model. These are typically theories that propose fundamental values for workplace learning, or general theories that are relevant to learning and its requirements. The restricted explanatory and predictive power of such theories is, of course, a main reason why theoretical pluralism flourishes in much social science thought.

This restricted explanatory and predictive power of broader social science theories is well illustrated by monotheories with their large reliance on single-factor explanation, for example the unconscious mind, inferiority feelings, economic relations. As noted already, history points to the limited success of monotheories. Popper (1963) offered a famous account of the limitations of monotheories in the social sciences. He pointed out that theories such as those of Freud, Adler and Marx had been developed by their adherents in such a way that they were no longer testable. That is, the theories had been elaborated in such a way that no actual state of affairs in the world could be inconsistent with them. Thus, they had been turned into '*post hoc*' theories, theories that can 'explain' anything that happens once it has happened. Popper argued that being consistent with whatever happens is not a virtue of a theory but a vice. He emphasised that only theories that make testable, specific predictions and are then modified, on the basis of how they fare in the testing, are worthy of support. He summed up his objection to theories that are made immune to refutation as 'a theory that explains everything explains nothing'. If Popper is right about this, then theories that at first sight seem to have very wide scope actually have none. The question needs to be asked whether Popper's criticisms are applicable to more recently fashionable theories that involve single-factor explanatory devices, such as human capital, power–knowledge and discourse. Certainly, from the way that some enthusiasts use these concepts in their writings, they appear to underpin theories that are compatible with everything. If so, this would tell against the worth of such a theory.

Alternative theories commonly focus on different aspects of a topic, thereby reflecting their very different basic presuppositions

In examining what aspects of workplace learning a theory signals as important and what aspects it neglects, we start to become aware of the basic assumptions of the theory. Disagreement with a theory's presuppositions provides one of the strongest grounds for questioning its worth. I will, by way of example, provide a brief discussion of the assumptions that underpin the two main views of the nature of experience that I have noted in the literature relating to workplace learning. In the process it will become clear which of these views I find most plausible.

The first theory of experience that I will consider is inspired by postmodernism and is well presented in various writings by Usher and colleagues (e.g. Usher 1989b, 1992, Usher *et al.* 1997). Broadly this theory argues that since experience can only be stated in discourse, therefore experience is inherently discursive.

As Usher puts it:

> language enters the picture. As a signifying system independent of individuals it provides meanings through which experience is interpreted. Language regulates and forms experience rather than simply being a device for naming it which is how humanistic discourse sees it.
>
> (Usher 1992: 208)

Language is neither a mirror of reality nor merely a tool for understanding it but constitutes the experience of reality.

(Usher 1989b: 29)

However, while this kind of view is very fashionable at present, it needs
further elaboration since in the form stated above it is highly ambiguous in
that it can be any of the following three very different positions:

1   All is language (naïve discursivism).
2   All that we can know or experience is language.
3   All that we can know or experience is *via* language, that is we can
     never be sure of the accuracy of our knowledge and experience of the
     world which is inevitably through the intermediary of language.

While some recent writers appear to be proponents of one or other of the
first two of the above options, a careful reading of Usher's work shows
him to be committed to the third option. It follows from this option that
workplace learning is an essentially discursive activity.

However, there is available a second theory of experience which rejects
some of the assumptions of the postmodernist theory. In attacking the work
of Rorty, who subscribes to the postmodernist theory just outlined, Thayer-
Bacon (1997) points to the different starting point of this second theory:

If Rorty is correct, this means that experience is not directly accessible
to us, our language acts as a filter, sifting and sorting through our
experiences and helping us to name and give meaning to what we
experience. Those experiences we do not have a language for, fall
through our filter and are lost as experiences.

(p. 243)

But, responds Thayer-Bacon:

Language affects how we view the world, and how we make sense of
the experiences we have. But it is also true that much of what we
experience remains unnamed, and cannot be reduced to its articulated
meanings. I urge people to be receptive and attentive to the inarticu-
late too, not just what is named.

(p. 244)

She goes on to commend Dewey's view of experience. According to
Dewey:

The nature of experience can be understood only by noting that it
includes an active and a passive element peculiarly combined. On the
active hand, experience is *trying* – a meaning which is made explicit in

the connected term experiment. On the passive, it is *undergoing*. When we experience something ... We do something to the thing and then it does something to us in return .... The connection of these two phases of experience measures the fruitfulness or value of the experience ... [which] is primarily an active-passive affair; it is not primarily cognitive.

(Dewey 1916: 146–7)

Thus, experience for Dewey is simply what occurs when humans carry out transactions with their environment, an acting and being acted upon, a doing and being done to. According to Dewey human thought (language) is something that has grown out of and been shaped by experience. He thinks of it as a tool that has evolved as humans have employed it and developed it to make sense of their experience and to shape subsequent experiences. Thus Dewey agrees with postmodernists that language is inherently contextual. In a very significant way, he thinks that it records human experience. But whereas postmodernists claim that language is *sufficient* for experience, that is language constitutes experience, Dewey argues that language is merely *necessary* for experience, that is language plus something else constitutes experience. This something else is the acting and being acted upon, the doing and being done to.

Dewey attacked various forms of positivism for assuming that our primary relation to reality is knowledge, a view he labelled 'intellectualism'. The error of 'intellectualism' is its assumption of a split between the mind and the world, thereby creating a 'spectator' view of knowledge'. However, for Dewey, positivism of various sorts is not the only form of 'intellectualism':

The only difference between its empiricist and rationalist (or idealist) varieties is whether the world or the 'mind' makes the larger contribution to knowledge.

(Garrison 1996: 4)

Those strands of postmodern thought that operate with the basic assumption that language constitutes experience, are, in Dewey's terms, a form of 'intellectualism'. By having linguistic practice determine experience, this type of postmodernism provides the latest version of the theory/practice dichotomy that has bedevilled understanding of vocational education and training. In its traditional form, the theory/practice dichotomy was responsible for the evident contempt for vocational education and training that has marked much of the history of educational thought. According to this view, workplace practice is to be understood as the application of theory to solve the problems that characterise the particular given workplace. To the extent that such theory is general, it comes from the traditional disciplines which are at the heart of education. To the extent that such theory is particular to the workplace, it is of no interest to educators. Hence, so the reasoning has gone, vocational education and training adds nothing to educational thought and can be safely ignored.

The recent interest in workplace learning has been an indicator that theory/practice understandings of vocational education and training are at last collapsing (Hager 1996). The problem, as I see it, is that some versions of postmodernism threaten to reinstate the theory/practice approach in a new guise. If experience is really constituted by language (or writing, text, discourse), then the latter is the means by which workplace learning is to be understood. This view certainly has significant support (e.g. Usher 1992, 1997, Usher *et al.* 1997, Garrick and Solomon 1997, Butler 1997). As was pointed out above, the traditional theory/practice dichotomy supported the assumption that happenings in the workplace were not worthy of investigation by educational researchers. The postmodern version of the dichotomy will keep its adherents in their studies since, on this view, the main prerequisite for understanding workplace learning is a knowledge of relevant texts. This is confirmed by the obvious remoteness from the details of everyday workplace practice that has been evident in the texts influenced by postmodernism that have been discussed in this chapter. In Deweyan terms, they largely ignore the acting and being acted upon, the doing and being done to, which are the central (and non-linguistic) components of human experience.

In this section, the different basic assumptions of two approaches to understanding workplace learning have been discussed. This has raised issues that call for further investigation. What this discussion has done is to illustrate the earlier point that differences in basic assumptions lead different theories to focus on quite different aspects of an issue. This further reinforces the earlier conclusion that, at best, any given theory will explain some aspects of workplace learning, whilst having little or nothing to say about other aspects of the topic.

Conclusion

The focus of this book is understanding learning at work. This chapter has argued that in order to do so we must have recourse to theories of some kind. To assist readers to make sense of the wide diversity of theories that are relevant to workplace learning, this chapter has described some main features and uses of different kinds of theories. The reader has been offered guidance on selecting from the range of available theories about workplace learning, as well as on identifying the different basic assumptions that underpin these theories. May our common endeavours to understand workplace learning better continue to grow and flourish.

References

Argyris, C. and Schön, D. A. (1974) *Theory in Practice: Increasing Professional Effectiveness*, San Francisco: Jossey-Bass.

Argyris, C. and Schön, D. A. (1978) *Organizational Learning: A Theory of Action Perspective*, Reading, MA: Addison-Wesley.

Berryman, S. (1993) 'Learning for the workplace', *Review of Research in Education* 19: 343–404.

Butler, E. (1997) 'Persuasive discourses: learning and the production of working subjects in a post-industrial era', in J. Holford, C. Griffin and P. Jarvis (eds) *International Perspectives on Lifelong Learning*, London: Kogan Page.

Dewey, J. (1916) 'Democracy and education', in J. A. Boydston (ed.) *John Dewey: The Middle Works, Vol. 9*, Carbondale, IL: Southern Illinois University Press.

Edwards, R. and Usher, R. (1994) 'Disciplining the subject: the power of competence', *Studies in the Education of Adults* 26(1): 1–14.

Foley, G. (1995) 'A framework for understanding adult learning and education', in G. Foley (ed.) *Understanding Adult Education and Training*, Sydney: Allen and Unwin.

Frankena, W. K. (1970) 'A model for analysing a philosophy of education', in J. R. Martin (ed.) *Readings in the Philosophy of Education: A Study of Curriculum*, Boston: Allyn and Bacon.

Garrick, J. and Solomon, N. (1997) 'Technologies of compliance in training', *Studies in Continuing Education* 19(1): 71–81.

Garrison, J. (1996) 'John Dewey's philosophy of education', Unpublished paper.

Hager, P. (1996) 'Professional practice in education: research and issues', *Australian Journal of Education* 40(3): 235–47.

Hager, P. (1998) 'Understanding workplace learning: general perspectives', in D. Boud (ed.) *Current Issues and New Agendas in Workplace Learning*, Adelaide: National Centre for Vocational Education Research.

Knowles, M. (1991) 'Creating lifelong learning communities', *New Education* 13(1): 69–75.

Marsick, V. and Watkins, K. (1990) *Informal and Incidental Learning in the Workplace*, London: Routledge.

Phillips, D. C. (1992) *The Social Scientist's Bestiary*, Oxford: Pergamon.

Popper, K. R. (1963) *Conjectures and Refutations*, London: Routledge and Kegan Paul.

Thayer-Bacon, B. J. (1997) 'The nurturing of a relational epistemology', *Educational Theory* 47(2): 239–60.

Usher, R. (1987) 'The place of theory in designing curricula for the continuing education of adult educators', *Studies in the Education of Adults* 19(1): 26–36.

Usher, R. (1989a) 'Locating adult education in the practical', in B. Bright (ed.) *Theory and Practice in the Study of Adult Education: The Epistemological Debate*, London: Routledge.

Usher, R. (1989b) 'Locating experience in language: towards a poststructuralist theory of experience', *Adult Education Quarterly* 40(1): 23–32.

Usher, R. (1992) 'Experience in adult education: a post-modern critique', *Journal of Philosophy of Education* 26(2): 201–14.

Usher, R. (1997) 'Seductive texts: competence, power and knowledge in post-modernity', in R. Barnett and A. Griffin (eds) *The End of Knowledge in Higher Education*, London: Cassell.

Usher, R. and Bryant, I. (1989) *Adult Education as Theory, Practice and Research: The Captive Triangle*, London: Routledge.

Usher, R., Bryant, I. and Johnson, R. (1997) *Adult Education and the Postmodern Challenge*, London: Routledge.

Wain, K. (1987) *Philosophy of Lifelong Education*, London: Croom Helm.

6 Past the guru and up the garden path

The new organic management learning

David Beckett

Managers' learning is increasingly influenced by what management gurus say it should be. This chapter recognises some helpful things gurus have said about managers' learning. It builds on these at several points, but by and large the message is that your workplace learning, if you are a manager, is best shaped by what you think and do, and how attentive you are, to your thinking and doing. If your 'generative' learning (Senge 1990) is of interest to you, read on.

The first parts of the chapter set this message out by outlining organic learning, using three examples of commonplace situations where managerial expertise is required. Organic learning is then placed in a wider organisational context, and ten suggestions by which a manager could support organic learning in an organisation are then listed. After that, the remainder of the chapter pushes organic learning into new areas, developing creative thinking and creative making as crucial to organic learning for managing within organisations in the next century.

What do we know about managers' learning?

This depends on what we know about what managers actually do.

Here we have to be careful of the factual and the folkloric. Mintzberg (1989) details this distinction, in his first chapter, luminously titled, 'The Manager's Job: Folklore and Fact'. The folklore is that managers 'plan, organize, coordinate and control'. However, Mintzberg goes on to say that

> the fact is that those four words, which have dominated management vocabulary since the French industrialist Henri Fayol first introduced them in 1916, tell us little about what managers actually do. At best, they indicate some vague objectives managers have when they work.
>
> (p. 9)

Mintzberg's own research findings (or what we know about managers) draw this conclusion:

Considering the facts about managerial work, we can see that the manager's job is enormously complicated and difficult. The manager is overburdened with obligations; yet he or she cannot easily delegate his or her tasks. As a result, he or she is driven to overwork and is forced to do many tasks superficially. Brevity, fragmentation and oral communication characterize the work. Yet these are the very characteristics of managerial work that have impeded scientific attempts to improve it. As a result, management scientists have concentrated their efforts on the specialized functions of the organization.

(p. 14)

Looking, then, at what managers actually do (the facts), not what they hope to do, nor what their organisational setting is doing, we can pick up how they learn. Not surprisingly, whilst at work, managers can learn powerfully through experiences which are intense, dynamic, uncertain and decisional. Like most white-collar jobs, and in particular, professionals' work, managers' work is 'hot action'. They share with teachers, nurses, lawyers, surgeons and the like the heat of the moment where decisions are taken on the run, case by case, and with the nagging doubt that action might be inadequate – superficial, hasty and inappropriate.

Brevity, fragmentation and oral communication characterise the work

'Brevity, fragmentation and oral communication characterize the work' says Mintzberg. And all in the context of 'hot action'. Hot action lends itself to rich possibilities of knowledge productivity (Beckett 1996). It is this perspective on managers' work which generates many possibilities for managerial learning.

After all, we know the old model of static, hierarchical command, with learning as the filling up of empty vessels with knowledge, is history. Schools threw it out about two decades ago. Traditional corporate training was based on this idea, where a trainer 'filled up' the skill deficit by running trainees around a set course of skilled behaviour again and again until they got it 'right' – then the assumption was that this new skill would transfer readily to the real work beyond the training classroom. We know now that these 'empty vessels' were often only temporarily filled with the required skill or knowledge, and that, even so, 'transfer' to real work was itself a deficiency in the whole approach.

Empty vessels have been replaced by an image of the learner as somehow embedded in a system. We read of systems, and how systematic training, with its inputs and outputs (based on 'empty vessels'), has been superseded by systems thinking (Senge 1990). While systemic thinking is undoubtedly important for leadership in organisations, this chapter takes up the individual manager's potential for what Senge has called 'generative' learning (in opposition to the more traditional coping mechanisms he called 'adaptive' learning). So we are interested in change and deliberation upon that change. Clearly management scholarship regards this as central to organisations and their leadership, as well as to managers' personal growth. Some time back, Argyris and Schön (1978) identified 'double-loop learning' as the kind that critically questions the suppositions of single-loop learning (the input–output, or linear, model). Asking 'what if?' questions invites a flexibility into decision-making, which, taken seriously, leads beyond adaptation, to the generation of change. Double-loop learning builds on the feedback possibilities of single-loop learning, but views the feedback more laterally. In the twenty years since they wrote together, both Argyris and Schön have separately continued to make substantial contributions to our understanding of the leadership of learning at work.

Argyris, for example, lists (1993: 5–6) some key assumptions of education for leading-learning:

1   Learning should be in the service of action, not simply discovery or insight. The evidence that managers know how to lead-learn is that they can produce action based on double-loop reasoning.
2   The competencies involved in leading-learning are the same when dealing with individuals, groups, intergroups, and organisational features such as culture.
3   The first key to leading-learning is not personality or style. Rather, the key is the theories of action, the set of rules that individuals use to design and implement their behaviour.

Argyris, in his first principle, recognises what we are calling hot action. His second principle clearly identifies the significance of managers' leadership in context. His third principle shows a preference for a set of rules that individual managers use, that is apply, in their workplaces. Yet 'theories of action' which issue in a set of rules for action is, as this chapter will show, not the best way to think of managers' learning. Rule-based approaches, such as Argyris's, are oriented towards problem-solving, which is of course what marks out a lot of the manager's daily life. That much is well recognised by Mintzberg. But rule-following amidst 'hot action' is too much like systems thinking – it does not reflect what daily life for managers is like. Therefore it is not likely to be of much help in advancing managers' learning in the workplace.

This chapter, then, moves beyond systems, networks and rule-following (which some have called a 'cognitivist' model). On the contrary, what follows is an appreciation of learning from the 'brevity, fragmentation and oral communication' of managers' work. In short, it replaces both the 'empty vessels' model and the 'cognitivist' model of workplace learning with what can be called organic learning.

What is organic learning?

Life at work is typically experienced as an integration of thinking, feeling and doing. Problems and issues, projects, and performances of various kinds fill the day. None of these go on without purposes, skills, resources, technologies and so on. And they go on, typically, in a social setting. There is a peer group of other workers somewhere nearby – from the same room or building, to the neighbourhood, to the international community of (say) similar professionals. Amidst this context of typical worklife, organic learning brings to awareness what is learned in the doing of the work, while the work is being undertaken. Deliberation upon experiences, whilst amongst the examples, is often provoked by coffee-break conversations, second opinions, dissent and conflict, and striving towards certain immediate successes. When a worker is aware that he or she is learning from these experiences (not merely undergoing them), we will call that an organic phenomenon. It presents as an integration of thinking, feeling and doing. The test of the experience having been learned from will be the contribution it makes to individual change, and, perhaps, to organisational change. Of course, workplaces will want to encourage positive changes, so the making of these experiences will ideally be creative. The latter part of this chapter takes up what that might be like.

We can clarify organic learning with three examples of activities now quite common at work:

- *Mentoring and coaching* programmes, which are most effective when they deal in the sociocultural experiences of the participants where there is a personal investment in 'fitting in' fast: this is integrative and growth conducive, and involves thinking, feelings and of course what is being done at work.
- *Projects* focus learning in outcome-driven ways, where there is an urgent requirement to achieve those outcomes before the sunset of the project: this drives the reliance on hot action simultaneously with an integrative purpose, especially since teams are often involved.
- *Competency structures*, which are most effective when breadth of judgement is recognised as a vital component of the performance indicators. Such judgement is best understood as an integrative experience, because in the midst of 'hot action' we bring to bear upon our decisions a wide range of thoughts and feelings, focused on the 'appropriate' response.

We will outline shortly how these three clarify organic learning. The central point, though, is to recognise in each of them the primacy of both the 'brevity, fragmentation and oral communication' generated by the real workplace, and also the drive to achieve a vision which is integrative. And what are being integrated are the thoughts, feelings and actions of the workers. Organic learning is advocated as the new concept which glues all this together, if it can be shown that some deliberate awareness of the experiences themselves is part of the work.

Surfacing organic learning

Deliberate awareness must be cultivated quite explicitly – it must be brought to the surface of worklife. So far we have identified characteristics of managers' work, and linked these to certain emerging characteristics of workplace learning. Managers in our three examples of settings conducive to organic learning would need explicitly to surface adult learning focused nonetheless on purposeful change. They could bear three simple questions in mind during 'hot action', such as these:

- *What are we doing?*
- *Why are we doing it?*
- *What comes next?*

Answers to these simple questions can provoke workplace learning for managers because they represent context-sensitive, yet visionary, responses to daily work experiences. These can be implicit in mentoring, in projects and in competencies. They provide the 'glue' which converts the brevity, fragmentation and oral communication of the typical managers' work day into focused learning. They operationalise organic learning, but in structures where the answers to these questions are readily available: the intention of the mentoring, the purpose of the project, and the evidence of the competent judgement.

After the following three examples are outlined, some shared characteristics are discussed, and the definition of organic learning pinned down.

Three organic examples

Mentoring

Alex has joined Humus Consolidated, an organisation specialising in land-care processes and products. All new employees are linked to more experienced staff in a mentor–mentee scheme, with the purpose of induction. Alex's mentor, Lee, who has agreed to assume this role, is not in a line of responsibility for Alex, and has undergone some training in the implementation of mentoring. Lee's knowledge of Humus extends over several years, and includes substantial specialist knowledge in an applied science. Nevertheless, in the mentoring scheme, Alex and Lee agree at the outset that induction is best pursued by way of more generic 'counselling' approaches, rather than specific 'coaching' approaches. Regular meetings (half an hour once a fortnight), with follow-up note-keeping and some tasks to carry out by Alex, have centred on discussions about what work

Alex is doing, why these actions are being performed, and the overall significance they may have at Humus. Answers to these questions emerge as Lee 'counsels' Alex in the development of a sensitivity to social and cognitive understandings as these present at Humus. Alex assimilates the culture of Humus ('the way we do things around here'). But more significantly, Alex is guided in that assimilation by Lee's skilful usage of questioning: How does x fit with y? What implication would doing b have for a and c? What would you need to bring to (certain tasks and events) to plan for success? These generic questions are powerful for Alex because they provoke a sense of ownership of the learning process at and through the workplace. They explicitly surface adult learning, in a particular context. Moreover, they deal in the values of Humus, of Lee and of Alex; they do not restrict the mentoring scheme to cognitive knowledge, but address the feelings and emotions inevitably generated by induction. In doing this, Lee is able to show Alex that there are more or less appropriate ways of dealing with the 'affective' as well as the 'cognitive' side of workplace learning, at least at Humus. If the counselling approach to mentoring is successful, Alex should be able to demonstrate in actions at work an understanding of the necessity for sophisticated interpersonal skills such as problem-solving, communicability, team membership and perhaps embryonic leadership.

Project management

Elsewhere at Humus, a large information technology (IT) project is in the offing. This involves many desktop computer and server upgrades, a new e-mail program for the whole staff, and the development of the organisation's first Web site. A project team has been formed, combining expertise from several sections of the organisation, such as IT support, human resources, marketing, applied science and so on, and there is an end of the year sunset for the project to look forward to. This is a unique project for Humus, and has been given a high organisational priority, with appropriate resourcing. The project team has been meeting for some weeks and is well into its 'life cycle', characterised in rather cheeky fashion in some literature (Robbins 1993) as: forming, storming, norming, performing, adjourning. At Humus, the team is somewhere in the 'storming–norming' range. Members have moved beyond the individuality of their discrete expertise (in 'forming' the team), but they have not yet reached that optimum level, 'performing', when work on the project is at its most effective. Rather, their meetings are often marked by conflict over the project's priorities and operations, and by grappling with their identity as a group. Leadership and the balance between perceptions of the project's needs and the team members' are prominent issues. Common ownership of the project has yet to emerge in the detail of how best to achieve its purpose. What is being done, and why, and what comes next are all negotiable. As a learning environment, the project team presents as a porridge of expertise, emotions, ideologies and energy. The development of certain 'people' skills, such as conflict resolution, task analysis and shared time management, as well as everything Humus's mentoring scheme is on about, will be essential. Establishing order will be important, but not at any cost. Ownership of the project by all involved implies that everyone will have to recognise strengths in others, and admit to compromise in themselves. This will probably happen. After all, the team members have invested their identities and energies in what they hope is a success story.

Competence

The staff cafeteria at Humus was rocked by a blazing row. Two prominent employees exploded in anger with each other, culminating in the accusation: 'You're completely unprofessional', with appropriate body language. People left the room, embarrassed. Certainly we feel the force of such an accusation, because so much competence is inferred on us at work when we regard ourselves and each other as professionals. At Humus, staff are involved in a Professional Development Plan, and there is a requirement that at annual appraisal time, evidence of achievement in the PDP be presented. Links with competence can be established in several ways: technically, practically, strategically and personally, skills can be identified and developed. New IT expertise, shown through completion of a formal course, would be technically relevant if Humus IT needed that expertise. But already, then, that becomes a strategic skill or competence, and perhaps also a practical skill or competence, if it arose in daily workplace experience at Humus. Personal skill or competence, in the 'people' skills we identified in the first and second examples, would be required if that new-found IT expertise involved performing it with other people, such as on a project team. Then, on a continuum ranging from 'technique' to 'values', we have moved across to the 'values' end, where there needs to be an integrated way to identify professionals' competence in the value-ladenness of work (Hager and Beckett 1995). Judgements about appropriate decisions (involving not only IT but also any other 'hot action' at work) require the marshalling, or integration, of a range of considerations: technical, practical, strategic and personal. Gluing these together with professional competence is a complex and elusive achievement; Humus has an appraisal scheme which invites evidence for that achievement. In effect it asks employees the same simple questions we have asked all through these examples: What have you done? Why have you done it? Where did it lead?

What do these three examples of organic learning share?

These three examples have shown that three simple questions (What are we doing? Why are we doing it? What comes next?) can be asked and substantially answered in particular settings. Managers as leaders can provoke organic learning by raising these questions in each of the examples just outlined. Those simple questions are intended to operationalise organic learning, because they integrate thinking, feeling and doing in particular ways. They lead from, and back into, actions. The mythical Humus Consolidated thus advances organic workplace learning if structures for mentoring, projects and competencies encourage the workers involved to develop their (adult) learning explicitly, in the ways they get on with the job! And simple questions like those proposed can be asked by those who lead or manage mentoring, projects and competencies programmes and structures.

Feelings and thinking are bound up in each of these examples. Mentoring was, in this example, induction into a culture. Project team membership was by definition a shared success story waiting to be told. Professionals' competence in this example centred on skilled judgement, inevitably involving people and their workplace feelings and location. In all three examples, organic learning centres on ownership of people's feelings about the work, both personally and interpersonally, as much as it centres on thinking (the old 'cognitivism').

Moreover, there was a strong sense of needing to reach a contextually sensitive outcome. In other words, each example required 'appropriateness'. For mentoring, the 'way we do things here' is just that – the 'appropriate'; for project teams, the way forward is the 'appropriate' way; and for professionals, judgements about what to do are decisions about the 'appropriate' course of action. Organic learning is shown in a focus on what is regarded in any particular situation as the 'right' (or 'appropriate') thing to do. The context, or location, will set up what that focus will look like. This, which defines what is focused about organic learning, and, as we noted earlier, feelings and thinking which are caught up in actions are the raw material for organic learning.

Organic learning in the organisation

It is one thing to spell out how an individual manager, in a specific context, can be encouraged to think and act in an integrated, focused way: that is, can take responsibility for his or her organic workplace learning. It is a larger task to show how this organic learning can be encouraged across an organisation. Nevertheless, there are some easily understood structural provisions which can be identified. Firstly, however, a little background is required.

Workplace learning has a dreary history. In brief, it has emerged from reactive and behaviouristic assumptions about adult learning at work – typically showing up in the traditional 'training classroom', and it is now dragged blinking and bewildered into a fast-moving 'enterprise' globalism, where what is required is proactive, strategically focused, non-classroom learning. This chapter so far has shown how organic learning presents a helpful umbrella under which individuals (managers, in this case) can generate all manner of experience-driven learning.

In that sense, human agency ('what I can do') has become an increasingly central and compelling feature of worklife – rather than the traditional 'skill-deficit' training ('what I can't do'). Our three examples are powerful and popular because they should advance the capacities of more people for more involvement in worklife than previously. In this sense, workers (such as managers) are actors in an increasingly demanding work environment: their agency is not only expected but required by the new workplace.

The traditional behaviourist approach to learning at work (the old 'inputs–outputs' systematic training we noted earlier) has been replaced by what is called a humanistic approach. This is a model of learning centred upon the holistic richness and individualistic integrity of human experience. That is, humanist psychology starts with the reasons, motives and values of the individual and seeks ways of structuring the experience we all inevitably undergo, so that better learning results. So formal or 'classroom-based' workplace learning is only part of the experiences people have at work from which they learn. Informal and incidental learning have emerged as significant concepts in the further development of workplace learning. Our three examples, above, are simply ways of structuring this learning, without obliterating the experiential integrity it has for the participants.

Apart from these educational innovations, globalisation and technological changes put pressure on productivity and profitability, injecting an urgency into workplace learning, especially for managers. Managers at middle and chief executive levels cast about for strategies that give a hope of that elusive market edge. Furthermore, and ironically, organisational restructuring since the early 1990s has shown amongst other things that middle-level management is disappearing. Without some new notion of the responsibilities of leadership for generating better workplace learning, it is hard to see where the authority for innovation is meant to come from. Who is around to articulate the strategic vision of the organisation in ways that make it accessible to the workforce in a range of learning modes? Those who are still around are those who can express and enhance organic learning, who can display it in their daily work, and who can support others in like fashion. In short, organic learning, supported and modelled across an organisation by sympathetic managers, offers some of the best ways to advance the sense of ownership of a specific part of the workplace, as well as advance the ownership of the whole, integrated, corporate culture.

How can managers support organic learning?

In the light of these 'background' issues, how can such managers show support for organic learning in organisational structuring? Here are ten suggestions:

1   Implement policies for specific strategies to make corporate work experiences tangible, such as mentoring and coaching, including stating dedicated time to engage these (hopefully also including common time and space).
2   Develop policies which acknowledge development of workers' individual strategies: career planning; input into annual appraisal; initiatives with particular assignments, projects or work problems; acquisition of competencies and new skills (languages, technology).
3   Restructure for peer collaboration through occupational teams, natural work groups (site-based rather than occupation-based) and off-site shared experiences, and reflection and review of all these in the light of productivity, both personally and organisationally.
4   Provide amenable workplace conditions such that access to the above is maximised (child care, flexible work practices such as rotation, opportunities for leadership development).
5   Institute incentives to learn which are tangible: promotion, articulation with formal study, study leave.
6   Articulate the need for strategically significant workplace learning and use this to shape programme design and structures (as listed in 1–5).
7   Articulate clear expectations of legal and ethical accountability.
8   Manage the work environment more collaboratively than consultatively, surfacing the 'people' competencies of conflict resolution, team-building, communicability and so on.
9   In particular, collaboratively establish a workplace 'mission', detailed in achievable and equitable objectives.
10 Link these to evidence of learning (journalling, conference and discussion chapters, project reports, presentations to peers, simulations, appraisals, formal study pathways).

Creative thinking – and feeling

At the heart of organic thinking is creativity. This is a ready development of the famous 'double-loop learning' well established in management and organisational literature. Creative double-loop learning does not just ask 'What if we try [something] this way?' but plays with possibilities hitherto untried: 'Let's see what this would be like.' We explore, here, the prospects for creative thinking in organic learning.

Consider the popular notion of an organisational 'vision' as a point of entry to this exploration. Managers, and all in a corporate workplace, are increasingly subject to, and hopefully participants in, 'vision' or 'mission' statements. Perhaps a sceptic would regard these as creative wish-lists at least in so far as they express mere hopes – something quite impractical. After all, someone might argue, what is practical at work is what works at work!

This is undoubtedly correct – we do want to achieve what 'works'. Vision statements have at least the virtue of directing us to some idea of the purposefulness of practical daily work, even if the grandness of the vision itself eludes us. In fact, in practical daily work, an action is the right action if it 'works' – if it turns out to be practical. So let us push on with this assumption: that our purpose at work is to achieve what 'works'. Creative thinking about organic learning at work will hinge on it.

In daily worklife, their 'rightness' or 'appropriateness' defines the practicality of judgements, decisions and actions. This rightness can be called, after Aristotle, phronesis ('practical wisdom'). How does this practical wisdom-at-work help us enhance organic learning?

Quinn, in his *Beyond Rational Management* (1991), reminds us that practical wisdom is not ditching rationality in favour of warm fuzzies. On the contrary, the manager of the future has to integrate thinking and feeling:

> Moving beyond rational management does not mean moving from the purposive to the holistic frame. It does not mean moving from Theory X to Theory Y or from a left-brain to a right-brain perspective. It does not mean in any way devaluing rational thinking....[One must] move to a metalevel that allows one to see the interpenetration and the inseparability of the two polarities. This third step takes us to a transformational logic. It allows for simultaneous integration and differentiation.
>
> (pp.163–5)

'Integrity' and 'integration and differentiation' are organic concepts in workplaces because they focus on the 'wholeness' of those experiences at work which are potentially educative and from which workers (in this case, managers) inevitably learn. Argyris, as we saw at the beginning of this chapter, like many of those exploring adult learning processes, such as his colleague, Schön (1983, 1987), has hit upon the power unleashed when adults are assisted in making their own learning more explicit to them. Double loops, reflection-in-action, meta-cognition, and all manner of strategies to provoke these, have in common the aim of bringing to awareness the very act of awareness. This is what is meant by our earlier statement that organic learning makes adult learning explicit. It is this unpacking of a sensitivity to one's own state of knowledge, in the workplace, which is driving the construction of a new sort of manager. Indeed, Argyris (1993) connects this explicit personal awareness with the broader picture when he states:

> Leadership education that focuses on theories-in-use and reasoning processes is more easily integrable with such managerial disciplines as strategy, managerial economics, management accounting, and management information systems. This is because these disciplines are themselves theories of action intended to help managers achieve specific goals. Moreover, their effective use requires productive reasoning. Managerial disciplines, in principle, eschew defensive reasoning.
>
> (p. 7)

It is 'right' that leadership takes what some call a 'helicopter' view, and to some extent it is rational, purposive action which is the principle of that integration, but, as we have seen, feelings are in there too. Wise action draws upon both how we think and how we feel. In this sense, 'practical wisdom' (phronesis) shapes organic learning. Aristotle is, then, some help here. But we need to look within the 'doing' of what is judged right – and the learning associated with that, described, so far as it goes, by phronesis.

So my argument goes further. Within phronesis, at the very basis of the judgement that some actions are the 'right' (effective, appropriate) ways to go, is a judgement of creative value. Such creative judgements require balance, tact, compromise and patience. It is true that all of these can reasonably be expected of phronesis. What I seek, however, is an improvement on this analysis, whereby we can acknowledge that workplace learning is a phenomenon deep within practical 'doing' (read: action) towards certain localised values. In short, can we find in the very exercise of practical wisdom (the creative thinking and feeling) an opportunity for organic learning?

Creativity itself – 'making'

Let us return to Aristotle (1941 ed. McKeon). In the *Nichomachean Ethics*, he writes extensively of various forms of knowledge, of which practical wisdom is the 'true and reasoned state of capacity to act with regard to the things that are good or bad for man' (p. 1026). But Aristotle has a separate category of knowledge for making:

> the reasoned state of capacity to act is different from the reasoned state of capacity to make...art is identical with a state of capacity to make, involving a true course of reasoning. All art is concerned with

coming into being, ie. with contriving and considering how something may come into being which is capable of either being or not being, and whose origin is in the maker and not in the thing made.

(p. 1025)

Art is essentially about making, but of course we need to acknowledge that there are myriad human 'making' activities which are not necessarily artistic: we can make love, make a mess, make a fuss, make amends and so on. In the workplace, making is the key to success. Many workplaces want to make a profit – they need to be productive! For managers, the job is essentially to make things work. Managers, as we saw, have to make the 'right' (read: good, effective, appropriate) decisions. These judgements contribute to an organisation's expectation that making a profit (or whatever) is essential. So, for a manager who is serious about his or her, and others', workplace learning, the query 'what if we try this?' is a creative act – an act of making. Double-loop questioning, reflective practices and generative strategies are, in Aristotelian terms, essential to organic learning.

Creativity at work shows up in actions which are 'tryings' or anticipations of good results. And this can be learned, largely because there is a significant role for skill in this. Making (or creating, or producing) is a human activity which by its very existence integrates aspects of our experiences in ways that are judged valuable. Integrative work activities are those judged to be both new and worthwhile and thereby they contribute to outcomes which may themselves be practically 'wise'. There is a beauty about the actions of highly skilled practitioners which transcends the exercise of the skill. We say of such expertise that 'they made it look effortless'. As in certain sport and musical performances, it is in the performative aspects of (say) managerial work which are recognisably skilled, rational and 'right' that we can see creativity is apparent.

Thus the very creativity of a manager's work practice is organic in two ways: at the heart of organic learning is, as Schön (1983, 1987) puts it, the 'artistry of performance'. This is encased by phronesis, a judgement of practical wisdom: such 'tryings' anticipate new ways of working.

In organisational settings, organic learning will be set up partly by the context (this is the 'given' for the manager, and connects with the vision, mission and leadership of the enterprise as we discussed earlier). We want, however, in all this emphasis on creativity, or artistry, in work to acknowledge the responsibility a manager or any other practitioner has to animate and develop this 'given'. Senge draws attention to this in the subtitle (*The Art and Practice of the Learning Organization*), and therefore the content, of his book (1990). He develops it later (Senge *et al.* 1994).

In fact, the 'given' context requires its expression in creative management. A vision unrealised is a waste of time: it is unintegrated into daily corporate life. It is in being 'worked upon' (Schön would say: in the artistry of performance) that management learning becomes organic. As Billett shows in Chapter 10, what psychologists call 'situated learning' is the most powerful workplace learning, because humans are immersed in their daily activities, from which they are especially susceptible to learning. Such immersion involves the totality of experience, which, as we noted at the outset, is central to organic learning.

Many philosophers, of whom Aristotle is one splendid example, similarly recognise the situation or context of human activities as crucial to the meaningfulness of those activities. Our personal identities are, perhaps, constructed first by each other (i.e. socially and emotionally), from which our individuality then flows. Organic learning takes this sequence seriously.

Leadership in organisational learning will be more apparent in those who understand their own 'context' or situation in daily social life at work – shared feelings, thoughts and actions at work construct us as workers. Those who can recognise this – who are open to their own organic learning possibilities – can then advance such learning in others. So it is with managers, who are frequently leaders in some way, working with other humans (say, team members, learners, patients, clients). Their creativity will show in their own performance of sophisticated 'people' skills. The current interest in 'emotional intelligence' has direct bearing on this (Goleman 1996). If managers can create amongst their peers and their clients a climate which nurtures everyone's creativity, they will have demonstrated the fusion of thinking, feeling and doing. They will have shown that organic learning is at the structural and cultural heart of the organisation in which they work. In terms of creativity, they will have made learning work – at work.

In the organisation of the next century, the making of learning will be more substantially recognised amongst work-based performance, and I have outlined how and why this richer notion of learning from workplace experience can be encouraged.

A new question: 'how can we/I do better?'

Organic workplace learning, because it addresses the making of decisions and judgements and their instantiation in action, perhaps issues in a fourth simple question, which we can add to our earlier three: *How can we/I do better?* The answers to this require a creative stance to thinking, feeling and doing, bound up together in particular workplaces, with all their problems and issues, projects and competencies. The really successful managers will be those who can take their organic learning capabilities even further. In provoking this question where they work, they will do so in such a way that their colleagues and associates will trust them to countenance a diversity of answers. Bennis (1997) argues that sophisticated leadership is partly shown in the generation of trust. In addition, this question will also encourage, in the best workplaces, flirtation with chaos. The creative potential of chaos is central to what Handy (1997) calls 'finding sense in uncertainty'.

This chapter has suggested that, for an organisation or an individual manager looking to advance organic learning, the signs are that what is needed is closer sensitivity to human experiences at work. In other words, more explicit structural and personal attention to adult learning, particularly learning arising from affective experiences (feelings, emotions), and on the particular context, or 'situation', of those experiences should be the focus of managers' learning. The task is, as the novelist, E. M. Forster urged, 'only connect'.

References

Argyris, C. (1993) 'Education for leading-learning', *Organisational Dynamics* 21(3): 5–17.

Argyris, C. and Schön, D (1978) *Organisational Learning: A Theory of Action Perspective*, London: Addison-Wesley.

Aristotle (ed. R. McKeon) (1941) *Basic Works*, New York: Random House.

Beckett, D. (1996) 'Critical judgement and professional practice', *Educational Theory* 46(2): 135–50.

Bennis, W. (1997) 'Becoming a leader of leaders', in R. Gibson (ed.) *Rethinking the Future: Rethinking Business, Principles, Competition, Control and Complexity, Leadership, Markets and the World*, London: Nicholas Brealey.

Goleman, D. (1996) *Emotional Intelligence: Why it can matter more than IQ*, London: Bloomsbury.

Hager, P. and Beckett, D. (1995) 'Philosophical underpinnings of the integrated conception of competence', *Educational Philosophy and Theory* 27(1): 1–24.

Handy, C. (1997) 'Finding sense in uncertainty', in R. Gibson (ed.) *Rethinking the Future: Rethinking Business, Principles, Competition, Control and Complexity, Leadership, Markets and the World*, London: Nicholas Brealey.

Mintzberg, H. (1989) *On Management*, New York: Free Press.

Quinn, R. (1991) *Beyond Rational Management*, San Francisco: Jossey-Bass.

Robbins, S. P. (1993) *Organisational Behaviour*, sixth edn, New York: Prentice Hall.

Senge, P. (1990) *The Fifth Discipline: The Art and Practice of the Learning Organization*, New York: Doubleday.

Senge, P. *et al.* (1994) *The Fifth Discipline Fieldbook: Strategies and Tools for Building a Learning Organisation*, London: Nicholas Brealey.

Schön, D. (1983) *The Reflective Practitioner*, New York: Basic Books.

Schön, D. (1987) *Educating the Reflective Practitioner: Toward a New Design for Teaching and Learning in the Professions*, San Francisco: Jossey-Bass.

7 Gendered workers and gendered work

Implications for women's learning

Belinda Probert

One of the most significant changes in the labour forces of countries like Australia and the USA and those of Western Europe has been their increasing feminisation in the last decades of this century. Well over half of the adult women in most member countries of the OECD are now in the paid workforce. In some countries their participation rate is almost equal with that of men, particularly under those welfare state regimes with an explicit commitment to promoting equality between the sexes. There are several factors which have played a role in this feminisation of the workforce. On the demand side, there has been the rapid expansion of a range of service industries relying heavily on women workers, such as the retail industry, and community and health services. On the supply side, there has been the rapidly rising levels of education among women within the OECD countries, together with the widespread cultural changes occurring in the wake of the women's movement of the late 1960s and early 1970s.

This feminisation of the labour force has been accompanied by almost continuous debate about the significance of gender in structuring men's and women's experience of work and the tenacity of sex-segregated labour markets. Attention has focused on the one hand on the phenomenon of horizontal segregation, where women remain concentrated in the lower levels of an occupational career structure (such as medicine, law or higher education) despite equal participation rates in relevant educational courses and entry-level credentials. On the other hand, there is persistent horizontal segregation with many occupations remaining strongly female (often with men in the highest positions) or male – such as nursing, primary teaching and most trades.

As the title of this chapter suggests, the focus here is not directly on workplace learning itself, but on the importance of a gendered analysis of the workplace for any understanding of the learning that may occur there. In this chapter the concept of workplace learning has been used to refer to a number of different practices, opportunities and dispositions, all of which may be shaped by formal and informal means. The questions to be asked concern the extent to which these practices, opportunities and dispositions are shaped by the gendering of both work and workers. The concepts of gendered work and gendered workers refer to the way social and behavioural attributes attaching to one or other sex are embedded in the construction of particular kinds of work and workers. For example, as many feminist writers have pointed out, work such as nursing and cleaning is closely linked to what are seen as natural feminine attributes rather than particular technical skills. This gendering of work has significant implications for what counts as learning or skill as opposed to natural talent.

While the conceptual focus of this chapter is on the need for a gender analysis of work and workers, this chapter is more about women than men. The reason for this is that much of what is written about work, and the organisations within which it is shaped, assumes an abstract worker who is in fact a man – not in any essentialist sense, but in the sense of a person with male social (and often psychological) attributes. Furthermore, the chapter builds on a history of feminist scholarship which shows that women are structurally disadvantaged in these gender relations. The purpose of this chapter is to identify not only gender difference but, more importantly, gendered inequity in access to and experience of opportunities for workplace learning. It should also be stated at the outset that such a focus does not assume that women constitute an undifferentiated social group, nor that women's workplace experience is something unitary. As will become clear, many of the factors driving rapid workforce change and an increased emphasis on workplace learning are leading to greatly differentiated experiences and opportunities for different groups of women.

Feminist perspectives

Discussion about the causes of gender differences and gender inequalities in the workplace have tended to polarise around two broad approaches. The first derives from the branch of economics designed to study social institutions like the family, namely rational choice theory, and specifically human capital theory. As Hakim puts it, 'it assumes people know what they value (have stable preferences) and act rationally to achieve their aims, to maximise or optimise their desires' (Hakim 1996: 13). From this perspective it is generally argued that women's concentration in particular low-paying occupations, or their location at the lower end of occupational career structures, reflects their lower levels of human capital – that is, their lower levels of qualifications and skills and fewer years of work experience. Researchers working within rational choice theory go on to argue that these lower levels of human capital are often the result of the choice that many women make to put their families before their careers. The kind of evidence that is cited in support of such arguments includes data on married women's preference for part-time work. Embedded, often implicitly, in this framework are a set of assumptions about women's attitudes to work which would have a major bearing on their attitudes to learning, defining them as less likely either to wish to learn, or to provide the same return on learning as men.

Over the last two decades feminist scholars have produced a substantial body of knowledge about the gendered dimensions of work that reveals the limitations of human capital theory, derived from sociological theories of gender relations in which power and inequality are central. For example, it is now almost twenty years since Phillips and Taylor (1980) published their article on the way definitions of skilled work have historically been constructed to exclude work done by women. As Phillips argued elsewhere, traditional hierarchies of skill to be found in the workforce reflect 'a system of male dominance in craft identity which is inextricably (if confusingly) linked with masculinity...jobs are created as masculine and feminine, with their skill context continually re-drawn to assert the dominance of men' (1983: 102). In their influential book, *Gender at Work*, Game and Pringle used a number of case studies ranging from white-goods manufacturing to banking to argue that the gendering of jobs was reproduced continuously within the workplace itself, in a remarkably flexible and adaptable manner. Jobs could indeed change their sex-typing, but what remained fixed was that there should be a distinction between men's and women's work. They argued that the distinction remains because 'gender is not just about difference but about power' (1983: 16).

This approach has been extended in feminist analyses of contemporary workplaces associated with 'flexible specialisation' that embody new forms of production with a greater emphasis on skill and workplace learning. As Jenson argues, 'restructuring the labour process to privilege skilled work and workers will further marginalize women unless political actors challenge long-standing processes which isolate women from machinery and which define women's skills as talents' (1989: 155).

While some studies focused on the way in which the workplace itself was a site for the reproduction of gendered difference and inequality, others continued to analyse the link between the gendered division of family responsibilities and women's particular patterns of workforce participation. The phenomenal growth in part-time employment, for example, which is characteristic of so many West European countries as well as Australia and the USA, is a highly gendered phenomenon that is widely seen as related to the increased workforce participation of married women. This differentiation of the workforce around marital status and working hours has obvious implications for workplace learning. From the employer's perspective, for example, assumptions about men's and women's commitment to work will play a major role in defining the need for learning opportunities and evaluating the likely return on them, not only in terms of the provision of training of various kinds, but also in the design of jobs and the introduction of new technologies. From the employee's perspective, the ability to take advantage of learning opportunities, be this in the form of training or new forms of work organisation, will also be sharply gendered.

Research on women and training contradicts the casual assumptions about women's attitudes to work and career made by many relying on human capital theory. Most women in feminised areas of work, having been excluded from the formal and economically rewarding paths of apprenticeships, have done their learning informally, on the job, 'sitting next to Nellie' (Butler and Connole 1992). Studies of clerical work, which is one of the largest areas of female employment, show that when women workers receive 'off-the-job' training this is generally highly task specific, and many are then expected to provide the same training for other workers (Liff 1993: 102). Furthermore, women undergoing such training generally remain employed in the same classification, and are denied the theoretical rewards of investment in their human capital.

Studies that have actually investigated women's commitment to work and attitudes to learning at work also consistently find high levels of interest in training and in mechanisms that would allow greater recognition of skills and accreditation of training (Lawrence 1994). However, at the same time, most discussion about the provision of opportunities for workplace learning is blind to the gender-specific constraints faced by women with family responsibilities. In other words women's attitudes to workplace learning are more strongly shaped by constraints deriving from the gendered division of labour in the family than by unproblematic choices between work and family.

Alongside a burgeoning field of academic study there has also been a sustained mobilisation by women demanding both equal access to male occupations and also the revaluing of feminised ones. Research on gendered inequalities in the valuing of skill, for example, lies behind the comparable worth movement which, in the USA in particular, has campaigned to have the different jobs that men and women perform compared in terms of requisite levels of skill, effort and responsibility. In Australia much feminist research has focused on the history of attempts to exclude women from parts of the paid workforce, and on the institutional practices that label and value women's work as unskilled. These practices are evident, for example, in the operation of the vocational education and training system (particularly the apprenticeship system), the decisions of industrial tribunals and the organising practices of male-dominated trade unions (Smith and Ewer 1995). They are sustained in the new vocational education and training agenda through the 'enduring masculine culture' of the sector that stems from 'the histories of trade training and (male) apprenticeships' (Butler 1997: 53).

The explanations for women's continued concentration in a narrow range of relatively low-status occupations have become more complex as the effects of gender as a central organising principle of both family life and the workplace itself are better understood. Sex segregation has not merely perpetuated the low-skill, low-pay status of women workers, but had a profound impact on the shape of feminised jobs and the technologies introduced around them (Appelbaum 1993). As Sonia Liff has argued, for example, 'saying that office jobs are women's work means more than just drawing attention to the fact that a lot of women work there. It also highlights the forms of work organisation and relations which operate' (1990: 44). Thus the element of personal service (making cups of tea, attending to non-work needs) which has been such a pervasive element of some kinds of clerical jobs is intimately linked to its definition as women's work, and would be unthinkable in the context of men's work. What is more, where critical elements of women's work involves capacities that can be defined as feminine (such as patience, communication or negotiation skills and so on), these are dismissed as natural female attributes rather than valuable workplace skills, and go unrewarded (Poynton 1993: 85–6).

These ideas have been developed in a number of ways over recent years, leading, for example, to the suggestion that organisational structure itself is not gender neutral. Acker argues that, 'In organisational logic, both jobs and hierarchies are abstract categories that have no occupants, no human bodies, no gender' (1990: 149). However, in reality a job already contains 'the gender-based division of labour and the separation between the public and the private sphere', precisely because job definitions refuse to recognise the different responsibilities and imperatives that men and women bring to the workplace from the domestic division of labour. Job definitions are designed around unspoken assumptions about an abstract worker which are in reality fundamentally gendered. As Acker concludes, the 'closest a disembodied worker doing the abstract job comes to a real worker is the male worker whose life centers on his full-time, life-long job, while his wife or another woman takes care of his personal needs and his children' (p. 149).

While women have been greatly increasing their participation in the workforce, this increase has been greatest among precisely those women who are most unlike the abstract worker of organisational and human relations theory – women with children and, increasingly, elderly dependents for whom they are primarily responsible. For as research is consistently showing, women's increased labour force participation has not been matched by any equivalent increase in men's family responsibilities (Bittman 1994). And within the workforce, a range of institutions and practices continue to devalue the skills and experiences of women, and to exclude them from positions of organisational influence.

A gendered view of post-Fordism and the new work order

Much of the contemporary interest in workplace learning, whether rhetorical or critical, derives from major changes in work organisation in the OECD countries promoting the growth of the 'knowledge-based' or information economy (Castells 1996). For some writers the changes associated with the demise of unprofitable Fordist production methods in high-wage countries are sufficiently radical to amount to the emergence of 'a new work order'. Central to the new work order is 'the (active) knowledge and flexible learning needed to design, market, perfect, and vary goods and services as symbols of identity, not on the actual product itself as a material good' (Gee *et al.* 1996: 26). As Catherine Casey puts it in Chapter 2, the emphasis now is on ' "empowered" team-playing employees maximally performing in participatory organizational "cultures" '; employees 'can exercise new forms of skill, knowledge, responsibility and commitment'.

Business consultants and managers are prominent among the authors of a spate of texts that celebrate and promote the new work order, such as Tom Peter's *Liberation Management* (1992), and Peter Senge's *The Fifth Discipline: The Art and Practice of the Learning Organization* (1991). In their highly critical review of this new work order, Gee *et al.* accept that these kinds of texts have been very influential in a short space of time. 'They are important not only in the domains of business and work – their vision and values have deeply informed contemporary calls for reform both in adult education and training and in schools across the developed world' (1996: 25). Perhaps not surprisingly, such texts have failed to pay close attention to the gendering of these new workplaces.

Women and the learning organisation

While feminist scholars have already warned of the need to subject the central concepts of post-Fordism, flexible specialisation and organizational culture to careful scrutiny, we have at least one empirical study of employment experience in what appears to be a highly successful organisation which points to new forms of female participation in the post-Fordist culture of work.

The US corporation 'Amerco', which is the focus of Arlie Hochschild's book *The Time Bind*, employs over 20,000 people across the USA. Over a third of these employees are women, and 25 per cent of its managers are women (1997: 15). Amerco has adopted a powerful total quality work system which emphasises 'autonomous work teams', 'enriched jobs', and a less obviously hierarchical work structure. The aim of this was 'to create more knowledgeable and company identified workers who would be invited to share with their managers a "common vision" of company goals and to talk over ways of implementing it'. Total quality 'presumes a worker is a capable adult, not a wayward child' (p. 17)

It is not my purpose here to focus on the learning culture in Amerco as such, but rather to draw attention to the apparently gender-inclusive practices and outcomes which Hochschild reports. Hochschild's interest in Amerco stemmed from its status as one of the ten most 'family-friendly' companies in the USA, but what she discovered was that hardly any parents took advantage of the policies designed to reduce their hours at work. For example, a tiny proportion of employees worked part time despite the availability of this option (p. 26). What emerged from this qualitative study of an 'ideal type' workplace was a new form of work commitment among its female employees, both those on the factory floor and those in white-collar and more senior positions. For the women in this study their employment at Amerco 'has become a source of security, pride, and a powerful sense of being valued'; they have 'absorbed the views of an older, male-oriented work world about what a real career and real commitment mean to a far greater extent than men have been willing to share "women's" responsibilities at home' (p. 247).

It is important to note that the example of how women have responded to opportunities at Amerco does not suggest that Acker's thesis about the gendered nature of organisations and jobs is becoming irrelevant. On the contrary it seems to suggest that organisations (and the jobs and hierarchies that appear as abstract categories within them) have succeeded in rendering workers' bodies and non-work lives even more invisible than before. To the extent that women wish to participate fully in the pleasures and rewards of the post-Fordist workplace they now find themselves behaving even more like men in relation to family responsibilities. While there is as yet little reliable data, we may expect more women to reduce their family commitments in a number of ways, from delaying having children to avoiding them altogether. Others, however, will deal with the conflict created by the demand that they become a 'company identified worker' by looking for alternatives. Anecdotal evidence abounds of senior women abandoning their careers in major law firms or successful corporations because of the impossible time demands, and seeking alternative work structures that are genuinely family-friendly. In Australia, for example, the very substantial increase in women running their own small businesses is partly attributed to this phenomenon.

The qualitative study of Amerco might be taken as typical of contemporary work organization precisely because of its consonance with the prescriptive content of so much management literature in the 1990s. Just as the car production line became the most studied workplace of Fordist industrial societies in the years after the Second World War, so Amerco and Hepheastus (Casey 1995) may be taken as exemplars of the post-Fordist era. But, just as the Fordist production line was nearly everywhere and always quite unrepresentative of the majority of workplaces, so Amerco and its new gender cultures may be but one rather small part of a much larger picture.

Gendered knowledge occupations

A characteristic of post-industrial societies is the strong expansion of what Castells calls information occupations (1996: 218), including the group

Reich so memorably labelled the 'symbolic analysts' (1992: 177). If we use the framework of occupational analysis we can see a strong expansion of employment in managerial, administrative, professional and technical jobs in which high levels of credentials and skills, together with continuous learning, are important. At the aggregate level there is clear evidence of women's increasing representation within this class. However, a more detailed British study of how women have fared in the expansion of these middle-class occupations argues that 'women have moved into positions of high *expertise,* but not into positions of high *authority*' (Savage 1992: 124). This research shows that women are still rarely able to advance their careers within bureaucracies by climbing an organisational ladder. 'Instead, these women who do manage to achieve careers within the middle classes tend to pursue "occupational" careers, usually within subordinate professional niches. Women's careers are usually based upon deepening their expertise, not on moving into organizational power' (1992: 125).

Savage argues that in situations where women cannot be prevented from acquiring relevant credentials (i.e. where these are gained externally, or in highly formalised ways available equally to men and women) they can gain expertise and professional employment. What such credentials cannot do, however, is ensure access to senior positions of organisational power and authority, since these are not dependent on such educational credentials. At this level management remains overwhelmingly male, and active in the exclusion of women (p. 148). What this study suggests is that opportunities for learning within bureaucratic organizations are still highly gendered, with women having to rely on external accreditation of expertise while men can move up within the organisation. This picture of women's unequal access to opportunities for workplace learning and reliance on self-help through external training is repeated at the other end of the employment spectrum. Butler and Connole have shown that in Australia the training offered to women in a range of feminised industries is 'unaccredited and narrowly task focused such as word processing or telephone techniques; or related to "emotional labour" such as client interaction, "aggression training", or "how to handle difficult people"' (1994: 9). To learn in ways that are of labour market advantage such women must look outside the workplace and pay for their own training.

While Savage's study of the gendering of the new knowledge occupations focuses on the exclusion of women from positions of real authority, it also points to the value of formal credentials to women in securing particular forms of career advancement – forms where their investment in human capital appears to bring good returns. The issue of the financial rewards to be gained from workplace learning and formal training of different kinds is one that is central to studies of gender pay equity. Human capital theory suggests a fairly straightforward relationship between pay and such measures of human capital as qualifications, skills and relevant work experience. However, a study of gender pay equity in Australian universities (Probert *et al.* 1998) found that this relationship was rather different for women working as academics compared with women working as general staff (such as administrative and library staff). For male and female academics the most important factor determining their career progression was the number of years they had worked full time in higher education. Also of considerable importance was the possession of formal postgraduate qualifications (1998:45). Women's lower income was, to a substantial extent, explained by their fewer years of experience and lower levels of formal qualifications. Inasmuch as women invested in the learning recognised by universities to the same extent as men, they tended to reap similar rewards.

For women working as general staff, by contrast, the relationship between their human capital and their income was far less straightforward. Men held significantly higher positions than women regardless of equivalent qualifications, suggesting that women are systematically underclassified according to their qualifications. A similar pattern was found in relation to the other central element of human capital, work experience, with men with the same amount of work experience in higher education reaching higher levels than their female counterparts (1998: 69–71).

Feminised career structures

A third example of emerging labour market structures is to be found in the internal labour markets in some of the new service industries where women are far more reliant on workplace training than formal qualifications. As Lovering has shown, 'in catering and retail, where employee–customer interaction is important to competitiveness, some large companies are also constructing new career ladders and promotion incentives to attract an "improved calibre of staff" ' (1990: 15). However, many of these new industries rely heavily on 'gendered jobs', and their new internal labour markets tend to be segmented accordingly. In banks and building societies, for example, there are new 'career clerical hierarchies' through which some women can rise to the position of branch manager, though few get any further. Employers are thus creating more segmented and truncated internal labour markets. Only a small group of employees will be targeted for training and promotion opportunities and management development programmes. For the majority the training provided will overwhelmingly be at the entry level for very task-specific skills.

In Australia, attempts to introduce structured training in feminised industries have failed to begin with an investigation of the unrecognised skills already being used in these areas, let alone any recognition of the skills which many women bring 'from previous life and employment experience' (Butler and Connole 1994: 13). Furthermore, there has been almost no development of middle-level skill development as opposed to entry-level skills training, which may create a 'cardboard' ceiling for women (Butler 1997: 49).

If we look at one of the main feminised areas of employment such as retailing, we find in Australia at least, a resolutely low-skill, low-pay model of work organisation prevailing (Probert 1995:11), which takes for granted the continuing oversupply of women, and particularly married women, willing to accept what Janet Siltanen has called 'component wage jobs' (1994: 77–9), in which a full-time workforce has been replaced with a largely part-time one. A similar story is to be found in the banking industry, where a sharp increase in the use of permanent part-time employees (mostly mature women with 'emotional labour skills') has been the result of a desire to retain valued employees who can be deployed with great flexibility. Most permanent part-time jobs 'provide indefinite employment in an area of the labour market that is segregated outside the career stream' (Junor 1998: 89). Women in the part-time workforce are acutely aware of the lack of career opportunities, and the lack of financial return on training.

Women learning in teams

The introduction of teams in such a way as to increase the autonomy of lower-level workers, reduce the role of supervision, provide greater variety of task, and treat employees as capable adults is a central component of the new work order. This form of work organisation implies both greater explicit opportunities for learning as well as the promotion of new attitudes to learning. In fact, its introduction is often associated with employee selection processes that are far more focused on attitudes or 'personality' than existing skills (Probert with McDonald 1996: 39). Some feminist analyses of gender structures in the workplace raise questions about the likely development of 'ungendered teams'. As Jenson puts it:

> What is unclear is whether such groups [teams] will mix together workers who are 'different' in ways which are relevant to the actors involved....In such tightly knit work collectives, the topic of group composition comes to the fore. Thus questions of difference – whether to include and cooperate with workers who are ethnically, racially or sexually 'different' – can appear in the workplace.
>
> (1989: 154).

Jenson concludes that 'the work teams that enthusiasts of flexible specialization predict with such relish are likely, under current workplace politics, to be single-sex groups, for which gender difference becomes a boundary' (p. 154).

In manufacturing, the new forms of teamwork and opportunities for learning have tended to benefit those already holding skilled jobs, who are overwhelmingly men. And there is likely to be little change in this since apprenticeships remain almost exclusively the preserve of men. In 1996 in Australia, for example, not many more than 10 per cent of apprentices were women, despite a great deal of activity designed to increase this proportion. Relatively few women work in high-level production jobs, and new forms of work organisation have seen the less skilled work separated out and redesigned for a contingent workforce. A Swedish longitudinal study of core and peripheral employment in industrial plants concluded that women whose less skilled jobs disappeared as a result of company cutbacks experienced a state of 'permanent temporariness' in which they were only able to land a series of temporary jobs. Men were significantly more likely to regain their footing in the labour market, finding full-time permanent employment (Gonas and Westin 1993). Similar trends have been found in US firms, with employers making 'significant investments in training male workers for secure, well-paid jobs, allowing them flexibility in task performance, job sites, and skill acquisition, while 'disinvesting' in female- and minority-dominated occupations where they need the cheapest, most variable, routinized, least politically demanding labour' (Smith and Gottfried 1997: 21).

Contingent or irregular and insecure workers appear to represent the antithesis of that multiskilled, company-identified employee described as integral to the new work order. The former may, however, be seen as the logical counterpart to the latter, providing much needed numerical flexibility. Since women form the vast majority of the contingent workforce in most countries, this raises profound problems for women's objective opportunities to learn at the workplace. The decline in opportunities appears, not surprisingly, to shape women's attitudes not only to the value of any learning linked to the workplace, but to the value of paid work itself.

While much of the interest in teams has focused on manufacturing work, they have equal relevance in some areas of feminised service work. Teams have, for example, been introduced among cleaning and domestic staff (largely female) in some Australian hospitals, and the response of some women (often migrants from non-English-speaking countries) confirms the enormous potential for learning. As one married woman, a migrant from Greece, put it: 'You learn all the time, you meet new people, learn different roles, different from before'. Another migrant woman from Yugoslavia said:

> it's not only the cleaning – we're involved with everything, it's inter-
> esting....You work like a team, all together. It doesn't matter if you are
> a PSA [Patient Services Assistant] or from the kitchen, nurses too – we
> help each other, discuss, never say no to each other.
>
> (Probert with McDonald 1996: 41–2)

The informal learning that is occurring through this form of work organisation is not recognised as learning by employers, nor is it in their interests that it should be. For these women, working in occupations that are low paid and where skills are likely to be undervalued because of their domestic nature, the learning opportunities provide powerful intrinsic rewards, but little in the way of economic rewards. The same women are acutely aware that they work harder as a result of the changes, and that the material benefits of this accrue to the employer. This example raises again the perennial problem of how feminised jobs can ensure equitable returns on learning. At the same time it should be noted that the shift to team-based work required all staff to move to full-time employment, thereby excluding part-timers from the benefits yet again.

Part-time work and workplace learning

Many writers have argued that the new labour market is one that presents increasingly polarised work opportunities, with a core and a periphery or diverging primary and secondary labour markets, almost defined by educational capital and opportunities for learning. Of particular concern has been the growth of casual and part-time work and evidence that it represents the expansion of less desirable forms of employment or the secondary labour market. In Australia the number of part-time jobs increased about 300 per cent between the early 1970s and the early 1990s, while full-time jobs increased over the same period by only 20 per cent. Part-time work has increased from 16 per cent of total employment in 1978 to over 25.5 per cent in 1997. This trend has not been a steady one, however, but rather an accelerating one, particularly since 1991. The most recent labour force statistics also show an absolute decline in the number of full-time jobs available. By far the most significant characteristic of part-time workers is their sex. In Australia almost 75 per cent of people working part time are women (and the majority of men who work part time are full-time students) (Australian Bureau of Statistics (ABS) 1997).

The conditions attaching to part-time work vary from country to country, as does the proportion of employed women who work part time. However, the gendered segmentation of the labour market around the distinction between part-time and full-time work is a significant feature of women's work experiences. A British study of employment in the retail and hotel industries shows that the construction of 'irregular' jobs and their association with inferior working conditions is inextricably linked to managerial perceptions of gender differentiation in the workforce. Employers justified the inferior working conditions associated with irregular cleaning and cooking jobs with explicitly gendered perceptions and valuations of skill. These jobs were ' "suitable for women" precisely because they "had experience", even an "inherent aptitude", based on domestic responsibilities' (Walsh 1990: 524).

A small proportion of part-time work in Australia is on a permanent basis, and in some cases the introduction of permanent part-time work has been the result of sustained campaigning from trade unions on behalf of their female members. Disappointingly, research suggests that for those women who take advantage of the opportunity to convert to part-time employment, their careers come to a halt. For example, a review of permanent part-time working in the Australian Taxation Office found that 'going part time means putting your career on hold' (URCOT 1995). Similarly, a review of permanent part-time work in case studies of banking, adult education and travel business concludes that those taking it up saw themselves as then being moved 'outside the career stream' (Junor 1998: 84). This is confirmed by a British analysis of the differences between part-time work and full-time work which concludes that the most important relate to employment-related benefits and opportunities for promotion (Rubery *et al.* 1994).

These findings are related to workplace learning in two kinds of ways. Firstly, they suggest that women working part time are somehow sidelined from the organisation's learning opportunities. They may, for example, find themselves unable to participate in job rotation schemes or opportunities to act at a higher level, both of which can be significant learning experiences for career development. Secondly, women simply find themselves unable to participate in training designed for the full-time workforce because such training is offered during non-working hours or without adequate supports such as the provision of child care. Since most women who work part time do so because of family responsibilities, it is hardly surprising that they are often excluded from learning activities designed around a full-time worker. In male-dominated trade areas women working part time are unable to participate since most apprenticeships are established on a full-time work model. The disadvantages in relation to training experienced by women working part time are even more strongly felt by those who are employed on a casual basis (who make up the vast majority of all part-time employees in Australia).

Gendered attitudes to work and workplace learning

The distinction between full-time and part-time workers is of prime significance for those with an interest in workplace learning, since data about these patterns are used to support competing and sometimes controversial claims about the nature of men's and women's commitment to work, and gendered identities in the workplace. Indeed, Hakim (1993) has argued from a rational choice theoretical perspective that women who work part time are very different from women who work full time, and that this difference is critical in explaining women's failure either to win equal rights in the workplace with men or to transform the workplace in women's interests.

In a review of the vast international literature on work orientations, work attitudes or work values, Hakim concludes that there has indeed been a decline in sex differences since the early 1980s (and this is partly due to men becoming less committed to work as well as women becoming more committed) (1996: 106). Once part-time workers are included, however, the picture is rather different and Hakim argues that 'the commitment of a part-time worker to their part-time job is not equal to the commitment of a full-time worker to their full-time job' (p. 106). In particular, women working part time are far less likely to see themselves having a career. According to rational choice theory, women's investment in the home leads them 'to choose jobs that are less effort intensive and are generally compatible with domestic responsibilities. It causes occupational segregation since wives will seek jobs that are less demanding even if they work full-time' (1996: 14). The implications of this line of argument for women's workplace learning are substantial, with very significant numbers of women workers being defined as relatively uninterested in opportunities for such learning, be they formal or informal.

Needless to say, Hakim's arguments have been strongly criticised by other researchers of women's labour market behaviour (Breugel 1996) on both empirical and conceptual grounds. Some studies have shown that men and women in similar occupations show remarkably similar degrees of work commitment (Bradley 1997), regardless of the presence of dependent children (Probert *et al.* 1998: 52).

Other responses to Hakim's arguments have focused on the unproblematic use of the concept of 'choice' to explain men's and women's different workforce participation patterns. Given that the choices women make appear to be strongly shaped by their previous experience of work as well as their current employment opportunities, there are powerful external influences at work. Qualitative research into women's decisions about the balance between work and family finds extremely diverse narratives of both necessity and choice (Probert 1997). In particular, many women thinking about returning to the workforce after a period of full-time responsibility for their families feel strongly that the skills and learning that go on outside the paid workforce are not only unrecognised, but that this time is seen by employers as *reducing* the level of their workplace skills. In this respect work commitment is reduced not by the preferences of married women but by their experience of employer attitudes and the contemporary double bind created by social values about full-time parenting, which on the one hand encourage maternal sacrifice in favour of family interests but on the other make full-time mothers feel they are 'some sort of imbecile' (Probert with McDonald 1996: 30). In Australia many such women actively seek out appropriate learning environments, in particular in the adult and community education sector, to develop work skills in order to overcome these disadvantages. Participants in this sector are estimated to be somewhere between 80 and

95 per cent women, with the majority aged between 35 and 54 years (Butler 1997: 32).

If we define work commitment not as some kind of fixed psychological disposition, but rather as the outcome of a range of experiences which may be strongly self-reinforcing or equally strongly undermining of confidence, we will look at workplace learning in a very different manner. For many women who have primary responsibility for their young children, returning to work is valued highly for its learning opportunities, for 'keeping the brain alive', and for providing the stimulation and satisfaction of increasing skills (Probert with McDonald 1996: 30–2).

Domestic commitments and in particular full-time responsibility for the care of children cannot be understood simply as constraints on women's labour supply behaviour and their commitment to work and workplace learning, since such commitments are themselves related to economic inequality. In particular poor employment prospects are a powerful disincentive for women.

Conclusions

In this chapter the concept of workplace learning has been defined very loosely to refer to a range of practices, opportunities and dispositions, all of which may be shaped by formal and informal means. The fact that women now make up a far greater proportion of the workforce in countries like Australia makes the need for a gendered analysis of these dispositions, practices and opportunities both more important and more complex. Indeed, it is increasingly meaningless to talk about 'women's work experience' as something unitary, or women workers as an undifferentiated group. At one extreme, for example, there has been an expansion in the proportion of jobs involving high levels of formal qualifications in professional, technical and managerial fields and this has created new opportunities for well-qualified women, while at the other, there is the well-documented growth in casualised and insecure employment where women are strongly overrepresented.

Data on the nature of the occupational structure of post-industrial economies are relatively simply to obtain, but what is more difficult is to explain the distribution of different groups between occupations. Nonetheless, it is worth recognising the continuities in women's unequal access to and benefit from workplace learning. These include the undervaluing of women's learning in feminised occupations and industries, the consistent pattern of task-specific training over career development learning, and the vital importance of women's access to formalised and accredited training that goes beyond the lowest-level skills if they are to be rewarded equitably for their investment in human capital. A gendered analysis alerts us to the fact that the very unequal distribution of men and women overall cannot be explained in terms of their historical investment in learning, or their commitment to workplace learning.

There are no grounds for believing that the new emphasis on workplace learning will do anything other than reproduce these inequities since the dominant discourses continue to rely on abstracted conceptions of work and workers that privilege men. More particularly, some of the forms of hiring and work organisation associated with the new work order may exacerbate gender segregation in the workplace on unequal terms. Both Lovering (1990) and more recently Castells (1996) have argued that in post-industrial or information labour markets recruitment practices frequently mobilise 'social criteria' (age, ethnic background and gender) rather than technical or competency-based criteria. According to Lovering an increased reliance on social criteria flows from the fact that workers are increasingly required to cooperate in a set of social relationships (1990: 17), while traditional internal labour markets are declining. This means that a smaller proportion of employees can make a career simply by following the rules, with employers increasingly using differentiated recruitment and training channels. Castells argues, similarly, that the inequalities in what he calls informational societies do not stem from any increased polarisation of the occupational structure itself, but rather from 'the exclusions and discriminations that take place in and around the labor force' – exclusions that focus on the 'gender/ethnic/age characteristics' of the labor force (1996: 220). As Jenson concludes:

> [S]tress on co-operation, on consultation, and on planning can make it seem compelling to find 'pals' with whom one feels comfortable. In this way, as a by-product of the new management form of work organization, internal lines of cleavage in the working class around very visible differences may be accentuated. Work groups, by their very form, foster 'we/they' feelings and relationships; boundaries are drawn which differentiate.
>
> (1989: 154)

The exclusions involving gender characteristics are inextricably linked to the wider sexual division of labour in society, and women's continued and unchanged responsibilities for the care of children and elderly dependents. There is now very substantial international evidence which suggests that women's increased labour force participation has not been matched by any significant increase in men's responsibility for the domestic sphere. The way in which opportunities for workplace learning are provided (for the abstract/disembodied worker), and the way women define and respond to these opportunities, is profoundly shaped by household structures and men's needs and interests within them. Women's domestic roles are used to justify their exclusion from equal financial rewards as well as training and career opportunities. At the same time, in occupations where formal educational qualifications are critical (higher education, law, medicine, accounting and so on), as opposed to managerial prerogative and selective fast-tracking, work intensification renders the work/family tension even more unmanageable. Meanwhile gendered jobs continue to be created in the secondary labour market, aimed at women who are defined as less committed than men. These jobs, which are increasingly casual and insecure, are expanding not just in the obvious sectors such as retailing, but also in professional but feminised sectors such as teaching. Here again, the destruction of secure career paths, and a growing reliance on one-year contracts, will have a major impact on the formation of human capital and the logic of learning.

The feminisation of the post-industrial workforce cannot be assumed to have reduced the significance of the concepts of gendered workers and gendered work, as well as gendered labour markets. An understanding of the way gender shapes the new jobs, organisations and labour markets is essential if we are to understand how workplace learning is structured and practised in contemporary workplaces.

References

Acker, J. (1990) 'Hierarchies, jobs, bodies: a theory of gendered organizations', *Gender and Society* 4(2): 139–58.

Appelbaum, E. (1993) 'New technology and work organisation: the role of gender relations', in B. Probert and B. Wilson (eds) *Pink Collar Blues: Work, Gender and Technology*, Melbourne: Melbourne University Press.

Australian Bureau of Statistics (various years) *The Labour Force Australia*, Canberra: Australian Government Publishing Service.

Bittman, M. (1994) *Recent Changes in Unpaid Work*, Occasional Paper, Catalogue No. 4154.0, Canberra: Australian Government Publishing Service.

Bradley, H. (1997) 'Gender and change in employment: feminization and its effects', in R. Brown (ed.) *The Changing Shape of Work*, Basingstoke: Macmillan.

Breugel, I. (1996) 'Whose myths are they anyway?', *British Journal of Sociology* 47(1): 175–7.

Butler, E. (1997) *Beyond Political Housework: Gender Equity in the Post-School Environment*, Sydney: Department for Women, New South Wales.

Butler, E. and Connole, H.(1992) 'Sitting next to Nellie', in *What Future for Technical and Vocational Education?*, International Conference Papers, Vol. 2, NCVER, Adelaide.

Butler, E. and Connole, H. (1994) 'Training reform and gender: reframing training for women workers', in *(re)Forming Post-Compulsory Education and Training: Reconciliation and Reconstruction*, Conference Papers, Centre for Skill Formation Research and Development, Griffith University, Brisbane.

Casey, C. (1995) *Work, Self and Society: After Industrialism*, London: Routledge.

Castells, M. (1996) *The Rise of the Network Society*, Oxford: Blackwell.

Game, A. and Pringle, R. (1983) *Gender at Work*, Sydney: Allen and Unwin.

Gee, J. P., Hull, G. and Lankshear, C. (1996) *The New Work Order*, Sydney: Allen and Unwin.

Gonas, L. and Westin, H. (1993) 'Industrial restructuring and gendered labour market processes', *Economic and Industrial Democracy* 14: 423–57.

Hakim, C. (1993) 'The myth of rising female employment', *Work, Employment and Society* 7(1): 97–120.

Hakim, C. (1996) *Key Issues in Women's Work*, London: Athlone.

Hochschild, A. (1997) *The Time Bind*, New York: Metropolitan Books.

Jenson, J. (1989) 'The talents of women, the skills of men: flexible specialization and women', in S. Wood (ed.) *The Transformation of Work?*, London: Unwin Hyman.

Junor, A. (1998) 'Permanent part-time work: new family-friendly standard or high intensity cheap skills', *Labour and Industry* 8(3): 77–95.

Lawrence, K. (1994) 'Valuing women: new approaches to/for the training reform agenda', in *(re)Forming Post-Compulsory Education and Training: Reconciliation and Reconstruction*, Conference Proceedings Vol. 1, Centre for Skill Formation Research and Development, Griffith University, Brisbane.

Liff, S. (1990) 'Clerical workers and information technology: gender relations and occupational change', *New Technology, Work and Employment* 5(1): 44–55.

Liff, S. (1993) 'Information technology and occupational restructuring in the office', in E. Green, J. Owen and D. Pain (eds) *Gendered by Design? Information Technology and Office Systems*, London: Taylor and Francis.

Lovering, J. (1990) 'A perfunctory sort of post-Fordism: economic restructuring and labour market segmentation in Britain in the 1980s', *Work, Employment and Society*, Special Issue, May: 9–28.

Peters, T. (1992) *Liberation Management: Necessary Disorganization for the Nanosecond Nineties*, New York: Vintage Books.

Phillips, A. (1983) 'Review of *Brothers*', *Feminist Review* 15: 101–4.

Phillips, A. and Taylor, B. (1980) 'Sex and skill: notes towards feminist economics', *Feminist Review* 6: 79–88.

Poynton, C. (1993) 'Naming women's workplace skills', in B. Probert and B. Wilson (eds) *Pink Collar Blues: Work, Gender and Technology*, Melbourne: Melbourne University Press.

Probert, B. (1995) *Part-Time Work and Managerial Strategy: Flexibility in the New Industrial Relations Framework*, Department of Employment, Education and Training, Canberra: Australian Government Publishing Service.

Probert, B. (1997) 'Choice and the structure of opportunity: the future of women's work in Australia', in P. James, W. Veit and S. Wright (eds) *Work of the Future: Global Perspectives*, Sydney: Allen and Unwin.

Probert, B. with F. McDonald (1996) *The Work Generation: Work and Identity in the 1990s*, Melbourne: Brotherhood of St Laurence.

Probert, B., Ewer, P. and Whiting, K. (1998) *Gender Pay Equity in Australian Higher Education*, Melbourne: National Tertiary Education Union.

Reich, R. (1992) *The Wealth of Nations*, New York: Random House.

Rubery, J., Horrell, S. and Burchell, B. (1994) 'Part-time work and gender inequality in the labour market', in A. M. Scott (ed.) *Gender Segregation and Social Change*, Oxford: Oxford University Press.

Savage, M. (1992) 'Women's expertise, men's authority', in M. Savage and A. Witz (eds) *Gender and Bureaucracy*, Oxford: Blackwell.

Senge, P. (1991) *The Fifth Discipline: The Art and Practice of the Learning Organization*, New York: Doubleday.

Siltanen, J. (1994) *Locating Gender: Occupational Segregation, Wages and Domestic Responsibilities*, London: UCL Press.

Smith, M. and Ewer, P. (1995) *The Position of Women in the National Training Reform Agenda and Enterprise Bargaining*, Department of Employment, Education and Training, Canberra: Australian Government Publishing Service.

Smith, V. and Gottfried, H. (1997) 'Flexibility and employment: the impact on women', Unpublished paper.

URCOT (1995) *Review of Permanent Part time Employment in the Australian Taxation Office: Report of focus group discussions*, Melbourne: Union Research Centre on Organisation and Technology.

Walsh, T. (1990) 'Flexible labour utilisation in the private service sector', *Work, Employment and Society* 4(4): 517–30.

Part III
Issues in practice

8 Culture and difference in workplace learning

Nicky Solomon

There is little argument that there has been enormous cultural change in the workplace. This has been accompanied by new interest in the use of culture as a management technology and a new interest in the productive potential of difference. Indeed the terms 'culture' and 'difference' have become central in workplace learning discourse. However while 'culture' and 'difference' are now part of everyday work language – organisational culture, team culture, a learning culture, cultural differences, celebrating diversity, cross-cultural training, culturally diverse workforce, crossing cultural boundaries – their meanings remain almost taken for granted and unexplored. This chapter, as part of a book whose purpose is to explore workplace learning, aims to surface some of the challenges that the terms 'culture' and 'difference' demand of workplace educators.

The chapter begins with a discussion of why 'culture' has become a central part of workplace discourse. This discussion is important as it not only considers the significance of 'culture' for contemporary work but also aims to demonstrate how the discourse of 'culture' has foregrounded issues of 'difference'. By considering learning in the workplace as a cultural practice, the relationship of culture and difference and the tensions around working within a common set of beliefs and attitudes while celebrating difference will be explored. This chapter will then examine 'difference' by considering the ways difference is spoken about and how this talk influences work and training practices.

The cliché-like usage of 'culture' and 'difference' suggests a common understanding about their meanings, implying that the practices and activities associated with them require little analysis or discussion. I suggest, however, that the unreflexive usage of these terms is superficial, counterproductive and inconsistent with their intention. The terms require discussion, problematisation and analysis. This is needed if we are to surface and unravel their complexities so that organisational and workplace learning dialogues and practices actually engage with matters of culture and difference.

This chapter is part of this engagement. It contextualises and problematises understandings about culture and difference. By articulating some of the complexities it aims to offer a way forward.

Culture in the contemporary workplace

As suggested above, an important workplace discourse is emerging around culture. Culture in this discourse signifies a number of changes in our understanding of culture as well as in the nature of contemporary work. Of course, workplaces in earlier decades did have a culture but they were not talked about as having a culture. There are a number of overlapping reasons for this related to the various meanings people have given to culture. The term culture has often had meanings related to lifestyle practices but until recently these mainly referred to lifestyle practices outside work – such as 'high' cultural activities related to the arts as well as everyday folk practices of 'ethnic groups'. It was outside of work where people made meaning of their lives. However, more recently the use of the term 'culture' has not been confined to life practices in a specific set of contexts but is more frequently used to describe 'a way of life'. Culture is used to describe how people group and identify themselves, that is the social human bonds, shared goals, belief systems and values that connect people. We now talk about groups and discourses in cultural terms, for example sports culture, youth culture, street-kid culture and workplace culture, in recognition of the lived experiences of groups of people as they relate to each other and make meaning of their lives.

> Culture is socially created forms of human interaction and cohesion. It arises through socialisation and learning; it is neither natural nor fixed. Culture entails multiple personal and social meanings, relationships, practices and values.
> (*Cultural Understandings as the Eighth Key Competency* 1994: 14)

Through the changes in post-industrial work and the accompanying changes in workplace practices, 'culture' has become central to workplace discourse. Industrial work practices had been organised around what has become known as a Fordist model of work. This model of work is characterised by scientific management, individual work tasks, roles and responsibilities, mass production of single products, where 'the human arrangement of the organisation is configured as if it were itself a machine' (Cope and Kalantzis 1997: 11). Over the last few decades this model has been critiqued as no longer relevant. Firstly, it is now recognised that people, particularly those in post-industrial countries, are less inclined to work in unrewarding jobs; secondly, the development of new technologies has enabled greater flexibility in the production of goods and services as well as in communication practices; and finally mass products (e.g. any car as long as it is black) no longer suits. Consumers now demand multiple choices and specialised goods and services. The combination of these factors has forced acknowledgement of the dynamic and human nature of post-industrial work – which is often referred to as the new work order or post-Fordism.

This understanding of the nature of contemporary work is reflected in the way work is described in both the literature, for example 'Gone then – except, again, in the backwaters of the old capitalism – are workers hired from the neck down and simply told what to do' (Gee *et al.* 1996: 19), and in the workplace itself, for example:

> The most critical task in this workplace is getting on with people. Dealing with people is the most important part of the job – these days it is the only way of ensuring that the technical operations run smoothly.
>
> (Joyce *et al.* 1995; data collected during research interviews with management and line supervisors)

With this foregrounding of the human, the primacy of the technical is being overshadowed by the social and the cultural.

It would be a mistake, however, to describe all workplaces or work practices as post-Fordist. Work practices in many workplaces still reflect the hierarchical, fixed horizontal and vertical relationships where many workers have narrowly defined job duties and responsibilities character-istic of a Fordist workplace. Nevertheless, in terms of contemporary management philosophy there is a movement towards teamwork and flatter hierarchies. When work is organised in this way employees at various levels participate in decision-making fora where the different back-grounds, experiences and different perspectives are understood to enhance the productive potential of teams. As employees engage in diverse social activities and new language practices, workplace culture and a valuing of difference is seen as the basis for employee motivation, public image and organisational effectiveness.

In recognition of the significance of social relationships at work it has been argued by Anthony (1994) as quoted in du Gay (1996) that:

> in order to compete effectively in the turbulent global economic envi-ronment, the foremost necessity is to 'make meaning' for people at work. 'Culture' is (therefore) accorded a privileged position in their endeavour because it is seen to structure the way people think, feel and act in organizations.
>
> (1996: 41)

In other words, 'culture' may be understood as the new technology for managing work and managing people.

Workplace learning as a 'cultural practice'

While learning has always been a feature of working, learning at work, like workplace culture, has a new status in contemporary workplace discourse. The emphasis on ongoing skills development in the context of the rapidly changing demands of work is reflected in the contemporary management literature with concepts such as the 'learning organisation' (Senge 1990, Field 1995), 'knowledge worker' (Gee *et al.* 1996, Reich 1991) as well as in the expanding training industry. Learning at work can no longer be described as a discrete activity for some, nor as an activity that occurs only at occasional moments in one's career. Rather in the productive workplace, learning is considered to be part of everyday work. Workplace learning can be understood as a cultural practice constructed by contemporary discursive practices of work. Learning is also constructing work discourses.

When considering the cultural practice of learning in the workplace it is important to examine the related social and economic factors that shape training in contemporary workplaces. As discussed earlier, work practices are undergoing considerable change as management strives to ensure efficiency and productivity in order to remain competitive in the local and global markets. These changes involve the development of a corporate culture through the development of mission and vision statements, an identification of workers with corporate aims and the conceptualisation of an organisation as a site of ongoing learning. The training associated with these changes is, however, not simply organisation specific. Over the last decade governments have played a major role not only in industry restructuring policies but also in accompanying education and training policies.

Contemporary training practices therefore, like work practices, differ significantly from those of a decade ago. While previously workplace training programmes were determined by local decisions made in response to local needs, training today in OECD countries is most frequently constructed within a competency-based training framework. This framework has been developed through government, industry and education partnerships resulting in policies and industry competency standards that represent institutionally recognised and legitimate knowledge.

A useful starting point therefore, in understanding the cultural construction of workplace learning in the current context, is to understand that competency training is not neutral, natural or objective. Indeed competency categories are intended to classify and measure, and the standards are there in order to judge who is competent and who is not competent:

> the discourse of competence reconstructs a technology of power within the education and training system as part of wider changes in the social formation, and does so in ways which construct individuals as responsible for their own position in the labour market and their

contribution to it. Power is exercised over and through them. As they become competent, they are 'empowered' and 'disempowered'.

(Edwards and Usher 1994: 7)

Industry competency standards, one of the key technologies for the construction of the skilled competent worker, can be understood therefore as a set of regulatory practices. This regulation is realised in the call for standardisation and benchmarking, and in the boundaries around 'units of work' and 'units of learning'. It could be argued that such prescriptions and boundaries run counter to contemporary discourse around difference and understandings about the 'organic nature of work' in workplaces that demand flexibility of production, service and work practices. They could therefore be seen as a technology for constructing 'sameness' that renders invisible the overlaps and complex relationships that allow for different ways of doing and being at work.

Importantly, though, at the same time difference can be seen as integral to competency training. Indeed part of the compelling philosophy of competency training is its 'learner-centredness' and the implications this has for difference through its design and focus on the 'individual learner'. The focus on the learners has many shapes and forms, an important one being the explicit 'transparent' descriptions that are comprehensible and thus 'accessible' to learners. Perhaps the most seductive quality of competency training, though, is that it is designed to meet the needs of individuals by placing learners at the centre thus giving them a sense of control over their learning (Usher 1997). This humanistic face suggests a sense of autonomy.

Furthermore this autonomous learner is situated within a particular set of pedagogical practices – learner-centred ones in contrast to teacher-centred ones. The latter is often characterised by predetermined content and activities, testing through exams, silent learners taking notes, and individual learning tasks/projects, while learner-centred pedagogical practices include negotiated content and activities, negotiated learning contracts and portfolios, oral participation, and group work. These learner-centred pedagogical practices resemble (at least in language) work practices in the post-Fordist workplace. Words such as *groups, participation, collaboration, negotiation* are key terms in the contemporary workplace discourse. This mirroring may or may not be coincidental but either way it takes us back to the earlier point about the multiple connected factors that influence the nature of workplace learning. As workplace learning becomes increasingly integrated into everyday work practices and further away from discrete classroom training programmes, the socialising of people to be certain kinds of workers is accompanied by a complementary socialization to be certain kinds of learners.

A recently completed commissioned research project (Joyce *et al.* 1995) highlighted this intimate relationship between the identity of the worker and the processes and goals of training. The project, which focused on communication practices in restructuring workplaces, investigated three food industry enterprises – each at different moments in the restructuring process. Senior management at each of the sites spoke emphatically about the relationship between the vision of the workplace and the role of training in the construction of particular kinds of workers. For example:

> The vision of this company focuses on teamwork and effective teamwork is dependent on three things: understanding and sharing of vision, commitment to it by all and underpinning all of this is training.

> The first task is to get teams and training started. People have to learn to accept the team concept.

The dialectical relationship of post-Fordist work practices and training was confirmed in interviews with middle management, although, as the following quotes demonstrate, a number of the tensions around the cultural changes also surfaced:

> Many people are scared of change – they don't want to change patterns, routines and familiar faces. They are worried about learning new skills.

> Teams are a good idea but everyone needs to learn and speak team kind of language. Everyone needs training about teamwork. You can't just throw people together and expect them to work as a team. However people are concerned about training and worried about their ability to handle it.

These quotes reveal the entanglement of the tensions around training and the changing work practices. Indeed they merge into one – each part of the same construction of particular kinds of workers.

Workplace educators therefore, whether HRD personnel or managers with learning as part of their briefs, need to exploit the blurred distinction between work and training. Importantly they need to work against the potentially repressive power of workplace learning where the management of training means differences are rendered invisible as learners' experiences are constructed/structured to fit a centrally controlled norm. Workplace educators and trainers, through their immersion within a particular culture, often understand training and learning practices as natural and predetermined. If, on the other hand, they have a greater reflexivity about the cultural construction of their own work, then they can exploit the potential openness of contemporary learning and work practices by 'unsettling the natural'. While learning may be a given within the culture of the workplace, the specific components of this given can be challenged.

Working with difference

Workplace learning, in the contemporary workplace, encompasses the complexities of working within a 'common workplace culture' at the same time as being able to negotiate effectively the meaning and values of differences amongst employees and with consumers.

Difference, within workplaces with shared belief systems, values and attitudes, is talked about in many ways. On the one hand the language of post-Fordist work with its flexible specialisation, teamwork, participatory and collaborative work and decision-making practices all problematise the notion of norms or normality. This is supported by the language of productive diversity (or the celebration of difference) where different knowledge and skills are recognised as valuable resources for the productive workplace in the competitive local, national and international marketplaces. However, on the other hand, in spite of the significance given to 'difference' in the post-Fordist workplace, it is often argued that very particular sets of norms continue to be upheld. Culture in the post-Fordist workplace, as discussed earlier, has meant that diversity, while inevitable and central to work and to the worker, still has to struggle against the seduction of sameness. Indeed it is often argued that in spite of the rhetoric there is still a presumption of sameness where those who are not the same (i.e. have different knowledge and skills) are seen to be in deficit.

This tension in working with difference in a framework that presumes sameness is part of the complexity of competency-based training. For example, recognition of prior learning (RPL) practices, which are considered to be one of the key conceptual shifts that mark the acknowledgement and accreditation of learning outside formal institutions, potentially provides the opportunity for giving meaning to individuals' diverse knowledges, experiences and skills – in other words, provide space and reward for 'the other'. However, when this meaning is recognised and assessed within monocultural classifications of competence, then as Michelson (1996) points out, 'each can only be understood in terms of sameness and conformity'. Recognition of prior learning therefore, while potentially a tool for recognition of difference, often has practices and procedures that assume particular kinds of experiences. Very often the learner's prior experience has to fit into particular categories that have been constructed in a way that determines what is legitimate and non-legitimate experience and knowledge. Moreover, learners have to know how to select and convert their experiences into such categories in order to be 'rewarded'.

While it may be inconsistent with the focus on flexible specialisation and diversity, Cope and Kalantzis (1997) argue that contemporary workplaces fail to manage diversity. They argue that post-Fordism has only fringe awareness of differences, as the focused centre of vision in an organisation is culture as similarity. They support their argument by drawing on

research findings which reveal the continued marginalisation and disen-
franchisement of the non-English-speaking background workforce. Their
interpretation of post-Fordist work as located within a culture of sameness
can be read as overly general in its critique and perhaps ignorant of the
complexities in the way different organisations manage 'difference'.
Nevertheless their work does highlight many of the tensions around sameness and difference in the contemporary workplace.

The tendency towards sameness has pedagogical implications for workplace educators in relation to the role of training. For instance, does
training have an assimilatory or cloning function or is it one that takes
advantage of different knowledge and experiences even when they do not
necessarily sit comfortably within a fixed prescriptive framework?

These tensions around sameness and difference are not new ones in
terms of educational theory and practice. Over the last few decades educators and policy-makers have grappled with quite contradictory desires – on
the one hand the desire is to use education to make people more alike and
on the other 'to serve the different learning styles and needs, the different
cultural orientations, and the different aspirations toward work and living
represented by the diverse population' (Burbules 1997: 98). Yet in spite of
the increased debate and dialogue between educators speaking from tradi-
tionalist positions and educators and theorists speaking from postmodern
positions, in most western countries the increasing shift towards
centralised curriculum and its explicit focus on very particular kinds of
knowledge point to the dominance of 'sameness', 'common' and 'normalising'. As indicated above, this dominance is reflected in vocational
learning and workplace discourses.

Nevertheless the normalising functions of training are often accompanied by an array of cross-cultural training packages – marketed as central
to the management of the diversity of the local and increasingly international workforce. Not surprisingly, the key focus of cross-cultural training
varies considerably in different countries. There is a cultural specificity
reflecting quite different histories and politics around government and
workplace policies to do with cultural differences. Cross-cultural training
in Australia, unlike, say, in the USA where cross-cultural training has a
strong anti-racist function, tends to adopt a 'strength in diversity' model
(ODEOPE 1995, HEROC 1994). This model connects with a productive
diversity policy designed to realise economically the potential of Australia's
culturally and linguistically diverse population. The following quote from
a speech given by the then Prime Minister of Australia demonstrates the
shift in the way government policy constructs cultural difference.

> There have been distinct phases in Australia's postwar response to its
> immigrants. The first phase was characterised by the expectation that
> immigrants would fit into the dominant Anglo-Australian culture. The
> second was characterised by the encouragement of tolerance and

respect for diversity, and the effort to ensure access and equity regardless of ethnic origin. And this effort will continue. But now we have the beginnings of a third phase. We must take advantage of the potentially huge national economic asset which multiculturalism represents. That is what Productive Diversity is about.

(Keating, 1993)

In this productive diversity discourse, cultural differences, usually described in terms of ethnic knowledge and practices, are considered to offer particular kinds of cultural capital that can give organisations a cutting edge in business whether in terms of their export possibilities, local ethnic markets or relationship with multinational partners.

In this kind of training, the focus is market oriented. In order to penetrate new markets the focus is on the content of differences by providing a description of facts about ethnic specificity – the particular attitudes, values and behaviours of particular groups of people that distinguish them from others. However, such groupings often suggest homogeneity within the grouping which in turn often reinforces stereotyping. For example, it is not unusual to hear that NESB (Non-English-Speaking Background) employees have the wrong attitude, or that Asians prefer lecture-style teaching methods, or that older people find it hard to learn or that women can negotiate better. These understandings focus on:

differences between groups, each having its set of characteristics and each set differing from the others. Cultural groups are described as if they were homogenous – differences are between groups and not within them.

(Cope *et al.* 1994: 27)

While information about specific cultural practices can be extremely valuable, at the same time its potential to encourage stereotyping needs to be acknowledged. Care is needed when dealing with specific cultural practices so that they are not seen as static or fixed or single ways of being. Such an understanding denies the dynamic process of culture that recognises the complex hybrid practices that evolve through social interactions. Moreover, this packaging of cultural difference often, even if unwittingly, carries the burden of conflicts between nations and ethnic groups. In addition, stereotyping can also deny the intersections between the various cultural categories, such as age, gender, socioeconomic status and ethnicity as well as the way local contextual factors, such as power relations and regulatory technologies, influence employees' working and learning styles.

Importantly though, training, with its description of the exotic distant other, often does not enable either managers or trainers to identify and work with the complexities around working (and learning) with difference. It is important to move away from the idea that difference is something that is either external or something to be 'fixed up', or even something that is a particular way of being that needs to be learnt as a separate body of knowledge.

All the discourses of diversity are problematic. For instance, Bhabha (1995), Rizvi (1994) and Burbules (1997) each argue that they give an illusion of pluralistic harmony and consensus thus masking the unequal power relations that they may well be perpetuating. Furthermore each asserts that difference in these discourses is seen as benign rather than as a site of struggle or disruption. Moreover, it is only by seeing difference as potentially disruptive that new ways of thinking and doing can emerge. It is after all the ongoing generation of new knowledges and practices that is one of the goals of contemporary work. In other words, rather than taking a view of conflict as one to be resolved, usually through consensus (win win), contemporary work and learning practices perhaps should engage with understandings about difference that challenge the idea that difference is something that needs to be worked through and/or resolved through consensus.

I support Burbules' argument that difference, rather than sameness, be recognised as the norm. This reconceptualisation of difference complements the notion of 'unsettling the natural' referred to in the previous section. It acknowledges that all workers not only have cultural identities but also are cultural boundary crossers as they constantly engage in new cultural contexts, learning new kinds of relationships within and outside the workplace.

Boundary crossing

The final section of this chapter offers a beginning to a more reflective consideration of ways to engage in the complex issues around culture and difference in workplace learning. In the spirit of the aims of the book and the earlier discussion, the intention is not to present a set of guidelines or procedures for working with difference. Rather I would like to suggest a few ideas that help workplace educators and learners to engage more reflexively with their conceptualisation of culture and difference and the accompanying workplace learning practices. These suggestions are organised around three areas: recognition of one's own cultural identity and assumptions about culture and difference; recognition of the culture of the workplace and its assumptions about culture and difference; and finally recognition of the cultural dimensions of workplace learning. The suggestions themselves need to be interrogated and challenged.

The contemporary privileging of 'cultural' and 'social competence' in the workplace provides a space for engaging with the political and social context of work and the complexities around working with difference. This provides an opportunity for workplace educators with their colleagues to recognise and articulate their own values and beliefs and how these have been socially constructed. It is important to question our own beliefs in terms of what they mean for ourselves and for other people, how this influences what one understands to be 'normal' or 'natural', and connected to this, how one views 'difference'. For example, are people with different cultural and language backgrounds seen either as an exotic other – and therefore external and distant – or as part of the 'norm'?

This reflection on one's own cultural understanding can be complemented by an analysis of the culture of the workplace, that is the structures, norms, beliefs and values that underpin certain expectations and behaviours in the organisation. This will involve interpreting the meanings that are displayed and constructed through various organisational 'texts' such as linguistic, behavioural and spatial ones, as well as visual images. It should also include an analysis of the composition of the workforce in terms of gender, age, educational, cultural and language backgrounds and the way these are distributed across the different levels of the workplace. It may also involve a consideration of the various decision-making contexts and the role of employees as well as consumers in shaping the nature of the product or the service.

Such an analysis can reveal the organisation's conceptualisation of difference. For example, if women are in senior management positions, if the contribution of all team members is taken into account, and if job roles and tasks are allocated according to the strengths and weaknesses of employees, then this perhaps demonstrates that difference is considered to be critical to the process of generating new knowledge and practices. However, on the other hand if participatory processes favour those who make their voice heard in 'mainstream' linguistic and cultural terms, if difference is only used in deficit terms, this suggests that difference is seen as something to be fixed up or filled in or even left invisible. Such a view of difference, operating within a presumption of sameness, contributes to maintaining the exclusive closed networks and the ongoing marginalisation of workers from various cultural and language backgrounds.

When grappling with concepts of difference in relation to consideration of learning, working or communication styles it may help to consider who is different to whom, how they are different and who identifies them as different. In other words, think through what differences make a difference and to whom, and compared with what (Burbules 1997). It is problematic to examine difference within a presumption of commonality, where differences are categorised in relation to a common standard. Perhaps a way forward is to consider that working with difference challenges our understanding of these categories by the very nature of who we think we are. Also it is important to consider differences not as stable categories but categories that have a dialectic relation with each other.

Another useful consideration is understanding the potential of workplace learning as a cloning exercise. As discussed earlier, culture as a management tool, and the implementation of competency-based training where standards focus on a very narrow cultural view of what is a good worker, can be part of this cloning. They can provide the basis for very exclusive and excluding descriptions that inform the allocation of job roles and criteria for job recruitment and promotion.

Learning in the workplace, where flexibility and difference in terms of roles, tasks, processes and people are the norm, may best be achieved by understanding learning as a concept of 'repertoire' rather than as a developmental concept. This signifies a shift from understanding learning as a vertical climb to a specific ideal goal towards a horizontal model where learning is an expanding broadening experience that draws upon and adds to employees' prior life and work experiences. This view of learning suggests collaborative learning relationships that involve dialogues and negotiations. These dialogues give learners the opportunity to explore the cultural as well as the technical significance of their work. It can involve a number of activities which include:

- comparing and contrasting previous and current experiences and the language of different contexts;
- examining the relationships between culture, context and texts and how language and other representations of meaning operate;
- problematising situations in order to address the issues around the 'collisions' that occur around the encounters;
- developing a broad repertoire of communication skills that help employees to engage in the new and various contexts, their ambiguities and the collisions that are likely to arise.

Conclusion

The management and delivery of workplace learning needs to recognise the potential assimilationist effects of two powerful technologies – competency-based training and a management philosophy underpinned by a workplace culture that in many ways promotes sameness. Those involved in designing and implementing workplace training consequently need to work hard in order to counter this possibility. Both of these technologies have themselves a potential for constructively working with difference. By engaging with an understanding of culture as an evolving dynamic rather than as a fixed state of being, workplace learning dialogues and practices can more easily be challenged and seen as openings.

References

Anthony, P. (1994) *Managing Culture*, Buckingham: Open University Press.
Bhabha, H. K. (1995) 'Cultural diversity and cultural difference', in B. Ashcroft, G. Griffiths and H. Tiffin (eds) *The Post-Colonial Studies Reader*, New York: Routledge.

Burbules, N. (1997) 'A grammar of difference: some ways of rethinking difference and diversity as educational topics', *Australian Educational Researcher* 24(1): 97–116.

Cope, B. and Kalantzis, M. (1997) *Productive Diversity*, Sydney: Pluto Press.

Cope, B., Pauwels, A., Slade, D., Brosnan, D. and Neil, D. (1994) *Local Diversity, Global Connections, Vol. 1: Six Approaches to Cross-Cultural Training*, Canberra: Australian Government Publishing Service.

Cultural Understanding as the Eighth Key Competency (1994) Final Report to the Queensland Department of Education and the Queensland Vocational Education, Training and Employment Commission, Brisbane: Queensland Department of Education.

Edwards, R. and Usher, R. (1994) 'Disciplining the subject: the power of competence', *Studies in the Education of Adults* 26(1): 1–14.

Field, L. (1995) *Managing Organisational Learning: From Rhetoric to Reality*, Melbourne: Longman Australia.

du Gay, P. (1996) *Consumption and Identity at Work*, London: Sage.

HREOC (1994) *Diversity Makes Good Business, Managing Cultural Diversity in the Workplace: A Training Manual for Manager Development*, The Human Rights and Equal Opportunity Commission, Canberra: Australian Government Publishing Service.

Gee, J. P., Hull, G. and Lankshear, C. (1996) *The New Work Order: Behind the Language of the New Capitalism*, Sydney: Allen and Unwin.

Joyce, H., Nesbitt, C., Scheeres, H., Slade, D. and Solomon, N. (1995) 'Effective Communication in the Restructured Workplace', Project of the National Food Industry Training Council, Carlton North, Victoria.

Keating, P. (1993) Prime Ministerial speech at the Productive Diversity in Business Conference, Melbourne.

Michelson, E. (1996) 'Taxonomies of sameness: the recognition of prior learning as anthropology', Paper presented at the International Conference of Experiential Learning, 1–6 July, University of Cape Town.

ODEOPE (1995) *Strength in Diversity: Integrating Cultural Diversity in People Management Training*, Sydney: New South Wales Office of the Director of Equal Opportunity in Public Employment and Ethnic Affairs Commission.

Reich, R. (1991) *The Work of Nations: Preparing Oursleves for Twenty First Century Capitalism*, London: Simon and Schuster.

Rizvi, F. (1994) 'The arts, education, and the politics of multiculturalism', in S. Gunew and R. Rizvi (eds) *Culture, Difference, and the Arts*, Sydney: Allen and Unwin.

Senge, P. (1990) *The Fifth Discipline: The Art and Practice of the Learning Organization*, New York: Doubleday.

Usher, R. S. (1997) 'Seductive texts: competence, power and knowledge in postmodernity', in R. Barnett and A. Griffin (eds) *The End of Knowledge in Higher Education*, London: University of London Institute of Education.

9 Technologising equity
The politics and practices of work-related learning

Elaine Butler

To put it simply, learning is the new form of labour.
Shoshana Zuboff (1988: 395)

There is no benign power which will dispense equality – the realisation will come from active participation and struggle.
Edna Ryan and Anne Conlon (1975: 175)

Work, workplaces, learning, equity. Each of these seemingly unproblematic words is called upon countless times in conversations, texts, media and practices of everyday life. At the same time, each also represents highly contested terrain, marked out with contradictory meanings, power relations and diverse visions of the future.

The challenge for this chapter is to interrogate meanings invested in notions of equity and workplace learning at this time in the late twentieth century which is described variously as 'new times' (Hall 1988), 'risk society' (Beck 1992) or 'the age of contingency' (Bauman 1996). Such a challenge requires calling into question taken-for-granted understandings about work, learning for work and equity as well as unravelling the troubled relationships between them. To centre equity entails investigating patterns, practices and issues associated with advantage/disadvantage, inclusion/exclusion.

To undertake this investigation, this chapter problematises understandings about equality and equity, work and workers in 'new times', before shifting the focus to learning work/workplace learning. This interrogation identifies enduring patterns of disadvantage that challenge the possibility of equity in industrialised/capitalist economies. It then displays how equity has been technologised,[1] repositioned to serve the agendas of the neo-liberal state and so the economic rather than the social, management rather than workers. I argue that given the contemporary political/economic and cultural significance of work-related learning, it is well positioned to act as a site for struggles around equity. However, its very situatedness within capitalist discourses of paid work and the materiality of workplaces enhances the potential for the cooption of 'learning' continually to improve productivity and profits and so reproduce inequities, rather than to engage with difficult but significant struggles for more equitable individual and collective futures.

Equity, as Poiner and Wills (1991: 7) argue, is an illusory notion, closely associated with ideas around social justice, equality and visions of a socially just and 'fair' world, most often located within liberal democratic understandings. While the liberal approach has been dominant in shaping understandings and practices around equity in many western industrialised countries, equity frameworks are now subject to ever-increasing critical scrutiny. In reviewing approaches to equity, and especially those of the last three decades, it becomes apparent that while analyses of equity/inequity have contributed to greater understanding of the complexity of these concepts and so enhanced the ability to 'name' inequitable practices and outcomes that impact on the 'disadvantaged', equity-related policies and activities have done little to challenge the privileges that accrue to the invisible/advantaged norm.

Those working to achieve equitable modes of governance and citizenship, as well as people still disadvantaged by the structures and systems of everyday life, are seeking new ways in which to advocate and implement change to enhance social, political and economic equality. At the same time, contemporary neo-liberal forms of governance based on faith in 'markets' as the ideal mechanism for distribution and redistribution of social goods view modernist equity strategies as both unnecessary and too costly.

While old paradigms and approaches are imploding, to discard indiscriminately either all value orientations informing equity or practices associated with equity work would be foolhardy, given the absence of viable practical, political or theoretical alternatives. From this uncomfortable and somewhat compromised position I utilise Frazer and Lacey's (1993: 190–1) strategic concept of equality as

> not merely formal equality or even equality of material resources, but rather a commitment to the idea that substantial differences in levels of power and well-being themselves raise issues of social justice wherever their correction is within the ambit of collective effort or social policy.

From such a position it is possible to raise questions about oppression and inequality, and to focus on ordinal equality – 'the absence of very great differences in the distribution of power, resources and levels of well-being'. As Frazer and Lacey argue, this stance offers the potential to move beyond the constraints of the modernist distributive paradigm to a reflexive position of critical scrutiny and correction of social political processes and structures implicated in practices of inequality. This then is the project for equity.

Work, workers and (not so) new times

To think about workplace learning, a necessary first step is that of reviewing 'work'. Beck (1992: 139) says 'the importance that work has acquired in industrial society has no parallels in history'. Despite the significance of work (or more likely, because of it), definitions of 'work' are prolific and often contradictory.

Patterns of inequity and disadvantage can be mapped from early industrial through modernist to 'new' times. Although work long precedes capitalism, it is the combined story of capitalism (especially industrial capitalism) and work that provides the most powerful narrative. Work is most often understood as paid employment, producing 'things', in the public sphere. This representation privileges the market while displacing the domestic/private. As Beck (1992: 139) explains, 'wage labour and an occupation have become the *axis of living* in the industrial age. Together with the family this axis forms the bipolar coordinate system in which life in this epoch is situated.'

The story of capitalism and work is most often read as a tale of contradictory 'facts' – about self-fulfilment and opportunity; about division, exploitation, oppression and contestation. What is striking is the similarity of many of the patterns over time and across national boundaries – categories of segregation, hierarchies of advantage/disadvantage, and the enduring and endemic nature of such patterns. While segregation and sex-typing of labour pre-date capitalism, 'capitalism has had a crucial role in maintaining, consolidating and reconstructing patterns of segregation' (Bradley 1989: 227). The adaptability of capitalism, premised as it is on the dualism of capital/labour and supported further by the public/private binaries discussed earlier, provides a resilient framework for divisions within labour/work that have come to be named as 'equity categories' – gender, race/ethnicity, class (including socioeconomic status), age, (dis)ability and religion.

It is the slippery notion of globalisation that is now centre-stage, in popular, political and theoretical debates about capitalism and work. This idea is frequently called on by those attempting to explain chaotic and complex changes associated with this period in our collective histories (Waters 1995). Most commonly, the term globalisation is used as a 'shorthand' for belief in the accession of global corporate power and the inevitability of a globalised economy (Wiseman 1996). Changes associated with economic globalisation and new technologies in the nature, regulation, organisation and distribution of work provide a deeply worrying scenario for issues of equity. As Bradley (1996: 13) advises, 'the spread of a globally based economy has been built upon existing hierarchies of class, gender, "race" and age, promoting new patterns of social and economic inequity'.

Although work orientations are diverse, global patterns can be mapped:

the predominance of women in service-related industries where skills are regarded as 'soft' or 'low' and paid accordingly; the predominance of women in part-time, casualised and precarious employment; the dominance of (white) men in managerial/executive positions; the prejudice and disadvantage experienced by many immigrant workers; the invisibility of workers considered 'less able' than the (mythical) norm that personifies the working body; the discrimination faced by many workers based on sexual preferences; the colonised labour experiences of many indigenous peoples. Finally, rather than providing the 'equalising' mechanism envisaged by writers such as Zuboff (1988) research illustrates that new technologies and information industries reproduce previous patterns of segregation (e.g. Webster 1996).

While the enduring and globalising nature of segmentation is noted, further divisions driven by neo-liberal economic policies calling on the inevitability of globalisation and so the need for 'flexibility' are evident. Most noteworthy are dividing practices such as those between high-skill and low-skill work, and the contraction and intensification of full-time work into 'core' jobs that is accompanied by the rapid increase of casualised, marginal, precarious jobs described as 'peripheral'.

Within this scenario, a paradoxical trend is that of the rapid feminisation of the labour force. The labour force is being 'feminised' in a number of ways, of which the increased proportion of women in (mainly part-time) paid work is but one aspect. Other trends connected with this phenomena are associated with the decline of manufacturing (male-dominated) industries and the increase of (female-dominated) service industries; the increased (rhetorical) status being accorded to skills associated with the feminine (communication, teamwork, cooperation); and finally, the gradual but steady shift of men to part-time and service work – men working like women.

While this highlights the continuation of old divisions and the emergence of additional inequalities in relation to work in the 'new' times of economic globalisation, less attention has been focused on shifts that implicate cultural globalisation. It is a paradox that while millions of workers are feeling insecure about their futures, stressed, working longer and faster (e.g. Morehead *et al.* 1997), 'workers' are being named as 'the most important asset' of corporations. Work-related learning is a central rallying point in this cultural shift.

Where the cultural dimensions of globalisation are overt is in human resource (HR)/management texts and practices. The task of management is to transform control-oriented organisations to commitment-driven enterprises (Cunningham *et al.* 1996), populated by 'new' workers who are to be highly skilled, flexible risk-takers, able to tolerate fear, uncertainty, cultural change and stress while still being able, productive and creative (Butler 1998a). The focus shifts from employment to employability. As posited by James (1994: 3):

this is the world of the mobile self: of constant retraining in all senses of the word; of being prepared to move anywhere according to the dictates of the labour-market; of continually refashioning one's pleasure and expressions of self.

The question must be asked whether in fact these are new times or an evolution of surveillance and control regimes that extend those of Taylorist/Fordist workplaces. Where (or what) is 'equity' here?

What, then, are the implications for equity, for worker–learners? What meanings are given to 'equity', by whom and why? Is it possible to talk about equity and work in the same breath, or to imagine equitable principles and practices shaping work and workplace learning? What will the relationships be between equity and workplace learning? What dimensions of power and control are inherent in workplace learning? Is it possible for workplace learning to be 'empowering' or 'liberating'? Is work-related learning being coopted solely to 'serve' capitalism and so inequity? Such critical questions comprise a direct challenge to policy-makers, bureaucrats, employers, unions, curriculum designers, workplace educators and trainers as well as worker–learners.

Learning work/workplace learning

Work-related learning has many histories, disparate pedagogies and notions of 'curricula', from medieval crafts and guilds to 'modern' apprenticeships and traineeships; from the 'brutalising school of labour' (Welton 1991: 13) to vocationally oriented modern universities; from women 'sitting next to Nellie' to children watching their elders. Hart in a 1993 review of workplace learning literature identified two main approaches – firstly a 'skill approach' that emphasises corporate/national skill requirements for the workforce, and a second that emphasises the workplace as a site of learning (pp. 20–1). Increasingly, the focus is shifting to the continual production of knowledge as a commodity, positioning workers as human capital, virtually immune to obsolescence – 'generic workers of the future' (Hart 1996: 107), a docile/disciplined labour force of the future (du Gay 1997, 1996, Butler 1998b). As 'knowledge' is increasingly elevated as the pivotal axis in distributing opportunities for both capital and labour, work-related knowledge and skills intensify as a site of political struggle.

Overwhelmingly, literature and texts concerned with workplace learning represent 'workers' as compliant and disembodied (Butler 1998a); 'work' as unproblematic – a naturalised concept that enjoys universal meaning. Embedded in this portrayal is work as paid employment in predominantly full-time jobs situated within 'workplaces'. As argued above, this seemingly neutral and untroubled notion of work is an 'invention of modernity or, more exactly, of industrial capitalism' (Gorz: 1994:

53). In obscuring differentiation between paid and unpaid work(ers), it negates embodied differences; it subjugates knowledges and learning silently to serve paid work/places; it denies power and division in work and the status of workers. Finally, most workplace learning texts assume that workers' knowledges and learning are commodities that belong to their 'learning organisations'/employers.

We now live in globally networked 'learning societies' (Castells 1996) comprised not only of citizens engaged in lifelong learning but also of 'learning economies' as neo-classical economic growth models shift to incorporate knowledge and technological change into their frameworks to enhance economic growth and development (Marceau *et al.* 1997). The dominant (western) discourse of work-related learning now focuses on individuals increasingly taking responsibility for their own learning. Such 'learning' is firmly located within the discourse of lifelong learning, which has been coopted over the last three decades to meet the needs of capitalism in crisis in the west (Butler 1998a, 1998b).

The blueprint in shifts to realign learning and capitalist economies – UNESCO's report *Learning to be* (Faure *et al.* 1972) – is pivotal in the promotion of learning societies and lifelong education. Although this report viewed lifelong education/learning as a democratic technology (Edwards 1997) this aspect of that vision has been replaced by a shift to

> a neo liberal functionalist rendition (OECD) orchestrated as a corollary of globalisation and hyper capitalism...[with an] emphasis on competition and the global economy and means whereby OECD members can position themselves to flourish in the global economy.
>
> (Boshier 1998: 47)

The worlds of education and work have been joined as never before, with the commodification of education and development of education markets to service the economy and the world of paid work through the production of 'positional goods' – knowledge and learning (Luke 1997, Marginson 1997a, 1997b). Within this (quasi-)market system learners are positioned as clients or customers (workers) ready, willing and able to exercise informed choice, purchasing or entering into contractual agreement to 'consume' learning. Knowledge is commodified, packaged, differentially valued and costed, not so much as a public (or even private) good, but as a traded good. Through workplace learning, knowledge is framed as a corporate good; learner/workers as human resources/capital.

Individuals as human resources and education as an investment in human capital have long histories. Both OECD and UNESCO have been highly influential in a (global) revival of a 'new brand of human capital theory penetrated by market liberalism that provides the routes for the restructuring and marketisation of education' (Marginson 1997a: 94). This 'new' human capital model assumes 'learners' (workers) have untroubled access to benevolent industry/enterprises that are eager to mediate in the development of individual workers' capital/ resource value.

The ascription to (reinvented) human capital theory interwoven with complementary discourses of human resource development (HRD) inherent in workplace learning has profound implications for equity. According to Bittman and Pixley (1997: 201–2) it reinforces the (erroneous) view of a level playing field – that the market is neutral to all, regardless of gender, race/ethnicity, class or age. The assumptions are that employers do not discriminate; that all humans have (equal access to equal) choices about the learning investment they can and will make, to add value to self.

Kell (1997), commenting on the reluctance of Australian industry and business to fund work-related training, notes that the shift in provision of education services (in 'partnership' with business) mirrors the divisions that characterise workforce/corporate reorganisation. Kell's (1997: 26) analysis identifies targeted provision of differentiated education services to

- the professional and technical elite located in the 'glamour' core sectors;
- 'just-in-time' skills training to refuel the 'reserve armies of workers... continually recycled through the disposable workforce'; and
- skills training to bolster the flagging work ethic of the unemployed.

In these ways then, and by reinforcing emergent forms of work organisation and distribution, non-critical workplace learning becomes complicit in (re)producing inequities in both the labour market and in workplaces. For those excluded unwillingly from workplaces the future looks grim. For those who participate provisionally, social inequalities and marginalisation are 'sharpened' (Probert 1997). For those who are (or aspire to be) 'core' workers, the production, commodification, management and 'trading' of knowledge are an ever-intensifying pursuit. To this end, the questions of who participates, who knows, who learns what and why, and who decides are central to issues of equity/inequity.

Managing to discriminate: the technologising of equity

The politics of equity and work-related learning in Australia during the last decade provide an informative and situated view of discursive shifts that shape realities for worker/learners. While this 'case study' is specific in its location, similarities with other western industrialised countries can be identified (e.g. Cameron 1996). Before analysing the politics of equity and work-related learning/training, it is helpful to consider the relationship between equity and the state. In Australia, the politics of gender contestation and those of the wider movement for 'equity' or equality have focused in the main on the public/policy sphere through direct engagement with the state. This engagement with its long history of collective/group and individual struggles has resulted in policy commitment to 'equity' regulated through equal opportunity/anti-discrimination complaints-based legislation in most arenas of Australian institutional life for the last twenty-five years.

This equity system is based on distributive rather than procedural justice. The mechanism invoked to redress marginalisation of various people was (and is) that of target groups – the colonisation of sectors of the population into supposedly homogeneous groupings – indigenous peoples, women, disabled, those from non-English-speaking backgrounds and so on. Rather than recognising and valuing difference *per se, category equity* conceals and contains differences, both within each 'group', and between and across groups where individuals may ascribe to multiple identifications. Moreover, such groups continually find themselves in competition with other equity groups in their efforts to obtain scarce resources, power or recognition; one group's 'victory' becomes a loss for others.

Foucault describes the use of classification systems as 'the art of distribution, to establish presence and absences, to know where and how to locate individuals' (1977: 143). This act of distribution results in three techniques for sorting and ordering – enclosure, positioning and then ranking – thus establishing further (shifting) differentiation among and between groups of the population. Categorisation techniques such as target groups both allow for continued protection of the norm from naming and analysis, and act as an organising principle through which 'equity' (or justice) can be measured out, distributed or redistributed, in order of perceived/constructed needs and political expediency, by political masters.

At best such a system offers the opportunity to become 'as the norm', which is ironic, given the rapid feminisation of the workforce mentioned earlier. Alternatively, the category equity system can also be understood as a technology of governance, to 'order' unruly differences (e.g. Bauman 1993, Luke 1997). While legislative target-based frameworks have provided public space for contestation by equity/advocacy workers and have established a useful 'bottom line', as Poiner and Wills (1991: 7) state:

> it is all very well to push for equity in distributive systems, but so long as wider interpretation of justice and equity are excluded, appeals to equity are ultimately useful primarily to those concerned to defend a fundamentally unequal and unjust social structure.

In Australia, work-related learning has been intimately connected with vocational training. The training reform agenda introduced into Australia in the early part of this decade was part of a national microeconomic reform strategy interconnected with processes of globalisation. From its inception the intent was that industry would drive this 'training' system, and that (accredited) training preferably be delivered in workplaces. This reform agenda has set in place a decade of sea-change in work-related learning in Australia.

The reform agenda, conceived and implemented by two successive federal Labor governments, was considered both an economic and a social justice strategy, informed by a subscription to human capital theory with a 'human face'. However, equity has never been centred as an organising principle, despite the opportunity of a 'greenfield site'. Rather, in line with state practice/s, the approach adopted without question was that of target groups labelled 'disadvantaged' according to underrepresentation in vocational education and training. All system planning was done with equity being kept firmly to one side: first get the system right, and then 'do' equity. This is *equity as appendage*. Thus equity is both a legislative/institutional requirement but also rendered vulnerable in its own marginality, mirroring the position of equity within the state.

The problem associated with the non-situatedness of equity was addressed by allocating target groups to the third of the National Strategy's four key themes – improved accessibility (ANTA 1996: 1). This resulted in the correlation of and confusion between equity and access, to the detriment of other significant considerations in the planning, delivery and monitoring of equitable public (and private) provision of work-related learning. This approach, which I frame as **equity as access**, is a significant moment in the process of technologising equity.

As a result of the impact of globalising strategies adopted by the state, and in keeping with the disadvantaged/target group approach and concerns focusing on accessibility, 'new' target groups continue to emerge: youth (perhaps the most significant, given the collapse of the youth labour market); males (young men considered to be 'at risk'); prisoners; people with psychiatric disability; selected mature-age workers; refugees; the homeless and the information-poor (ANTA 1996: 3). Given that the collective groups identified as 'target/disadvantaged' represent well over two-thirds of the population, the question must be asked: who or what is the system serving? Is this 'equity'?

Bacchi (1996) in her discussion of 'category politics' recognises the tensions inherent in the interaction between equity, unifying or homogenising groupings (categories) and the necessity to develop ways of working that do not conceal, contain or patronise heterogeneity or difference. This challenge to reconceptualise equity is profound, as category equity both establishes the legislative frameworks that make equity 'sayable and seeable', while simultaneously disciplining equity. The disciplinary technologies are acted out through providing contradictory spaces for groups and/or individuals, positioned as 'disadvantaged' and so in need of patronage/protection and special treatment, while at the same time they are demanding the right for full and equal participation as citizens. The 'art of distribution' constitutes the act of disciplining and hence operates as a mechanism of governance while claiming to share economic/societal benefits with the 'disadvantaged'.

Bacchi (1996) argues that the categories themselves are not the problem; rather it is the deployment of categories for political uses that is highly problematic, describing this as 'category politics'. It is this approach that is evident in the discursive practices that occur between the rhetoric of equity policy for vocational and workplace education and training, and its material/actual outcomes – *equity as category politics.*

The emergence of an ever-increasing number of equity groups illustrates the fragmentary nature of Beck's (1992) risk society, both pushing at the boundaries of understanding and limiting what can be achieved through liberal approaches to equity. Analyses of equity outcomes continue to illustrate the inability to achieve even the modest goals set for categorised groups. In part this can be associated with a lack of political will, a lack of conceptual clarity about equity, and non-recognition of *equity as expertise.* That is, anyone can 'do' equity. While bureacracies continue to seek easy ways to 'do' equity, the everyday practices of equity workers intensify in demands and increase in complexity.

The emergence of *equity as diversity* that embraces the marketised neo-liberal approach of *equity as equal treatment of all* is now prevalent in Australia. Both these approaches silently support the winding back of state-based commitment to equity. These merging approaches also inform current efforts to 'mainstream' difference (named as 'diversity'). The seductive rhetoric of the associated discourses masks a number of inherent dangers for equity. International studies relating to gender mainstreaming illustrate it as highly problematic in the absence of systemic and structural change to support such a shift (Razavi and Miller 1995). Equally problematic is the colonisation of concepts of difference and diversity and the way these coopted discourses are being positioned to dislocate 'equity', and especially gender equity.

An emergent and problematic extension of the equity/diversity approach is that of *equity as productive diversity*, that accommodates converging interests of the state and public policy, business, some 'target groups' and equal employment opportunity (EEO) practitioners. It is promoted through the persuasive liberal/modernist rhetoric of equity as 'equal treatment for all', as easy to implement, manage, and 'better' (less problematic and not tied to legislation) than equal opportunity, EEO and affirmative action. Given its flawed assumption of an existing 'level playing field' and the dangers inherent in individualisation in situations of unequal power so evident in workplaces, its political use illustrates yet again an approach of 'managing' diversity in the interest of increased productivity (Bacchi 1996) – managing to discriminate.

The next factor of significance to equity and workplace learning is the relationship between state/legislative equity mechanisms for the provision of work-related education, and the equity cultures and practices of industry/business. The need to interrogate this relationship is based on the privileged status ascribed by the state to industry: that of 'driver and client' of the vocational education and training system, and recipient of public resources both to implement training and to benefit from it. In most workplaces equity is framed as *equity as legislative necessity*, resulting in a plethora of workplace training initiatives usually at managerial and supervisory level to enhance compliance with the law and so avoid litigation. Unless there is genuine commitment to equal opportunity and affirmative action, such workplace learning is of little consequence and can indeed be mis-educative through outcomes associated with resultant covert resistance to equity.

Research continues to highlight the general reluctance of industry to engage proactively with equity beyond legislative requirements, based on a belief that equity is a public sector issue (Thornton 1994, Barnett and Wilson 1995). The emergence of *equity as a cost*, while not a new phenomenon, is reoccurring more frequently. One strategic response to this has been the efforts of equity groups (especially women) to represent themselves as untapped HR/capital potential. However, while the jury is still out on whether training is a cost or an investment, this perceived double burden of cost works against equity initiatives. In terms of economic crisis or restructuring, the 'good of the market' becomes the public good, triumphant over issues of equity.

A similar strategy utilised to persuade business to embrace equity by calling on the language inherent in discourses of economic rationalism is evident in both the HR and lifelong learning literature – that of representing *equity as efficiency and effectiveness*. In this framing, the exclusion of equity groups from the national skills base is presented (again in HR/capital terms) as an act of national and/or corporate inefficiency. It is also an illustration of repositioning through 'talking the talk' – to politicise equity agendas from both within and without the dominant discourses of neo-liberalism and managerialism. However, the effectiveness of discursive games remains problematic, especially when alluding to apparent compliance with agendas that, despite seductive rhetoric, are fundamentally oppressive and alienating in social and workplace settings.

A recent policy-related document concerning equity and vocational education and training (VET) in the Australian context illustrates the colonisation of both training and equity by neo-liberal ideals of the free market:

> Considerable national effort and expenditure has been invested over the past ten to fifteen years to increase the participation in VET to targeted population groups. In the emerging training market, where the purchaser buys outputs, a key question will be how to best purchase activity to produce equitable outcomes.

> (ANTA 1997: 4)

Here we see clearly illustrated the technologising of equity – acknowledgement of 'equity' (albeit grudgingly), a shift in the 'policing' of equity (passive and disembodied target groups) to the marketplace, which is viewed as context free and an equalising mechanism. The purchasing agent (industry/workplace assisted by trainer/training provider) 'buys outputs' (training effort) to produce skilled flexible workers through 'activity' (pedagogical discourses of learning work).

This then is *technologised equity* – colonised, subjugated and outsourced to business as a commodified marketable training 'output'. The warning by Sawer (1989: 15) that 'giving responsibility for equity programmes to those whose faith is in the market has been compared to putting mice in charge of the cheese shop' is timely indeed. New discursive games are not ends in themselves, but representations of struggles around belief systems. Moreover, they provide signs for the future. These discursive shifts mark a critical moment in the politics of equity that must be taken seriously.

So – whither equity in workplaces and workplace learning? It appears that workplaces are far from becoming democratised and that work-related equity, already highly compromised, faces an even more precarious future. Similarly, equity is positioned as increasingly problematic within the texts, policies and practices of work-related learning. It is apparent that the converging discourses shaping both work and education/learning for work are complementary in their intent. Mindful of the power inherent in the intersecting of their respective practices, both work and work-related learning are perhaps best viewed as human technologies – 'hybrid assemblages of knowledges, instruments, persons, systems of judgment, buildings and spaces, underpinned at the programmatic level by certain presuppositions about, and objectives for, human beings' (Rose 1996: 132). Within this troublesome scenario, it is highly likely that any notion of 'equity' will continue to be coopted into an emergent regime of truth – that of productive culture (Stockley and Foster 1990, du Gay 1996, 1997), a culture being (re)constructed through changing work orientations, practices and work-related learning to smooth the trajectory of 'new' capitalism.

Like most panaceas about learning constructed for public consumption, productive culture with its attendant practices and outcomes can sound utopian. However, as Casey (1995:132) argues, 'the new cultural discourses of production...are now as essential to production as labour and machine technology were in traditional industrial production'.

This claim is echoed in Zuboff's (1988:395) prophetic statement that

> learning is no longer a separate activity that occurs either before one enters the workplace or in remote classroom settings. Nor is it actively preserved for a managerial group. The behaviors that define learning and the behaviors that define being productive are one and same –

learning is not something that requires time out from being employed in productive activity; learning is at the heart of productive activity.

While the interconnectedness between workplace learning and productive culture is apparent, what is far less certain is how (and if) practices of equity can be inserted. Indeed, as Stockley and Foster (1990: 317–18) argued:

> 'social justice' associated with calls for equity lacks the rigour needed to combat the productive culture scenario and currently has no discourse or agenda able to cope with the necessary redefining of concepts such as access, equity and participation.

The marketised platform of 'new' capitalism, where the social and the cultural perform and produce for the economic, is a location more hostile than conducive to notions of equity. However, as intimated at the beginning of this chapter, times of chaos, uncertainty and change offer dangerous opportunities for reflexive action, to reaffirm, discard or rework values and practices to enhance democratic social and economic life.

Reading the signs – uncertain futures

I have argued that equity and workplace learning are located firmly within the discourses of globalisation and lifelong learning, and are imbued with the enhancement of productive culture. Such a culture embraces increased productivity, consumption and individualisation. Certainly, globalisation and 'the global encounter' constitute a new logic of economic, political and cultural interrelationships and development (Robins 1997) that is experienced differently by different groups. While local manifestations of globalisation and attendant shifts in work and work-related learning differ, an interrogation of the literature indicates that the potential for sharpening inequities along lines of old social divisions is high. Similarly, new divisions of advantage/disadvantage are apparent and reflected in the further polarisation of workforces, with the polarisation intensifying segregation based on differences of gender, race/ethnicity, able-ness, age, sexualities and geography. Questions of equity must focus on who will benefit, at whose or what cost. Equity questions are also intimately linked with issues of sustainability, and the kind of global/local futures we desire.

Globalisation is an unfinished project that is both contradictory and contested. Continuities with modernity and industrialisation are disrupted rather than negated. Despite the 'reinvention' of corporations as imagined communities for heroic workers and willing servants (Salaman 1997), the motive behind reinvention continues as that of increased productivity and profitability. The shift from a Fordist hierarchical organising logic to the

productive logic of quality, service, teams and learning is neither a dichoto-
mous relationship nor a break with the past (Gherardi 1995). Workers still
labour in differentiated conditions and for differentiated rewards. Changes
in labour processes still have the power to 'strip', ignore, displace or
punish workplace learning. Human capital is still imbued with assumptions that (de)value 'attributes' according to cultural capital,
gender/sexuality and so on (O'Loughlin and Watson 1997: 147).

Despite the gloom, the potential to democratise work and workplaces
(albeit with vigilance, caution and strategy) through contemporary cultural
shifts beckons. Workplaces are represented in such a way that illustrates
them as 'amenable to deliberation, argumentation and invention' (du Gay
1997: 287). If organisations are to 'make meaning' at and for work,
perhaps such an opportunity can be used not only to compete in turbulent
global markets but also to 'replace meaning stripped from work by
Taylorist–Fordist techniques of production and control markets' (du Gay
1997: 286). A prerequisite here will be the need to read out, understand
and politicise new forms of power and governance that both extend
previous struggles around labour power, and seek to obscure conflict
between 'the pursuits of productivity, efficiency and effectiveness on one
hand, and the humanisation of work on the other' (Rose 1990: 56).
Labour no longer exists outside of culture.

Challenges to equity are profound. Again, continuities exist. While it is
now recognised that issues of race, class, disability and gender cannot be
so easily separated, that the distributive paradigm is no longer adequate to
capture the complexities of injustice and the politics of difference (Taylor
et al. 1997: 148–50), equity-related legislation remains as a baseline for
policy and workplace negotiations. Similarly, the category equity approach
can be seen to provide a shaky and imperfect platform from which to 'hold
ground' and continue informed activism while working towards new
forms of politics.

Within this bleak scenario, a number of potential strategies are
emerging from various local/global locations and from differing theoretical–practical positions, in the quest to 'resurrect the mobilising power of
arguments about justice'. Many such ideas seek to embed both general
(normative) principles and the politics of difference, to bridge the legacy of
modernising universal principles and the 'fragmenting particularities' of
these new times (Harvey 1993: 102). Such strategies include strong recognition of the need for a systemic critical global analytic to interrogate new
material/cultural conditions of alienation and exploitation, where
rescripted 'systems for domination...open up new frontiers for capitalism,
patriarchy and colonisation' (Hennessy 1993: 16).

Theorists and activists are endeavouring to construct new frameworks
for understanding capitalism, patriarchy and colonialism, oppression and
exploitation, to move to new ways of thinking about democracy (e.g.
Benhabib 1996, Fraser 1997, Yeatman 1994). Fraser (1996) suggests a set

of principles for gender equity in post-industrial states (anti-poverty; equality principles of income equality, leisure time equality, equality of respect; principles of anti-marginalisation and anti-androcentrism). Bradley (1996) identifies four forms of fragmentation that, along with global polarisation, produce complex and fluid patterns of inequality (internal, within a collectivity or workplace; external, gender, age, ethnicity, region and so on; general processes of social change; fragmentation through individualism). Each of these four forms provides a platform for political activism and education around work and life. The above theorists acknowledge that there are many ways of being human (Fraser 1997), that while social inequalities exist redistribution is still necessary, but that strategies are needed to connect these within a reconceptualised framework that does not rest on any one axiom of 'difference'.

Also of interest are emergent if tentative texts exploring reconceptualised forms of ethics and ethical behaviours in postmodern times (Bauman 1993, 1996, du Gay 1996, Foucault 1997, Rose 1996, Minson 1998). James (1994: 4), for example, writes in an editorial comment for a collection of articles on critical politics, of 'ethics based on living with *productive tension*, a politics which seeks to *reflexively engage* with *principles-in-tension* rather than resolve them out of existence or find the bland middle way'. Finally, the new information technologies so intimately linked with globalisation also provide new possibilities for linking local politicised action with global strategies, reconnecting individual/collective through fleeting or ongoing alliances in practical and theoretical ways that transcend confining temporal–spatial boundaries.

Workplaces are social–material spaces that mirror and shape new global–local relations and processes interconnecting the economic, political, social and cultural. In this way, the converging practices of work and workplace learning provide discursive and material spaces for constructing a politics of equity in work and workplace learning. Through reading the signs, it is obvious that the challenges are profound. It is fitting, I believe, to conclude with the words of Pat O'Shane (1996: 11):

> We have to take stock now and ask ourselves what sort of society we want to build for ourselves in the (new) millennium. What are our guiding values and principles? The proposal I put forward is that we reaffirm the principles and values of equity and participation; that we reaffirm we are a society of human beings, not numerals....There will be extraordinary pressure brought to bear.

If, as workers, learners, educators and humans, we seek equitable and sustainable futures, and enhanced potential 'to live, to love and to work' in ways where profit does not count more than people, then the interrelated political, material and discursive practices of equity, work and work-related learning comprise a significant site for energetic intellectual and practical struggles.

Notes

1 In using the term 'technologisation', I am drawing on Fairclough (1996: 73) who identifies five characteristics of technologisation (of discourse): the emergence of expert 'discourse technologists'; a shifting in the policing of the practice; the design and projection of context-free technologies; strategically motivated simulation; and the pressure towards standardisation of practices. Further, I incorporate the idea of social/discursive technologies as forms of governance (e.g. Rose 1996, Dean and Hindess 1998).

References

ANTA (1996) 'An approach to including access and equity in vocational education and training. Issues paper', Brisbane: Australian National Training Authority.

ANTA (1997) *Australian Training. Special Edition*, June, Brisbane: Australian National Training Authority.

Bacchi, C. L. (1996) *The Politics of Affirmative Action. Women, Equality and Category Politics*, London: Sage.

Barnett, K. and Wilson, S. (1995) *Separate Responsibilities: A comparative equity focused study of commercial and community training providers*, Canberra: Australian Government Publishing Service.

Bauman, Z. (1993) *Postmodern Ethics*, Oxford: Blackwell.

Bauman, Z. (1996) 'Morality in the age of contingency', in P. Heelas, S. Lash and P. Morris (eds) *Detraditionalization, Critical Reflections on Authority and Identity*, Oxford: Blackwell.

Beck, U. (1992) *Risk Society: Towards a New Modernity*, London: Sage.

Benhabib, S. (1996) *Democracy and Difference. Contesting the Boundaries of the Political*, Princeton, NJ: Princeton University Press.

Bittman, M. and Pixley, J. (1997) *The Double Life of the Family, Myth, Hope and Experience*, Sydney, Allen and Unwin.

Boshier, R. (1998) 'Edgar Faure after 25 years: down but not out', in J. Holford, C. Griffin and P. Jarvis (eds) *Lifelong Learning: Reality, Rhetoric and Public Policy, An international perspective*, London: Kogan Page.

Bradley, H. (1989) *Men's Work, Women's Work. A Sociological History of the Social Division of Labour in Employment*, Cambridge: Polity.

Bradley, H. (1996) *Fractured Identities. Changing Patterns of Inequality*, Cambridge: Polity.

Butler, E. (1998a) 'Persuasive discourses: learning and the production of working subjects in a post industrial era', in J. Holford, C. Griffin and P. Jarvis (eds) *Lifelong Learning: Reality, Rhetoric and Public Policy, An international perspective*, London: Kogan Page.

Butler, E. (1998b) 'Equity and workplace learning: emerging discourses and conditions of possibility', in D. Boud (ed.) *Current Issues and New Agendas in Workplace Learning*, Adelaide: National Centre for Vocational Education and Research, 89–109.

Cameron, B. (1996) 'From equal opportunity to symbolic equity: three decades of federal training policy for women', in I. Bakker (ed.) *Rethinking Restructuring: Gender and Change in Canada*, Toronto: University of Toronto Press.

Casey, C. (1995) *Work, Society and Self. After Industrialism*, London: Routledge.

Castells, M. (1996) *The Rise of the Network Society, The Information Age. Economy, Society and Culture*, Vol 1, Oxford: Blackwell.

Cunningham, I., Hyman, J. and Baldry, A. (1996) 'Empowerment: the power to do what?', *Industrial Relations Review* 27(2): 143–54.

Dean, M. and Hindess, B. (eds) (1998) *Governing Australia. Studies in Contemporary Rationalities of Government*, Cambridge: Cambridge University Press.

du Gay, P. (1996) 'Organising identity. Entrepreneurial governance and public management', in S. Hall and P. du Gay (eds) *Questions of Cultural Identity*, London: Sage.

du Gay, P. (1997) 'Organising identity: making up people at work', in P. du Gay (ed.) *Production of Culture/Cultures of Production*, London: Sage.

Edwards, R. (1997) *Changing places? Flexibility, Lifelong Learning and a Learning Society*, London: Routledge.

Fairclough, N. (1996) 'Technologisation of discourse', in C. R. Caldis-Coulthard and M. Coulthard (eds) *Texts and Practices. Readings in Critical Discourse Analysis*, London: Routledge.

Faure, E. *et al.* (1972) *Learning to Be. The World of Education Today and Tomorrow*, Paris: UNESCO.

Foucault, M. (1977) *Discipline and Punish: The Birth of the Prison*, London: Allen Lane.

Foucault, M. (1997) *Ethics. Subjectivity and Truth*, trans. Robert Hurley *et al.*, (ed.) Paul Rabinow as *Ethics. The Essential Works of Michel Foucault 1954–1984. Vol. One*, London: Allen Lane.

Fraser, N. (1996) 'Gender equity and the welfare state: a post industrial thought experiment', in S. Benhabib (ed.) *Democracy and Difference. Contesting the Boundaries of the Political*, Princeton, NJ: Princeton University Press.

Fraser, N. (1997). *Justice Interruptus. Critical Reflections on the 'Post Socialist' Condition*, New York: Routledge.

Frazer, E. and Lacey, N. (1993) *The Politics of Community. A Feminist Critique of the Liberal-Communitarian Debate*, New York: Harvester Wheatsheaf.

Gherardi, S. (1995) *Gender, Symbolism and Organisational Cultures*, London: Sage.

Gorz, A. (1994) *Capitalism, Socialism, Ecology*, trans. C. Turner, London: Verso.

Hall, S. (1988) 'Brave new world', *Marxism Today* October: 24–9.

Hart, M. (1993) 'Educative or miseducative work: a critique of the current debate on work and education', *Canadian Journal for the Study of Adult Education* 7(1): 19–36.

Hart, M. (1996) 'Educating cheap labour', in P. Raggatt, R. Edwards and N. Small (eds) *The Learning Society. Challenges and Trends*, London: Routledge.

Harvey, D. (1993) 'Class relations, social justice and the politics of difference', in J. Squires (ed.) *Principled Positions. Postmodernism and the Rediscovery of Value*, London: Lawrence and Wishart.

Hennessy, R. (1993) *Materialist Feminism and the Politics of Discourse*, New York: Routledge.

James, P. (ed.) (1994) *Critical Politics. From the Personal to the Global*, Melbourne: Arena.

Kell, P. (1997) 'Teaching in the fast lane: fast capitalism, knowledge, labour and organisations in vocational education and training', *Education Links* 55: 24–37.

Luke, A. (1997) 'New narratives of human capital: recent redirections in Australian education policy', *Australian Educational Researcher* 24(2): 1–22.

Marceau, J., Manley, K. and Sicklen, D. (1997) *The High Road or the Low Road? Alternatives for Australia's future. A report on Australia's industrial structure for Australian Business Foundation Limited (ABF)*, North Sydney: ABF.

Marginson, S. (1997a) *Markets in Education*, Sydney: Allen and Unwin.

Marginson, S. (1997b). *Educating Australian. Government, Economy and Citizenship since 1960*, Cambridge: Cambridge University Press.

Minson, J. (1998) 'Ethics in the service of the state', in M. Dean and B. Hindess (eds) *Governing Australia. Studies in Contemporary Rationalities of Government*, Cambridge: Cambridge University Press.

Morehead, A. *et al.* (1997) *Changes at Work. The 1995 Australian Workplace Industrial Relations Survey*, South Melbourne: Addison Wesley Longman.

O'Loughlin, T. and Watson, I. (1997) *Loyalty is a One Way Street. NESB Immigrants and Long-term Unemployment*, Sydney: ACIRRT/University of Sydney.

O'Shane, P. (1996) 'On the slide to barbarism?', *The Advertiser* (Adelaide), 4 July: 11.

Poiner, G. and Wills, S. (1991) *The Gifthorse. A Critical Look at Equal Employment Opportunity in Australia*, Sydney: Allen and Unwin.

Probert, B. (1997) 'Gender and choice; the structure of opportunity', in P. James *et al.* (eds) *Work of the Future, Global Perspectives*, Sydney: Allen and Unwin.

Razavi, S. and Miller, C. (1995) *Gender Mainstreaming. A Study of Efforts by the UNDP, the World Bank and the ILO to Institutionalise Gender Issues*, Geneva: United Nations Research Institute for Social Development (UNRISSD).

Robins, K. (1997) 'What in the world's going on?', in P. du Gay (ed.) *Production of Culture/Cultures of Production*, London: Sage.

Rose, N. (1990) *Governing the Soul. The Shaping of the Private Self*, London: Routledge.

Rose, N. (1996) 'Identity, genealogy, history', in S. Hall and P. du Gay (eds) *Questions of Cultural Identity*, London: Sage.

Ryan, E. and Conlon, A. (1975) *Gentle Invaders: Australian Women at Work*, Ringwood: Penguin.

Salaman, G. (1997) 'Culturing production', in P. du Gay (ed.) *Production of Culture/Cultures of Production*, London: Sage.

Sawer, M. (1989) 'Efficiency, effectiveness and equity?', in G. Davis, P. Weller and C. Lewis (eds) *Corporate Management in Australia*, Melbourne: Macmillan.

Stockley, D. and Foster, L. (1990) 'The construction of a new public culture: multiculturalism in an Australian productive culture', *Australian and New Zealand Journal of Sociology* 26(3): 307–28.

Taylor, S., Rizvi, F., Lingard, B. and Henry, M. (1997) *Educational Policy and the Politics of Change*, London: Routledge.

Thornton, M. (1994) 'The seductive allure of EEO', in M. Grieve and A. Burns (eds) *Australian Women. Contemporary Feminist Thought*, Melbourne: Oxford University Press.

Waters, M. (1995) *Globalisation*, London: Routledge.

Webster, J. (1996) *Shaping Women's Work. Gender, Employment and Information Technology*, London: Longman.

Welton, M. (1991) *Toward Development Work: The Workplace as a Learning Environment*, Geelong: Deakin University Press.

Wiseman, J. (1996) 'Life on the global race track: the nature and implications of globalism', *Just Policy* 6: 26–34.

Yeatman, A. (1994) *Postmodernism Revisions of the Political*, New York: Routledge.

Zuboff, S. (1988) *In the Age of the Smart Machine. The Future of Work and Power*, New York: Basic Books.

10 Guided learning at work

Stephen Billett

Most adult workers would agree that they have learnt a lot through their experiences in the workplace. When they are asked how they have learnt in the workplace they usually say that it is 'just by doing things', 'other workers', 'observing and listening to others' and 'the workplace' itself (Billett 1996). It is tempting to dismiss these kinds of comments as being naïve. Such a temptation is never more likely than in countries where there is an emphasis on formal learning within educational institutions which enjoy legitimisation through certification. From such situations have come associations between teaching and learning. Nevertheless, most of us are not so easily fooled. We frequently have a strong sense of how we learnt to do particular vocational tasks, and from whom and where we gained insights and understandings. This chapter shows how learning in the workplace occurs and proposes how we should best organise learning experiences in the workplace to maximise their impact. The key premises advanced here are quite simple. Firstly, the kinds of activities that individuals engage in determine what they learn. Secondly, the kinds of guidance they access when engaged in that learning will determine the quality of that learning. Hence, the title for the chapter attempts to capture both the circumstance and utility of guided learning in the workplace as part of everyday productive activities.

The chapter has three aims. Firstly, it aims to advance understanding of learning as part of everyday thinking and acting as portrayed by the comments above. Secondly, the strengths and limitations of learning in workplaces are examined to identify contributions which are both likely to be valued and to be guarded against. Thirdly, a model of organising learning for the workplace is proposed. The arguments advanced in the chapter are as follows. It is through everyday activity in the workplace that individuals learn. Workplace contributions to learning are held to be different in kind to those furnished by educational settings. These contributions are not necessarily better or worse, but they are different. Moreover, particular workplace settings offer experiences and guidance premised on their goals and activities. Hence, learning is structured by the everyday activities and goals of the workplace. Given that these activities are necessarily important to the workplace, these learning experiences and their outcomes cannot be considered to be incidental, *ad hoc* or informal. Rather, they are authentic and rich opportunities to reinforce and extend individuals' knowledge. Importantly, workplaces also provide ongoing direct and indirect guidance which can assist learning in ways quite different from what happens in educational settings.

In addition, workplaces offer to many workers prospects for vocational development which would otherwise be denied. For workers in many industries, the workplace is the only place in which, they are likely to acquire knowledge because there are no available courses. Moreover, with the increased specialisation of workplace knowledge through technology or unique production requirements, the enterprise may be the best (perhaps only) site to develop that specialised knowledge (Harris and Volet 1996, 1997). Furthermore, with changes to work practice which include less hierarchical but more complex workplace relationships and which afford greater discretion to workers (Berryman 1993, Rowden 1997), the workplace provides the only possible environment which authentically integrates learning and provides access to the different kinds of knowledge required for workplace performance.

In order to discuss the propositions outlined above, a concept of learning as part of everyday thinking and acting is discussed first. Next, this idea is used to consider how workplaces structure activities and guid-ance for learners in ways that assist their learning by drawing on studies which identify the strengths and weaknesses of learning in workplaces. Following this, a model of a workplace curriculum is proposed. The model involves learners moving from fewer to more accountable activities in the workplace. This movement is guided directly by experts (i.e. those with skill and understanding of the task at hand), and indirect guidance provided by other workers and the workplace itself. Guidance both by those who have expertise and by others during participation in everyday workplace activities reinforces the identified strengths of learning in work-places and provides a means to address its weaknesses.

Learning as everyday thinking and acting

Learning is a product of everyday thinking and acting, including that occurring in the workplace. Learning is not something we switch on and off. It is ongoing. This is not a new idea. Piaget's concepts of equilibrium, accommodation and assimilation support and illuminate this view of learning. *Equilibrium* comprises individuals' attempts to integrate new information with what they already know (their existing knowledge struc-tures) (Piaget 1968). It is about making sense of the things we encounter throughout our lives. So, for instance, when faced with a new software package we might attempt to understand how to use it by considering other software programs. In this way, the task of understanding new knowledge or seeking equilibrium between what is known and what is being presented draws on individuals' existing knowledge. Assimilation and accommodation are two processes which underpin individuals' search for equilibrium. *Assimilation* is the process of linking existing knowledge to an activity or stimuli. For example, using a set of existing work procedures to undertake a workplace task which seems to be of similar kind to those with which these procedures have been previously successful. *Accommodation* is the process of developing new knowledge when faced with a novel situation. So, for example, in a move to self-managed teams, individuals' existing views about and implementation of management practices may need to be transformed, and new views, goals and procedures developed. Because assimilation involves less effort than accommodation, learners prefer to engage in assimilation, rather than accommodation. This is because their knowledge is organised in particular ways which have been purposeful in previous circumstances. Hence, learners prefer to use existing knowledge because engaging in knowledge building is demanding and challenging. Accordingly, there has to be sufficient motivation to engage in accommodation. This is particularly the case if the task is novel, requiring effort and potentially reorganisation of existing knowledge. Workplace tasks may well provide the interest and motivation to engage in accommodation. The point here is that workplace activities routinely engage us in combinations of assimilation and accommodation.

To refine this view further, recent work proposes that learning occurs through problem-solving (Anderson 1993, Shuell 1990). This problem-solving is of two sorts, routine and non-routine, which are analogous to assimilation and accommodation, respectively. Routine problem-solving is what we do thousands of times a day (e.g. changing gears when driving, making keystrokes on computers, carrying out standard workplace procedures) and these activities reinforce what we know and can do. So, more than just achieving goals in places such as work, this routine problem-solving reinforces and refines our existing knowledge. Each time we change gears or conduct some other highly routinised procedure, reinforcement and refinement of those procedures occur. Non-routine problem-solving, on the other hand, develops new knowledge because in dealing with new tasks and activities individuals extend their knowledge. When faced, for example, with technological applications of work processes or movements to self-managed teams, we engage in non-routine problem-solving resulting in the construction of the new knowledge required to be successful in those activities. So when engaging in workplace tasks we reinforce our existing knowledge and also construct new knowledge. In this way we learn throughout our lives by participating in everyday activities through moment-by-moment learning (Rogoff 1990).

However, there are likely to be different outcomes from engaging in different activities. Consider the difference in outcomes through learning about coal mining or farming by working either in a coal mine or on a farm, or alternatively by engaging in classroom activities associated with farming or coal mining. Equally, consider the different goal-directed activities that individuals will engage in, for example, in open cut or underground coal mines or in farms with different climates, locations, soils and so on. Therefore, what we learn through this problem-solving will be very much influenced by the particular problem-solving opportunities which these circumstances present.

Even then it would be mistaken to believe that learners construct knowledge in a uniform way. Rather than merely 'internalising' knowledge from social sources, or being 'socialised' as behaviouralists would have us believe, an interpretative process of knowledge construction occurs (Rogoff 1995, Valsiner 1994). Individuals are meaning-makers. This simply means that individuals' construction of knowledge is based on their existing knowledge, including their beliefs and values. Even though there may be dominant procedures or beliefs in a particular workplace, it does not mean that individuals will uniformly construct knowledge associated with those beliefs and procedures. Workers exposed to, for example, unethical activity or unsafe working practices are unlikely either to develop a uniform belief about those activities or to construct their views and procedures unquestioningly. For example, in using a manual to understand a piece of machinery or engaging with an acknowledged workplace expert, not only will individuals construct knowledge from these interactions, but their view about the social source (manual, workplace expert) will be transformed. Through this process, individuals may develop a greater appreciation of the potency of the expert's insights or the manual's utility. Alternatively, they may find the utility of one or the other lacking. So learning is an active and interpretative process based on individuals' existing knowledge. This idea is important because belief about direct instruction and 'training solutions' are often based around text-based resources premised on the view that individuals will learn uniformly from these sources. Indeed, the often favoured approach to workplace learning through text-based materials has been shown to have limitations and compares unfavourably with workers' construction of knowledge through everyday activity (Billett 1994).

Hence, workplaces furnish experiences which are purposeful in the construction of knowledge required for workplace performance. However, it is the type of activities individuals engage in and the guidance they experience which influence the robustness of that knowledge. Knowledge secured in workplaces is likely to be different from that constructed in the schoolroom because the knowledge-constructing experiences are different. Moreover, workplaces develop more than practical knowledge. Knowledge structures have propositional, procedural and dispositional dimensions which are not separable in this way. Propositional knowledge includes facts, statements, assertions – inert knowledge – whereas procedures are what we use to think and act with. Dispositions comprise values, attitudes and interest (Perkins *et al*. 1993). In different settings, knowledge is developed which has different propositional, procedural and dispositional characteristics (Billett 1997).

Workplaces as sites for learning

The activities in which individuals engage in the workplace influence what knowledge they construct. These activities are framed by the workplace's norms and values. They include both the types of activities which take place in the workplace ('what we do here is...') and also how they are undertaken ('how we do things here is...'). Knowledge gained goes beyond the immediate scope of vocational activities to include knowledge about power relationships and divisions of labour. So there is a 'hidden curriculum' in workplaces just as there is in educational institutions. That is, unintended learning results from such engagement. Some of these unintended outcomes are undesirable. Short-cuts, inappropriate behaviour, the reinforcement of restrictive practices such as non-inclusive behaviour, and problems associated with the development of understanding have been identified as problems associated with workplace learning (Billett 1996, Harris *et al*. 1996a). Vigilance is always required to ensure that workplace activities do not promote undesirable outcomes.

Knowledge required for expertise in work is most likely acquired through a combination of engagement in work tasks of increasing accountability, the close guidance of other workers and experts, and the more indirect ongoing guidance provided by the setting. This combination appears to be the basis for the development of robust (i.e. transferable) knowledge in the workplace (Billett 1996). It is not difficult to illustrate the potency of workplace activities in developing and reinforcing knowledge. What happens in workplace learning is analogous to the aims of immersion programmes for second-language development. It has been recognised that a few interludes a week are inadequate for students to develop their Japanese, Chinese or French. Consequently, students are immersed in the second language with it being used as a vehicle to teach other subject matter (e.g. geography, maths, history). Analogously, immersion in everyday workplace activities provides opportunities to develop models for performance through observation, to generate tentative solutions to workplace tasks and to secure those solutions directly or indirectly guided by others. As individuals use the procedures they are tested, are modified by the cues they receive and are reinforced by success with workplace tasks. This ongoing immersion in workplace activities engages workers in both routine and non-routine problem-solving leading to the development of the knowledge which permits expert performance in that particular workplace. This activity results in knowledge being·constructed and organised in ways that are purposeful in securing workplace goals, and it may permit transfer to other similar situations and circumstances.

Both direct and indirect guidance enrich this engagement in workplace activities. Direct guidance by experts and other workers is reported as guiding learners' choice of solutions to tasks, and securing goals and permitting learners to engage successfully in increasingly mature conduct of tasks (Billett 1994, Harris *et al.* 1996a). That is, they provide models, clues and cues to aid and refine performance with workplace tasks (e.g. how a task is done, to what degree and standard). Equally, the provision of joint problem-solving with experts and others provides staged access to increasingly accountable activities (Billett 1996, Harris *et al.* 1996a). This notion is grounded in Vygotsky's concept of the zone of proximal development (ZPD). This idea holds that task accomplishment is likely to be far greater when assisted by another, than by individuals' solitary experience and discovery alone (Vygotsky 1978). For example, to ease the difficulty of a task a more experienced colleague might provide suggestions to guide success – 'if it won't print, check the default setting' – because the learner might be unaware of such information. Alone, through discovery, the learner might never secure that knowledge and thus experience needless frustration. Experts and other workers can provide such access to knowledge as they engage in joint problem-solving with the learner. For example, in one secondary processing plant (Billett 1994), production staff worked alongside overseas experts during the commissioning phase. In doing so, the workers engaged in a range of activities to set up the plant. Participation in these joint problem-solving tasks permitted these workers to take responsibility for the plant's operation when the experts left. This responsibility included addressing ongoing production problems and refinements to plant operation. Access to guided experiences is particularly important when knowledge for performance is not accessible (e.g. when it is hidden by 'black-box' technology), or when it remains unavailable to the direct awareness of learners (e.g. stress factors in construction, bacteria in food preparation). However, the quality of interaction between expert and learners is very important. Learners have to do the thinking. If the expert merely tells rather than models, questions and demonstrates, the outcomes will be quite weak (Harris *et al.* 1996a) because the learner has not engaged in the thinking and acting required to construct and reinforce his or her knowledge.

From investigations of workplace learning, it is evident that indirect guidance available in the workplace is an important source of knowledge. In these studies, 'observing and listening to other workers' is consistently reported to assist learners with the conceptualisation and approximations of workplace tasks (Billett 1996). A unique and potentially potent contribution of workplaces is the authenticity of indirect forms of guidance. For example, a warehouse worker commented on the library of resources provided by her workplace for the various arrangements for packing pallets (Billett 1994). In sum, everyday work experiences immerse individuals in thinking and acting, and hence learning. The contribution of these activities is augmented by both direct and indirect guidance. In combination, these social sources transform and reinforce individual knowledge. However, the same investigations revealed shortcomings which need to be addressed when organising a workplace curriculum.

Role of guidance in workplace learning

The potency of workplace learning is premised on access to guided workplace experiences. Therefore, if learners are denied guided access to both routine and non-routine activities, weak learning outcomes may result. For example, doing the same routine tasks repeatedly over time is likely to provide less rich learning experiences than combinations of new and routine tasks over the same period. Conversely, if learners are asked to complete tasks outside of what they can achieve without guidance, this could lead to confusion and reluctance to engage further. For instance, workers with a low level of skilfulness in a particular area may find it difficult to do what others can do with ease. This is because they lack the prior knowledge which permits others to complete the tasks. It is therefore necessary to provide guidance to structure workplace experiences to take the learner from engaging in activities that are increasingly accountable (Harris *et al.* 1996a) yet in ways that are within their ZPD. This concern is the foundation of the 'learning curriculum' which is advanced below.

The goal for workplace learning is securing those forms of knowledge which permit workplace performance – non-routine problem-solving. This includes values which are likely to encourage participation and acceptance of other workers' views and contributions, regardless of ethnic or gender differences. The particular values embedded in workplaces determine the types of knowledge that are constructed, what is prized and what is de-emphasised (Harris and Volet 1996, 1997). Individuals may well secure inappropriate forms of knowledge through workplace experiences, particularly if certain knowledge, attitudes and values are accessed and rewarded in the workplace (e.g. 'this is not work for women'). Bad safety habits are also learnt through workplace experiences (Harris *et al.* 1996b). Such outcomes may not be inevitable, because, as proposed above, the construction of knowledge is not socialisation or internalisation. This means individuals interpretatively construct concepts and practice. Nevertheless, the dominant values of the workplace are likely to be influential, because relationships are rarely based on equal standing and novices will feel the need to comply. There is also, as Harris *et al.* (1996a) report, confusion sometimes about what is the 'right way' of doing a task. These concerns again emphasise the direct guidance of experts and other workers in order to manage goals for learning and appropriate workplace procedures. More than participation, structured guidance is required to address the shortcomings of the negative aspects of workplace culture.

A particular problem identified for workplace learning is to secure the understanding required for non-routine work activities (Billett 1994). Gott (1995) in addition doubts the ability of current approaches to learning in apprenticeship to secure the conceptual knowledge associated with 'high-tech' tasks. Such concerns need to be addressed because, as Berryman (1993) and Gott (1995) report, and Barnett in Chapter 3 argues, the increasing complexity of work makes the knowledge required for many workplace tasks more difficult to access. This means the very knowledge required for workplace performance is becoming more complex and less easy to learn. Berryman (1993) holds that conceptual knowledge is increasingly being required for workplace performance. However, much of that knowledge is hidden. Being hidden means it is not observable and is therefore more difficult to learn. The use of instructional interventions such as questioning dialogues, analogies and diagrams as part of everyday work activity can be used to address this problem (Billett and Rose 1996). Instructional strategies such as these can be used as part of everyday work practice to engage learners and to make accessible what is hidden or simply unavailable.

Guidance in the workplace is therefore a key factor for the development of robust knowledge and a means of addressing the shortcomings of workplace learning. The direct guidance of experts is likely to be an important factor in workplace learning, and therefore limits to guidance may diminish the quality of outcomes. In studies of workplace learning, those working alone or in remote locations emphasised the importance of gaining access to relevant expertise (Billett 1994). However, the workplace learner determines who is a credible source of knowledge (Volkoff 1996). Therefore, appointed mentors and trainers might not be seen as credible by the learners. Also, if the expert merely tells, rather than models and demonstrates, the outcomes might be quite weak (Harris *et al.* 1996a) as the learners will not be engaged in the problem-solving activity of thinking and acting. Lack of available expertise has a negative impact upon workplace learning.

Ideally, the knowledge secured through workplace learning will be more or less transferable to other circumstances (new tasks) and across settings in which the same vocational practice is conducted. In these ways, workplaces provide rich environments for the construction of the knowledge required for expertise. So a potentially important role for experts in the workplace is to maximise the prospect for transfer. This prospect is most likely to be realised if the learners have a rich base of knowledge in a particular context, with links and abstractions being made to other situations. For example, questions such as 'however, if this factor were to be different what would you do?' are likely to be important to disembed knowledge from a particular application thereby maximising its transfer to another. Tennant discusses this issue in greater depth in Chapter 11.

However, organisational factors may also inhibit guided learning in workplaces. Firstly, not all other workers or experts may be willing to share their knowledge, particularly if they are concerned about being displaced by those whom they have guided and supported (Lave and Wenger 1991). Workers may be reluctant to show another how to do a particular task, if they believe it is against their own interest. Secondly, they may fear challenges to their status (Moore 1986). Experts who are not rewarded or fear displacement may be unwilling to provide guidance and access to tasks if their own standing is threatened. It is within these concerns that a key limitation of workplace learning can be found. In Japanese corporations, for example, supervisors pass on their knowledge to subordinates, confident of not being displaced by their subordinates because promotion is based on seniority (Dore and Sako 1989). In the workplace learning studies mentioned above, it was evident that sharing of knowledge within organisations varied. Those organisations in which workers enjoyed broader discretionary roles and experienced fewer barriers to work practice offered environments with greater opportunities for workplace learning. It was in these environments also where there seemed to be less concern about the sharing of knowledge. Lynch (1993) argues that this complex of factors marks one of the differences in the relationship between individuals participating in educational institutions and workers learning in the workplace. According to Lynch (1993) the two workplace agents, the company and the individuals who work for it, have different goals, different access to resources and preferences, which means that the nature of what is to be offered may be less negotiable than in educational environments. What experiences a company is willing to make available to workers are associated with its strategic or even short-term goals.

Given the unequal weighting in this relationship it is not possible to be confident that individuals' interests will always be considered. Significantly, current work in HRD is suggesting that enterprises and their workers have never needed each other more than they do now. A key factor in the long-term survival and development of enterprises has been shown to be associated with the levels of enterprise-specific skills and individual workers' engagement with the enterprise (Rowden 1995, 1997). Moreover, Sefton (1993) has demonstrated the high degree of satisfaction and levels of participation realised when workers are given a say in training arrangements within the workplace. This suggests that a workplace curriculum needs to address both the requirements of the productive activities of the workplace and the involvement of individuals within it, as well as those factors associated with participation and guidance outlined above.

Workplace curriculum

Factors which influence workplace learning have been mentioned above. However, they need to be brought together to focus on the organisation of a workplace curriculum. In this section a model of workplace curriculum is proposed which takes account of both the organisational and pedagogical requirements of learning in the workplace and which leads to the development of expertise or full participation in the workplace. The four elements are discussed below.

1   *Movement towards full participation in workplace activities*   It is necessary to identify a pathway of workplace tasks learners need to access and become successful in as they move towards expertise. Delineating this learning pathway involves determining how best learners can move from the work activities undertaken by novices to those of experts. This pathway is founded on the principle of movement from peripheral activities to full participation in work activities. That is, from those activities which are less accountable and complex, to those which are more complex and may carry greater accountability (see Lave and Wenger 1991). The development and sequencing of this pathway should accommodate two general requirements. The first is to sequence workplace activities of increasing complexity and accountability. This permits the learner to participate in and secure knowledge incrementally while gaining confidence in undertaking more accountable tasks and securing more accountable goals. Secondly, the pathway has to enable learners to access procedures and processes, and importantly, the products of workplace activities. This access to processes and products enables the development of understanding about the goals for and standards of those completed tasks.

Identifying a learning pathway might be as simple as determining the sequence in which experts had acquired their skills and comparing this with the experiences of recent trainees. This sequence can be refined and ratified by workplace experts in the development of a pathway of learning tasks. Once identified, the pathway can be used to manage the sequencing of tasks to which novices will have access in their own journey towards expertise.

The pathway from peripheral to full participation in the expertise of the workplace is not required to be a fixed sequence of activities undertaken in a step-by-step fashion. Rather, it consists of groupings of activities which can be accessed and undertaken by learners as opportunities arise in everyday practice. Movement through the pathway is premised on the novice's ability to complete the tasks without the direct guidance of experts and others. Ability to successfully complete tasks independently suggests a readiness to move on to the next task.

2 *Access to the product (goals) of workplace activities* Access to both the product and the process of learners' workplace activities permits the development of understanding about what aspects of learners' performance are contributing towards standards associated with those activities. For example, as part of their training, warehouse workers at one site were taken in a delivery truck to supermarkets to see the goods they had packed onto pallets being delivered (Billett 1993). This experience allowed these workers to appreciate the importance of care and thoroughness in packing the pallets to withstand the rigours of long road journeys and the importance of arriving in a presentable condition. Making the goal accessible is an important consideration in all vocational practice. Through this, learners understand the basis on which their performance is judged. Equally, workers could be provided with access to the outcomes of their activities or those they are to learn about in other ways such as visits to different work areas.

3 *Direct guidance from more expert others* The investigations into workplace learning and theoretical ideas referred to above emphasise the importance of learners' interaction with expert others in the development of skilful knowledge. Those fellow workers acknowledged by others as being experts were seen as credible sources of knowledge. As noted above, there is no guarantee that someone titled 'the trainer' or nominated workplace mentor would be granted this status by workplace learners. The workplace expert's guided learning role may include establishing and monitoring the learner on the pathway of tasks, providing direct guidance in the form of questioning, direct instruction and making knowledge accessible. In addition, the expert models and coaches workplace procedures and then monitors the progress of the learner. The key principle in this joint learning activity is to press learners into doing the thinking and acting, as it is through that ongoing problem-solving activity that they will construct knowledge. However, judicious use of direct instruction will always be necessary, particularly when the learners do not possess the knowledge by which they can engage in purposeful problem-solving.

4 *Indirect guidance provided by others and the physical environment* Ongoing everyday vocational activity engages workplace participants in both routine and non-routine problem-solving as the basis for the development of vocational knowledge. This experience is essential for the development of robust vocational knowledge. Indirect guidance, such as learners listening to and observing other workers, is an important part of this experience. Models of practice, and standards against which learners can measure their progress, are provided by this indirect form of guidance (Lave 1990). Equally, the structuring of experience by the workplace and the cues and clues provided in the physical environment provide another form of indirect guidance. This form of guidance is often provided gratuitously by the

workplace. Its role in assisting with the structuring of workers' knowledge should not be underestimated as it grounds ongoing thinking and acting in a particular situation from which the learners construct knowledge.

So in sum, it has been advanced in this chapter that learning is a product of engaging in everyday activity. Workplaces furnish activities which provide learners with combinations of problem-solving experiences which assist them to extend and reinforce their knowledge. Workplaces may provide aids to learning in the form of the physical environment, other workers and experts who can model activities and provide guidance. However, to overcome some of the inherent weaknesses of workplaces as learning environments, guidance is necessary to limit the learning of inappropriate knowledge, to make accessible what is hidden, to sequence activities which avoid placing the learner outside what he or she can learn without the assistance of another and also to provide ongoing joint problem-solving which takes the learner from being a peripheral to full participant. So, in order to realise the full potential of workplaces as learning environments, experiences have to be structured and guidance provided to learners in ways that provide access for them and press them into problem-solving (thinking and acting), and collaborative and guided approaches to learning. The model of a workplace curriculum advanced here aims to secure this goal.

References

Anderson, J. R. (1993) 'Problem solving and learning', *American Psychologist* 48(1): 35–44.

Berryman, S. (1993) 'Learning for the workplace', *Review of Research in Education* 19: 343–401.

Billett, S. (1993) 'Authenticity and a culture of workpractice', *Australian and New Zealand Journal of Vocational Education Research* 2(1): 1–29.

Billett, S. (1994) 'Situated learning – a workplace experience', *Australian Journal of Adult and Community Education* 34(2): 112–30.

Billett, S. (1996) 'Towards a model of workplace learning: the learning curriculum', *Studies in Continuing Education* 18(1): 43–58.

Billett, S. (1997) 'Dispositions, vocational knowledge and development: sources and consequences', *Australian and New Zealand Journal of Vocational Education Research* 5(1): 1–26.

Billett, S. and Rose, J. (1996) 'Developing conceptual knowledge in the workplace', in J. C. Stevenson (ed.) *Learning in the Workplace: The Hospitality Industry*, Brisbane: Centre for Skill Formation Research and Development, Griffith University, 204–28.

Dore, R. P. and Sako, M. (1989) *How the Japanese Learn to Work*, London: Routledge.

Gott, S. P. (1995) 'Rediscovering learning: acquiring expertise in real world problem tasks', *Australian and New Zealand Journal of Vocational Education Research* 3(1): 30–68.

Harris, L. and Volet, S. (1996) 'Developing workplace learning cultures', in *Learning and Work: The Challenges. Proceedings of the 4th Annual International Conference on Post-Compulsory Education and Training*, Vol. 2, Centre for Learning and Work Research, Griffith University, Brisbane, 83–94.

Harris, L. and Volet, S. (1997) 'Developing a learning culture in the workplace', Murdoch University, Western Australia.

Harris, R., Simons, M., Willis, P. and Underwood, F. (1996a) ' "You watch and then do it. They talk and you listen": on and off-job sites as learning environments', Paper presented at the Australian National Training Authority Research Advisory Council's Third Annual Conference, 'Researching and Learning Together', Melbourne, 31 October–1 November.

Harris, R., Simons, M., Willis, P. and Underwood, F. (1996b) 'Pandora's box or Aladdin's cave: what can on and off-job sites contribute to trainees' learning?', in *Learning and Work: The Challenges. Proceedings of the 4th Annual International Conference on Post-Compulsory Education and Training*, Vol. 2, Centre for Learning and Work Research, Griffith University, Brisbane, 7–19.

Lave, J. (1990) 'The culture of acquisition and the practice of understanding', in J. W. Stigler, R. A. Shweder and G. Herdt (eds) *Cultural Psychology*, Cambridge: Cambridge University Press, 259–86.

Lave, J. and Wenger, E. (1991) *Situated Learning – Legitimate Peripheral Participation*, Cambridge: Cambridge University Press.

Lynch, L. (1993) *Strategies for Workplace Training: Lessons from Abroad*, Washington, DC: Economic Policy Institute.

Moore, D. T. (1986) 'Learning at work: case studies in non-school education', *Anthropology and Education Quarterly* 17(3): 166–84.

Perkins, D., Jay, E. and Tishman, S. (1993) 'Beyond abilities: a dispositional theory of thinking', *Merrill-Palmer Quarterly* 39(1): 1–21.

Piaget, J. (1968) *Structuralism*, trans. and ed. C. Maschler, London: Routledge and Kegan Paul.

Rogoff, B. (1990) *Apprenticeship in Thinking: Cognitive Development in Social Context*, New York: Oxford University Press.

Rogoff, B. (1995) 'Observing sociocultural activities on three planes: participatory appropriation, guided appropriation and apprenticeship', in J. V. Wertsch, P. Del Rio and A. Alverez (eds) *Sociocultural Studies of the Mind*, Cambridge: Cambridge University Press, 139–64.

Rowden, R. (1995) 'The role of human resources development in successful small to mid-sized manufacturing businesses: a comparative case study', *Human Resource Development Quarterly* 6(4): 335–73.

Rowden, R. (1997) 'How attention to employee satisfaction through training and development helps small business maintain a competitive edge: a comparative case study', *Australian Vocational Education Review* 4(2): 33–41.

Sefton, R. (1993) 'An integrated approach to training in the vehicle industry in Australia', *Critical Forum* 2(2): 39–51.

Shuell, T. J. (1990) 'Phases of meaningful learning', *Review of Educational Research* 60(4): 531–47.

Valsiner, J. (1994) 'Bi-directional cultural transmission and constructive sociogenesis', in W. de Graaf and R. Maier (eds) *Sociogenesis Re-examined*, New York: Springer, 101–34.

Volkoff, V. (1996) 'A shared endeavour: the role of mentors in work-based professional development', in *Learning and Work: The Challenges. Proceedings of the 4th Annual International Conference on Post-Compulsory Education and Training*, Vol. 2, Centre for Learning and Work Research, Griffith University, Brisbane, 71–82.

Vygotsky, L. S. (1978) *Mind in Society: The Development of Higher Psychological Processes*, Cambridge, MA: Harvard University Press.

11 Is learning transferable?

Mark Tennant

A view frequently voiced by governments, industry and commerce is that the contemporary workforce needs to be highly skilled, adaptable and flexible. This is a response to increasing technological and social change, global competition, economic restructuring, and changes in the nature and organisation of work. An 'adaptable and flexible workforce' implies one which can quickly and willingly apply existing knowledge and skills to new situations, and one which is prepared and capable of engaging in new learning as circumstances warrant. There is an expectation that both formal education and workplace training should produce the kind of learning which allows this adaptability and flexibility. Formal educational institutions are under scrutiny to provide education that is more 'relevant' – that is, pertinent to the needs of employers, which often means learning which is less abstract and discipline bound and closer to the problems and issues found in work contexts. In terms of workplace training, the expectation is that it eschew narrow skills-based learning (which is specific only to the particular job at hand) in favour of learning which is more broadly applicable. A common issue then, for both formal education and workplace training, is how to ensure that the learning which occurs is transferred or applied to new contexts. This is what is meant by 'transfer of learning': it is concerned with how knowledge acquired in one situation applies (or fails to apply) in other situations.

Knowledge and skill which apply across a range of situations (i.e. that 'transfer') are said to be more 'generic' than knowledge and skill which are confined in some way to the context in which they were acquired. From an educational perspective, the practical interest in transfer is to identify the conditions under which generic, transferable knowledge is more likely to occur.

This chapter begins with an overview of psychological research on the transfer of learning. The question initially posed is: 'does transfer occur?' The answer is 'yes' if the concept of transfer adopted allows the possibility of some learning and assistance in the new or 'transfer' situation. The second question posed is: 'what is the source of transfer?' This question is addressed implicitly by exploring three different perspectives: cognitive psychology, 'situated learning', and the perspective offered by the literature on practical intelligence and expertise. Finally a view of transfer is presented which draws on both the situated and cognitive perspectives, and which offers a range of strategies for the practitioner.

Psychological research on transfer

There have been a number of recent reviews of the psychological literature on transfer. After a review of research from Thorndike and Woodworth (1901) to the present, Singley and Anderson comment:

> A recurring observation on the study of transfer is that knowledge acquired in one situation fails to transfer to another...such failures are an inevitable consequence of the limited power and generality of human knowledge. Just having knowledge that logically implies a solution to a task is not enough. One must learn how to apply that knowledge to the task in specific situations.
>
> (1989: 2)

Detterman (1993: 21), in a similar review, supports the above observation:

> Transfer has been studied since the turn of the century. Still there is very little empirical evidence showing meaningful transfer to occur and much less evidence showing it under experimental control.

Detterman's view, which he claims is shared with other reviewers, is that little transfer occurs. He observes that after nearly a century of experiments on transfer, the consensus is that Thorndike and Woodworth's original assertions are close to the mark: that transfer is uncommon, and when it does occur, it is because of common elements in the two situations.

The problematic nature of transfer seems to me quite amazing. This is because educational discourse is imbued with the language of transfer; the idea that what is learned has some generic application is a fundamental tenet of education. Casual observation of everyday learning also confirms that transfer appears to be the rule rather than the exception, as some commentators would have us believe. As users of professional and other skilled services, we expect that a generic expertise will be brought to bear on our particular, unique situation, with all its contextual complexities, whether it is building a home or seeking legal advice. Why is it that the research findings seem to conflict with everyday observations, expectations and common educational practice? The answer, I believe, is to be found in the tendency of psychological experiments to adopt an over-rigorous view of transfer as something which cannot be assisted in any way. For example, Detterman claims that instructing subjects in a transfer experiment to apply the principles used in one situation to a new situation is not legitimate transfer:

> The main idea of general transfer is that subjects can and do use a previously learned principle in a new situation. Teaching the principle in close association with testing transfer is not very different from telling subjects they should use the principle just taught. Telling subjects to use a principle is not transfer. It is following instructions.
>
> (1993: 10)

While such a rigorous (and narrow) definition of transfer may be appropriate to some purposes, it is clearly not appropriate when the main interest is in how educators and trainers can assist with 'transfer' in a broader sense. Surely instructing students or trainees to apply an already learned principle is far more economical than teaching them from the beginning without any reference to their prior knowledge? The results clearly demonstrate that transfer can be assisted in this way.

My argument is that an over-rigorous view of transfer is not relevant to the interests of educators and workplace trainers. A broader, more pragmatic view of transfer is to regard it as something which occurs with assistance, and most often with the assistance of a teacher or trainer. The task then is to identify the conditions under which transfer is enhanced. As a first approach to understanding transfer of learning in the workplace, Anderson *et al.* (1996) provide a good summary of the general findings of cognitive psychology, at least as they are relevant to training design and delivery:

1 The amount of transfer depends on where the attention is directed during learning or at transfer. Attending to the possibility of transfer increases its likelihood.
2 Transfer is enhanced when training involves multiple examples and encourages learners to reflect on the potential for transfer.
3 Transfer is improved when there is instruction and training on the cues that signal the relevance of an available skill.
4 Different amounts of transfer occur depending on the amount of practice with the target task.
5 Transfer between tasks is a function of the degree to which the tasks share cognitive elements.
6 Combining abstract instruction with specific concrete examples is better than either one alone in producing transfer.
7 Training which focuses on both the whole task and its component parts is more effective than either one alone.
8 Training for skills to be used in complex social environments is best done with a combination of individual training and training in social settings.

Notwithstanding the above points, there are several limitations in applying the cognitive psychological findings to the issue of transfer in the workplace. Firstly, much of the research uses hypothetical or highly decontextualised problems and tasks which are removed from everyday workplace settings. At best the findings should be used as a tentative guide for workplace trainers, or as a point of departure for investigating transfer of learning in the workplace. Secondly, the educational debate surrounding transfer of learning studies has been primarily focused on schooling, and the relationship between school and work. There is now an interest, not only in transfer from school to work, but in the transfer of learning from work and life experience to formal education (as in the recognition of prior learning), from workplace training to work, and in the transfer of both formal and informal learning from one workplace context to another. There is also a need to identify a wider range of referents when talking about transfer. In the literature to date there has been insufficient attention given to the kind of knowledge or skill being transferred (e.g. procedural, propositional and dispositional knowledge), and there has been no attention given to the transfer of attitudes or general capacities like 'learning how to learn'.

There now exist a number of studies of transfer in the workplace, which are within a psychological framework, but which address some of the limitations of the traditional cognitive literature. Not only is there a focus on workplace settings, but there is a recognition of multiple sources of transfer. For example, following a comprehensive review of the literature on the transfer of training, which included studies which looked at a range of skills in areas such as handling employee complaints, plate welding, radio code use, safety, shipbuilding, policing, time management, supervision, record keeping and basic military training, Baldwin and Ford (1988) categorise the research as focusing on trainee characteristics (such as ability, personality, motivation), training design (content, sequencing, principles of learning used, strategies employed) and the work environment or what has been termed the 'transfer climate' (the supports provided and opportunities available to implement training).

A recent study of the impact of 'transfer climate' (Rouiller and Goldstein 1997) exemplifies this literature. This study looks at the relationship between learning and organisational transfer climate to transfer behaviour. The training programme is for assistant managers who work for a large food chain. The content covers administrative procedures for payroll development, appropriate food handling and preparation, shift management, and customer facilitation and service. Classroom instruction is combined with hands-on performance. Organisational transfer climate is defined as 'practices and procedures used in an organisation that connote or signal to people what is important' (1997: 332). The climate measure is divided broadly into 'situational cues' and 'consequences'. Situational cues serve to remind trainees of their training or provide them with an opportunity to use their training once they return to their jobs (e.g. the setting of goals which imply the application of training, new equipment or procedures which demand the use of learnt skills). There are also a number of consequences resulting from the application of learning to the job, such as positive or negative feedback, or no feedback, or perhaps even punishment (such as ridicule from fellow workers for adopting new techniques). Using such measures, Rouiller and Goldstein find that transfer is more likely to occur when the transfer climate is positive. Holton *et al.* (1997) have validated an expanded version of this transfer climate measure, which identifies seven elements of the work climate relevant to transfer:

1 Supervisor support (e.g. assistance and positive feedback).
2 Opportunity to use (e.g. resources and information to support use of newly acquired skills).
3 Peer support (e.g. assistance and positive feedback).
4 Supervisor sanctions (e.g. indifference or opposition of supervisor).
5 Personal outcomes – positive (e.g. advancement, career development).
6 Personal outcomes – negative (e.g. reprimands, overlooked for raises).
7 Resistance (e.g. group norms discouraging the use of new skills).

Research such as this is valuable in that it identifies the multiple ways in which transfer can be assisted, and it does so in a workplace setting: it provides clear guidelines for improving the workplace climate so that transfer is more likely to occur. But a shortcoming is that it imitates cognitive psychological methodology, and is therefore always in danger of falling into investigating only that which can be quantified (hence the development of an 'instrument' to measure organisational climate, together with an operational measure of transfer). Baldwin and Ford (1988) point out that many of the studies of the impact training design rely on simple motor tasks and memory skills with transfer being measured by learning and retention rather than the generalisation and maintenance of skills in workplace settings; and most studies of the effect of trainee and environmental characteristics used self-perceptions and self-reports of the extent of transfer rather than behavioural observation or ratings.

If research concerning transfer is confined to the psychological perspective then the issues investigated will clearly be narrowed to developing more sophisticated measures of transfer; such as behavioural ratings, observation schedules and interview protocols, with the purpose of relating such measures to factors such as the prevailing organisational climate and the nature of training interventions. While this is valuable, it is unlikely to capture the complexity of the situation in which transfer occurs. Within the psychological tradition, the very notion of transfer rests upon a conceptual separation of learning and the contexts to which the learning may be 'applied'. This fundamental separation is rejected by what has come to be known as the 'situated' learning perspective, which reframes the question of transfer, and in so doing potentially addresses some of the shortcomings of the psychological tradition.

Towards situated learning: studies of expertise and practical intelligence

Situated learning can be seen as a reaction to the privileging of the general and the abstract over the particular and the practical in the history of western culture. Historically, there has been a greater value placed on decontextualised knowledge; it is something which is abstract and general and which can be applied across a range of contexts (i.e. in a sense the context does not matter or it is trivial), and the most appropriate means to acquire such knowledge is through formal schooling. This view has found expression in contemporary times in the way we measure achievement at school and, indeed, the way we measure the potential for achievement through the use of tests of intelligence and aptitude.

'Situated learning' rightly seeks to redress this historical imbalance. There is no single situated learning perspective: the term refers to a broad collection of work which shares an emphasis on the importance of context in acquiring knowledge and skill. Some common propositions are the following:

1 High-level or expert knowledge and skill can be gained from everyday experiences at work, and in community and family life.
2 Domain-specific knowledge is necessary for the development of expertise (i.e. much of expertise relies on detailed local knowledge of a workplace, locality or industry).
3 Learning is a social process.
4 Knowledge is embedded in practice and transformed through goal-directed activity.

The emphasis on context in the situated learning perspective is justified through reference to studies of real-life situations where learning has occurred at a high level without formal schooling. One area upon which the situated learning perspective has drawn is the research on practical intelligence and expertise. This research highlights the role of context, and explores the nature and development of the generic attributes of expertise and practical intelligence.

The interest in practical intelligence can be seen as a reaction to the abstract and decontextualised nature of traditional tests of intelligence. It fits well with the everyday observation that there are persons who are not in conventional terms academically successful or considered 'intelligent', yet are quite capable of negotiating their own pathway through the world and mastering those things or topics which are of interest to them. In the literature on practical intelligence and expertise there is a shared presupposition that expertise is built upon the knowledge and skill gained through sustained practice and experience. In all instances there is an interest in documenting the performance capabilities or qualities of the expert or skilled practical thinker. Not surprisingly the most common technique is to contrast the performance of experts with those of novices with a view to developing a model of the nature of expertise and practical intelligence. Studies have sampled a range of professions, trades and skills such as waiting, canoe building, the magistrates' bench or chess playing, or particular functions such as decision-making and problem-solving in everyday milieux.

Some of the best-known and often cited work in this area are the 'Milk factory' studies of Sylvia Scribner (see Scribner 1984a, 1984b, 1986). Scribner contrasts practical thought with 'academic', 'formal' and 'theoretical' thought. The framework of practical thinking that Scribner developed was the result of more than two years' research work in a milk processing plant situated in a large city in the Eastern USA. The plant employed some 300 workers in a range of job categories (product assembly; wholesale delivery drivers; inventory and office clerks). Scribner's studies resulted in a challenging formulation of thought in context, in which skilled practical thinking is characterised by its flexibility (solving the same problem different ways yet with each way finely fitted to the particular occasion on hand), fine-tuning to the environment (aspects of the environment, be they people, things or information, are drawn into problem-solving), economy (where least-effort strategies are used), a dependency on setting specific knowledge, and the capacity to formulate problems (rather than solve given problems).

The best attempt to date at summarising the generic qualities of experts is that of Chi *et al.* (1988), as outlined below. (Other useful commentaries can be found in Lesgold 1984, Glaser 1987, 1985, Perkins and Salomon 1989, Ericcson and Smith 1991.)

1   *Experts excel mainly in their own domains.* Experts have a good deal of domain knowledge upon which their expertise is built and this cannot easily be transferred to another domain.

2   *Experts perceive large meaningful patterns in their domain* The organisation of the knowledge base is such that 'meaning' operates at a higher-order level (e.g. lower-order data are 'chunked' into meaningful wholes – such as when we see the number plate APE-246, we do not remember the individual letters and numbers, we 'chunk' them into the word 'ape' and the rule 'progression by twos'). This is illustrated in studies of chess (Chase and Simon 1973), typing (Gentner 1988) and taking inventory in a milk processing plant (Scribner 1986).

3   *Experts are faster and more economical* Experts often arrive at a solution without conducting an extensive search (e.g. Schmidt *et al.*

1990) and they are good at anticipating required actions and events (e.g. Gentner 1988).

4 *Experts have superior memory*   This capacity is restricted to a particular domain. Even if the domain itself is 'skilled memory' expertise is restricted to the problem types encountered in experience. Memory capacity is considered by Schmidt *et al.* (1990) to be the key to medical expertise. Nearly all investigations make some reference to the superior memory of experts. It appears that the phenomenon of 'chunking' only partially explains this observation – even Chase and Simon (1973) observe that the master chess player recalls both larger chunks and *more* chunks (which they are at a loss to explain).

5 *Experts see and represent a problem in their domain at a deeper, more principled level than novices*   Both experts and novices use conceptual categories, but those of the former are more 'principled' or 'abstract'. Certainly Ceci and Liker (1986) and Gentner (1988) demonstrate this. There is some doubt cast on this by Schmidt *et al.*'s (1990) study.

6 *Experts spend a great deal of time analysing a problem qualitatively*   That is, problem formation is a feature of how experts approach their task. This is especially the case with so called ill-structured problems where there is a need to create structure (for example, building a home, writing a piece of music or an essay on a given topic).

7 *Experts have strong self-monitoring skills*   That is, they are aware of their errors, mistakes and the need to re-evaluate solutions, more self aware and aware of the complexity of the problems confronting them.

The acquisition of expertise is tantamount to the acquisition of transferable, generic skills. What is not clear from the research is how such skills develop. We know that experience is important, but how is experience utilised to gain expertise and what is the role of the teacher or trainer? In this regard it is crucial to distinguish between expertise as an outcome and the acquisition of expertise as a process. For example, in Chi *et al.*'s (1988) summary of the generic qualities of expertise they note that experts are faster and more economical, partly because they do not conduct an extensive search of the data or information available. This does not imply that novices should be warned against conducting extensive searches of the data or urged to take short-cuts. Quite the contrary, extensive searches of the data (using standard, abstract algorithms – perhaps learnt 'out of context') are presumably important at the novice stage, and in this sense expertise is built upon the experience of being a novice.

Educators are concerned with how experience is used to become 'expert'. It is the approach to this question which serves to demarcate some of the differences among those who subscribe to a situated learning perspective.

Reframing the transfer question

The studies of practical intelligence and expertise go some way towards reframing the issue of transferability. A persistent theme is the central role attributed to domain-specific knowledge in expert performance and how this is gained from experience. This highlights the importance of the context or situation in which expertise is built, and, as such, supports the 'situative' position. The research allows scope for the role of the teacher or trainer and also draws attention to the importance of a more principled or higher-order representation of problems among experts. While knowledge is seen as domain specific, there is at least considerable transferability within each domain, and it is clear that expertise is built on a number of generic capacities that can be utilised in different contexts: such as problem formation, self-monitoring skills, higher-order principled thinking, and flexibility and adaptability to the environment in problem-solving.

A very different approach is that of Lave and Wenger (1991), and Greeno (1997). These authors, in their conception of situated learning, provide a radical departure from traditional ways of conceiving learning and the development of knowledge. For Lave and Wenger, the essential thing about learning is that it involves participation in a community of practice, which is essentially a community engaged in a common set of tasks, with its associated stories, traditions and ways of working. At first this participation is peripheral (hence the term 'legitimate peripheral participation'), but it increases gradually in engagement and complexity until the learner becomes a full participant in the sociocultural practices of the community (an 'old timer' rather than a 'newcomer'). They cite studies of communities of practice and comment on the way in which participation in the activities of these communities mediates learning. The interest is in how learners in quite divergent communities move from peripheral to full participation. Their examples range from the quite informal and family-oriented apprenticeship of Yucatec midwives, where the learning is almost invisible, to the high-technology and formal recruitment and training of quartermasters, and to the more recognisable master–apprentice relationship in the training of butchers. They point out the importance of having effective access to what is to be learned, and how the physical layout and the culture of work enhance or constrain participation by opening or closing opportunities for observation, mentoring, guidance and collaborative work. They emphasise access to practice as a resource for learning rather than instruction, and the value of relevant settings and strong goals for learning.

Their conception of learning entails quite a different mindset: away from the individual and towards the community. They are keen to distance themselves from the individualised psychological tradition which emphasises learning by doing, reflection on experience, and a decentring from the teacher to the learner, emphasising the view that learning is an 'integral and inseparable aspect of social practice' (Lave and Wenger 1991: 31). Similarly, they claim that the idea of reflection on practice or action is misconstrued; this is because there is a difference between talking about practice from the outside and talking within it:

> In a community of practice, there are no special forms of discourse aimed at apprentices or crucial to their centripetal movement toward full participation that correspond to the marked genres of the question-answer-evaluation   format   of   classroom   teaching....For newcomers then the purpose is not to learn from talk as a substitute for legitimate peripheral participation; it is to learn to talk as a key to legitimate peripheral participation.
>
> (pp. 108–9)

The idea then of discourse about practice as somehow distanced from practice or standing outside it is alien to their analysis. Learning is not so much a matter of individuals acquiring mastery over knowledge and processes of reasoning, it is a matter of coparticipants engaging in a community of practice. The focus is thus on the community rather than the individual. Allied to this view of the learner is a rejection of the idea that learners acquire structures or schemata through which they understand the world. It is participation frameworks which have structure, not the mental representations of individuals.

It is not surprising to find that Lave and Wenger reject the idea that knowledge can in any way be general, abstract or decontextualised. They argue that

> even so-called general knowledge only has power in specific circumstances...abstract representations are meaningless unless they can be made specific to the situation at hand....Knowing a general rule by itself in no way ensures that any generality it may carry is enabled in the specific circumstances in which it is relevant. In this sense any 'power of abstraction' is thoroughly situated, in the lives of persons and in the culture that makes it possible.
>
> (pp. 33–4)

From this perspective, the transfer of learning is conceived quite differently, as illustrated by Greeno *et al.* (1993: 100):

> knowing is the ability to interact with things and other people in a situation, and learning is improvement in that ability – that is getting better at participating in a situated activity. The question of transfer, then, is to understand how learning to participate in an activity in one

situation can influence one's ability to participate in another activity in a different situation.

Transfer is not a matter of learners acquiring abstract knowledge and procedures which are applied to many situations, rather it is a matter of 'learning to participate in interactions in ways that succeed over a broad range of situations' (Greeno 1997: 7). Thus 'teaching for transfer' is not enhanced through teaching abstract decontextualised concepts, or of building simple component skills in isolation until the learner is prepared for the complexities and 'wholeness' of practice; it is enhanced by taking into account the 'kinds of activities in which we want students to learn to be successful, and develop learning environments in which they can develop their abilities to participate in the general kinds of practices that are important to them' (Greeno 1997: 13). It is therefore possible to arrange learning situations that support more general learning – but the emphasis is on the 'situation' in which the learner participates, not on the knowledge and skill 'acquired' by the learner.

But there are some problems with adopting an extreme 'situated' learning position, and they stem from the proposition that learning can only occur through participation in communities of practice. Firstly, while the research certainly justifies a shift in *emphasis* towards the context or situation as being an important aspect of learning, it does not provide grounds for dismissing abstract, decontexualised learning as valueless. Secondly, on their account, there seems to be no role at all for teaching outside a community of practice: preparing learners for practice at 'arm's length' so to speak. For example, it would seemingly make no sense to create 'authentic' situations or *de facto* 'communities of practice', because they would need to be real communities, not artificial ones. Finally there seems to be no scope for critique and change in communities of practice – for standing outside the framework and taken-for-granted assumptions of the community.

The situated learning approach of Billett described in Chapter 10 offers the best attempt to date at reconciling the cognitive and sociocultural perspectives, thereby overcoming some of the shortcomings and limitations of the research and theory hitherto discussed. For Billett it is goal-directed problem-solving in particular situations which provides the means for constructing knowledge:

> as individuals engage in goal directed activities, they access, manipulate, and transform cognitive structures.
>
> (1996: 271)

Billett departs from the cognitive tradition in his acknowledgement that different forms of social practices lead to different ways of appropriating and structuring knowledge. His working out of this idea is quite elaborate, but basically he is saying that there are a variety of knowledge sources in a community of practice (such as other workers, hints, reminders, explanations, observations, listening, dealing with authentic problems, one's personal history), and that these have an impact on the way knowledge is appropriated and structured. Billett (1994) investigated workplace learning in a mining and secondary processing plant. He interviewed fifteen shift-workers and gathered data about how participants interacted with both the structured learning arrangements at the plant and the unstructured learning resulting from daily work practice. He documented the perceived utility of different learning resources: learning guides, computer-based learning, video, mentors, direct instruction, observing and listening, other workers, everyday activities and the work environment. He found that the informal elements of the learning system were the most valued by operators in assisting with workplace tasks and the resolution of problems encountered. An interesting aspect of this study is the rating of the utility of different learning resources for the development of different types of knowledge:

- propositional knowledge
- procedural knowledge, and
- dispositional knowledge.

The data obtained support the perceived potency of 'everyday activities', 'observing and listening' and 'other workers' as sources of all three types of knowledge. Billett, however, warns that, while informal learning clearly supports the development of higher-order procedural knowledge, workers express concern about the possibility of developing conceptual (propositional) knowledge through informal means only. There is therefore scope for making the tacit understandings of skilled workers more explicit, which may mean periods of formal instruction.

Billett's approach exemplifies one of the kinds of research needed to flesh out processes underlying the development of expertise because it documents how workers utilise their experiences (and resources available to them) for learning which has some general applicability. His approach adds a much needed 'learning dimension' to the studies of practical intelligence and expertise.

Strategies for enhancing transfer

Transfer of learning clearly occurs where there exists supplementary learning and assistance in the new context. The real issue is not so much whether transfer occurs, but how to locate its source and thereby provide appropriate assistance. For cognitive psychologists, its source is the development of cognitive structures, and the acquisition of higher-order, more principled understandings and procedures. Such cognitive structures are built through a balanced learning environment, which includes individual and group instruction, part and whole instruction, practice, exposure to a range of situations, and learning abstract principles in conjunction with many concrete examples. For the situational learning theorists, its source is in the kind of participation in communities of practice which results in effective participation in other situations – and so it is a matter of identifying the conditions which enhance learning in communities of practice, such as a transparent sociopolitical organisation, access to mature forms of practice, and symmetrical master–apprentice relations. The literature on expertise suggests that it rests on the kinds of generic attributes gained through experience and the way that experience is analysed, which is of course consistent with a more cognitively oriented approach to situated learning (see Billett in Chapter 10 and Garrick in Chapter 14 for further analyses of this issue).

At present, however, research in understanding learning in the workplace is still in its infancy, and considerable theoretical and empirical work needs to be done. In the meantime, the best approach for the practitioner is to be familiar with the debates and to extract from the evidence and their particular 'community of practice' those principles and strategies which, on balance, are good candidates for enhancing transfer.

Using this approach, transfer is more likely to be enhanced when:

1   Learners are exposed to 'authentic' activities, with the opportunity to access the full range of learning resources.
2   Learners are exposed to multiple situations and multiple examples.
3   Attention is drawn to the potential for transfer by highlighting the generic nature of the skill being acquired.
4   The higher-order skills and principles being acquired are identified and made explicit.
5   A supportive climate exists in the transfer context (e.g. supervisor support, opportunity to use learning, peer support, supervisor sanctions, positive personal outcomes, encouragement of further learning).
6   There is a capacity to 'learn how to learn from experience', that is practice in analysing experience and developing strategies for learning.
7   There exists a community of discourse (i.e. a common way of talking) in which all members are actively engaged in learning through communicating.
8   Learners have 'lifelong learning' skills and dispositions (the capacity to be self-directed and control and regulate one's own learning).

Each of the items in the above list is, of course, problematic, and can be elaborated or represented in different ways according to one's theoretical orientation.

This chapter began with posing questions about the transfer of learning, namely 'does it occur?', and if so, 'how can it be enhanced?' The issue of transfer goes to the heart of the educational enterprise, because it has to do with whether we can learn anything in a general way, and if so, how this is made possible. The difficulty with research and theory in this area is that it is politically charged: questions about the nature and sources of knowledge cannot be separated from questions about the control and legitimation of knowledge. These broader issues are never far away from the theoretical debates, and for this reason alone, it would be very naïve to imagine that the issue of transfer will ever be resolved in any final sense.

References·

Anderson, J., Reder, L. and Simon, H. (1996) 'Situated learning and education', *Educational Researcher* 25(4): 5–11.

Baldwin, T. T. and Ford, J. K. (1988) 'Transfer of training: a review and directions for future research', *Personnel Psychology* 41: 63–105.

Billett, S. (1994) 'Situated learning – a workplace experience', *Australian Journal of Adult and Community Education* 34(2): 112–31.

Billett, S. (1996) 'Situated learning: bridging sociocultural and cognitive theorising', *Learning and Instruction* 6: 263–80.

Ceci, S. and Liker, J. (1986) 'Academic and non-academic intelligence: an experimental separation', in R. J. Sternberg and R. Wagner (eds) *Practical Intelligence: Nature and Origins of Competence*, Cambridge: Cambridge University Press.

Chase, W. and Simon, H. (1973) 'Perception in chess', *Cognitive Psychology* 4: 55–81.

Chi, M. T. H., Glaser, R. and Farr, M. J. (eds) (1988) *The Nature of Expertise*, Hillsdale, NJ: Lawrence Erlbaum.

Detterman, D. K. (1993) 'The case for the prosecution: transfer as an epiphenomenon', in D. K. Detterman and R. J. Sternberg (eds) *Transfer on Trial: Intelligence, Cognition and Instruction*, Norwood, NJ: Ablex, 1–24.

Ericcson, K. and Smith, J. (1991) 'Prospects and limits of the empirical study of expertise: an introduction', in K. Ericcson and J. Smith (eds) *Towards a General Theory of Expertise*, Cambridge: Cambridge University Press, 1–38.

Gentner, D. R. (1988) 'Expertise in typewriting', in M. Chi, R. Glaser and M. Farr (eds) *The Nature of Expertise*, Hillsdale, NJ: Lawrence Erlbaum.

Glaser, R. (1985) *The Nature of Expertise* (Occasional Paper No. 107), Columbus, OH: The National Center for Research in Vocational Education.

Glaser, R. (1987) 'Thoughts on expertise', in C. Schooler and K. W. Schaie (eds) *Cognitive Functioning and Social Structure Over the Life Course*, Norwood, NJ: Ablex.

Greeno, J. (1997) 'On claims that answer the wrong questions', *Educational Researcher* 26(1): 5–17.

Greeno, J., Moore, J. and Smith, D. (1993) 'Transfer of situated learning', in D. K. Detterman and R. J. Sternberg (eds) *Transfer on Trial: Intelligence, Cognition and Instruction*, Norwood, NJ: Ablex, 99–167.

Holton, E., Bates, R., Seyler, D. and Carvalho, M. (1997) 'Toward construct validation of a transfer climate instrument', *Human Resource Development Quarterly* 2: 95–114.

Lave, J. and Wenger, E. (1991) *Situated Learning: Legitimate Peripheral Participation*, Cambridge: Cambridge University Press.

Lesgold, A. M. (1984) 'Acquiring expertise', in J. R. Anderson and S. M. Coastline (eds) *Tutorials in Memory and Learning: Essays in Honor of Gordon Bower*, San Francisco: Freeman.

Perkins, D. N. and Salomon, G. (1989) 'Are cognitive skills context-bound?', *Educational Researcher* 18: 16–25.

Rouiller, J. and Goldstein, I. (1997) 'The relationship between organisational transfer climate and positive transfer of training', in D. Russ-Eft, H. Preskill and C. Sleezer (eds) *Human Resource Development Review*, London: Sage, 330–47.

Schmidt, H. G., Norman, G. R. and Boshuizen, H. P. A. (1990) 'A cognitive perspective on medical expertise: theory and implications', *Academic Medicine* 65(10): 411–21.

Scribner, S. (1984a) 'Studying working intelligence', in B. Rogoff and J. Lave (eds) *Everyday Cognition: Its Development in Social Context*, Cambridge, MA: Harvard University Press.

Scribner, S. (1984b) 'Cognitive studies of work', *The Quarterly Newsletter of the Laboratory of Comparative Human Cognition* 6: Issues 1 and 2.

Scribner, S. (1986) 'Thinking in action: some characteristics of practical thought', in R. J. Sternberg and R. Wagner (eds) *Practical Intelligence: Nature and Origins of Competence*, Cambridge: Cambridge University Press.

Singley, M. K. and Anderson, J. R. (1989) *The Transfer of Cognitive Skill*, Cambridge, MA: Harvard University Press.

Thorndike, E. and Woodworth, R. (1901) 'The influence of improvement in one mental function upon the efficiency of other functions', *Psychological Review* 8: 247–61, 384–95, 553–64.

12 Competency-based learning

A dubious past – an assured future?

Andrew Gonczi

Over recent years there has been increased interest in the relationship between education, learning and the workplace. Countries in almost every part of the world have undertaken substantial reforms of their vocational education and training (VET) systems – most of them designed to link learning and work. Commonly, these have included the development of occupational and employment-related competency standards. Such standards have influenced the content of the curriculum in both general and vocational learning and the nature of workplace training.

Many western countries are now committed to a competency-based approach to VET, though what 'competency-based' means differs substantially between countries. What many of the reforms have in common is that the content of VET courses as well as workplace training and assessment is based on occupational competency standards. That is, courses are defined in terms of outcomes to be achieved by students, and assessment of learners is based on the criteria expressed in competency standards. What is different between countries is how competency standards are conceptualised, how and by whom they are developed and the degree to which the standards shape curriculum and assessment. In many places 'core' competencies have been developed. These are competencies regarded as essential for any form of working life. This chapter discusses reasons for these developments and suggests some desirable future directions for competency-based learning.

The attraction of a competency-based approach is easy to understand. It promises clarity of purpose and certainty of assessment. By analysing and specifying with precision the outcomes, standards or criteria that learners need to demonstrate, many educational problems can be addressed: what to teach, how to teach it and how to ensure that it has been learnt. Advocates of competency approaches argue that traditional approaches are cast in terms of unnecessarily broad and vague aims, that they focus on what knowledge trainers and teachers will try to teach students and that there is seldom clarity about what it is that is being assessed.

Critics of the competency approach suggest that the attempt to construct unambiguous outcomes for learning is a futile attempt to make simple what is complex. All education and training, they have argued, needs to allow for the unexpected and mysterious outcomes of the meeting of minds: that one can never predetermine all the outcomes of an educational process and that seeking to do so will place severe limits on what might be achieved.

Background to competency-based approaches

There have been previous attempts to introduce competency-based learning. As early as the 1930s, assessment theorists suggested that there was a need to measure students against clearly specified criteria. In the 1970s in the USA there was a brief flowering of competency-based approaches in teacher education programmes, where under the pressure of criticism of the quality of teachers, revolutionary approaches were trailed in some states. Rather than basing the curriculum on what academics felt students needed to know, it was felt that the curriculum should be based on what teachers actually needed to do in the classrooms. These then became the subject of intense analysis. The result was that many thousands of individual tasks were identified – many of them of the utmost triviality. As critics of this work pointed out, this attempt to specify outcomes with extreme precision collapses, in Wolf's evocative phrase, into 'a never ending spiral of specification' (1993). This descent into the most primitive behaviourism where individual behaviours associated with simple tasks (and subtasks) could be observed and ticked off on a checklist became the hallmark of competency approaches. Unsurprisingly, they quickly became disreputable as it was realised that even when teachers could do all the (trivial) things which were capable of being specified unambiguously, this did not make them successful teachers.

Given the failure of these approaches in the past, how can we explain the current popularity of competency approaches? There are four interconnected reasons. Firstly, the desire to make the complex simple continues to be a basic desire. This need not mean oversimplification, but it often can descend into this. Secondly, the increasing complexity of our world and the increased competitiveness of the global economic environment have produced a deep anxiety in many societies. Thirdly, education historically has always been seized upon as both a major cause of and solution to wider societal concerns. Certainty associated with the specification of learning outcomes is one step in the direction of addressing anxieties and reassuring such concerns. Finally, there have been considerable advances in thinking about the nature of competency which are linked with increasing acceptance that the old dichotomies between knowing and doing – the basis of much educational thinking in the western tradition – are false. There is now the possibility that competency approaches can address an enduring educational dilemma.

As Raven (1996) has recently pointed out, the literature on competency-based learning which has appeared recently is also a reaction against 'something that is sensed to be wrong' (p. 74). But what this is, what needs to be achieved and how this could be done are not clear. Raven suggests that contemporary competency literature lacks a conceptual and analytical base. It demonstrates little recognition of the need for a better understanding of the nature of competence, how it might be developed in individuals, how it might be assessed and what impact this would have on individuals, organisations and society generally. This chapter addresses some of these issues.

The argument that emerges here is that a 'holistic' or 'integrated' competency-based approach has many advantages over traditional approaches:

- It provides a curriculum and training framework which links practice to theory in more coherent ways than currently exist.
- It potentially provides a way of breaking the old dichotomy between 'knowing that' (knowledge/theory) and 'knowing how' (skills/practical) which has characterised Anglo-American education and which has resulted in the belief that education which is practical is both different from and inferior to that which is theoretical.
- It provides the basis for approaches to teaching and learning which could enhance students' adaptability and flexibility over their lives.

That is, despite its dubious past characterised by its excessive behaviouralism, a competency-based approach has an assured future so long as it adopts the integrated framework outlined below.

Reconceptualisation of competency-based learning

Philosophical approaches

Competence is a concept which can be explained and interpreted in a variety of ways. As Stevenson (1996) has argued, 'constructions' of competence alter in different contexts. The meanings given to competence in everyday life, in VET settings and in other academic settings are quite different. What is more, they are likely to change over time *within* each of these contexts and also to alter according to different value positions within them.

The competency of individuals derives from their possessing a set of attributes (such as knowledge, values, skills and attitudes) which they use in various combinations to undertake occupational tasks. Thus, the definition of a competent person is one who possesses the attributes necessary for job performance to the appropriate standard. Some tasks in some contexts will be quite specific and will require simple specific combinations of attributes. In other contexts, similar tasks will require more complex combinations of attributes because they have, say, to be completed more quickly or in more difficult circumstances. All occupations contain fairly general tasks, for example planning an activity, which will require different combinations of attributes. This conceptualisation of competence has become known as the integrated approach to competency and is discussed in more detail in a number of publications: Gonczi *et al.* (1990), Gonczi and Hager (1991), Hager and Gonczi (1993).

What is suggested in these publications is that the nature of competency is complex, bringing together personal attributes and the contexts in which they are used, within one conceptual framework. In doing this, competency goes beyond traditional conceptualisations, which concentrate only on the tasks that need to be performed or on the generic attributes or capacities that are said to underpin competency irrespective of the contexts in which these need to be applied. These two traditional approaches, the behaviourist and the generic, are discussed below.

Another way to think about the integrated approach to competency is in terms of the distinction between holism and reductionism. Competency standards and the learning based on them can be holistic in the sense that they bring together a multitude of factors in explaining and developing successful occupational performance. There are a number of ways in which the integrated approach to competency can be said to be holistic. Firstly, combinations of attributes are linked with tasks. Secondly, tasks themselves are often holistic. The usual way of thinking about competency, however, is within a behaviourist framework. There the approach is to break down (or reduce) tasks into their subcomponents in the hope of unveiling their essence or of achieving 'complete transparency', as Wolf (1993) has described it. The holistic approach to competency argues that tasks need to be thought about at a more general level. As, for example, when a basic education teacher 'modifies student's programmes as a result of continual monitoring' or when a family lawyer 'obtains relevant information from sources other than the client'. The third way in which the integrated approach is holistic is that tasks, even when thought of in this more general way, are rarely isolated from other tasks in the real world of occupations. In the case of lawyers, for example, while they are gathering facts from clients, they are *at the same time* developing a relationship with them. Similarly, in the case of teachers, while they are communicating effectively with students in the classroom, they will also often be managing time and monitoring learning.

Another important aspect is the normative nature of competence. As practitioners engage in work they increase their understanding of the culture and content of their occupation and of their workplace. As their participation in work moves from being peripheral to becoming more central, they are increasingly capable of meshing this cultural understanding with their technical knowledge and their skills and attitudes. This combination of attributes enables them to make increasingly informed individual judgements about how they should act. Such judgements clearly have a normative aspect. They are answering the question: 'how ought I to act in this situation?' Effectively, practitioners are clarifying the nature of competency in their occupations every time such decisions are made. Thus, rather than being a prescribed and predetermined set of behaviours, competency will be an ever-evolving reality which allows for critique and improvement of currently accepted ways of acting. This highlights the distinction between the potential richness of the notion of 'competent performance' and the tendency towards the behaviourist reading of 'competence *as* performance'.

Individual judgements will necessarily be guided, at a general level, by the set of competency standards developed for any given occupation. These standards represent the best attempts of a representative group of stakeholders to state the attributes needed to perform the major tasks in the occupation at a particular point in time. They are, however, necessarily quite general and do not claim to exhaust the possible contexts in which these attributes will be employed. What actually constitutes competence in an occupation constantly evolves as new situations are encountered and dealt with.

This approach to competency incorporates ethics and values, the need for practitioners to engage in reflective practice and to come to terms with context and culture. It also allows for the fact there will almost always be more than one way of practising competently.

Psychological approaches

The concept of competence also has a psychological dimension. Studies in the field of cognition add weight to claims that there is a need for a holistic approach to competency and that contextual and cultural awareness are vital aspects of what needs to be considered.

Recent scholarship in learning theory is increasingly undermining the generally accepted view that there is a separation between knowing and doing and that learning is an individual cognitive experience. See, for example, Lave (1988), Brown *et al.* (1989), Raizen (1994), Greeno (1997). This assumption of separation has formed the basis of the teaching of abstract, decontextualised concepts in secondary and higher education for a very long time. It has also been the basis of the separation of theory and practice in vocational curricula. That is, it has previously been commonly accepted that in order to be able to understand, learners need to be taught abstract concepts before, and distinct from, the context in which these concepts might be applied. However, evidence has been accumulating which suggests that learning and cognition are fundamentally contextual or 'situated'. That is, understanding develops through learners engaging with the social and cultural context, that performance and understanding are one and the same thing. This scholarship is strikingly in line with the ideas of the early twentieth-century educationalist John Dewey, who suggested that competency is the capacity to perform in a context (Dewey 1958).

While the psychological literature as a whole does not yet provide a comprehensive theory about the nature of competence or its acquisition, there is much recent literature which links with the integrated notion of competence outlined in this chapter. It provides directions for a new way of regarding workplace expertise with hands-on implications. The capacity to bring together knowledge, values, attitudes and skills in the actual practice of an occupation is the kernel of the integrated concept. As research in cognitive psychology suggests, an understanding of the culture of the workplace, and of the occupation, is an important ingredient in how these attributes are able to be brought together. Experience seems to be a necessary though not sufficient part of the process of becoming competent, a process which also incorporates an affective dimension. Clearly there is a good deal more to be done, but this concept of competence and its acquisition is able to unite philosophical and psychological approaches and clarify both the relationship between thought and action and the normative issues involved.

Arguments against the competency approach

There are a number of arguments against competency-based approaches which have emerged in the literature over the last few years. These can be classified into four categories:

1 Arguments against behaviourist approaches to competency. Such arguments are based on the assumption that a behavioural approach is the *only* approach to competency-based standards.
2 A more sophisticated version of this anti-behaviourist argument is the claim that all competency approaches, irrespective of their intention, are necessarily behaviourist. The proponents of these arguments, unlike those in the first category, are aware that there are other approaches, but they claim that any attempt to set predetermined standards or outcomes for learning cannot avoid being behaviourist.
3 Arguments against the generic approach to competence. These suggest that competence is only able to be understood within particular contexts or fields of practice.
4 Arguments against any competency approach on the basis of its normative assumptions about the nature of 'the good'. These arguments are often also about the aims of vocational education – the extent to which it should meet the needs of industry/professions (as *opposed to* the individual).

Both Gonczi and Hager in various joint and individual works (e.g. 1991, 1993, 1996) accept that most objections to competency-based approaches are an attack on a particular construction of competence. They make the further point that many of the objections to the narrow behaviourist approaches to competency-based learning are justified, as are the warnings that the competency agenda, in the wrong hands, could see the development of a kind of educational Taylorism.

The psychological literature discussed previously suggests that there is no evidence for the existence of generic competencies. Essentially this literature, and also that in the area of critical thinking, suggests that people cannot simply transfer expertise across domains of knowledge. Put another way, it demonstrates empirically that the so-called higher-order competencies (e.g. problem-solving) cannot be transferred from one context to another, without at least some relearning.

The second and fourth arguments against competency approaches outlined above are a direct challenge to the integrated approach presented in this chapter. Both, however, can be refuted. The argument that *all* approaches to competency are behaviourist is rejected by Hager and Beckett (1995) who point out that the fallacy of this argument is the assumption that all evidence gained from performance is behaviourist. It is in fact possible to infer knowledge, values and attitudes from performance if samples are carefully chosen. Further, inferences made about such values, knowledge and attitudes are no different from any other inferences about student knowledge made on the basis of an academic test or practical class in any educational institution. Almost all assessment uses the specific to make inferences about the general. There is also the essential point that an understanding of culture and context is essential to competence and that coming to terms with this means that predetermined standards are no more than a guide to what Walker (1993) has called 'situational understanding'.

The fourth argument against competency approaches has been advanced by writers such as Stevenson (1994, 1996), Newman (1994) and Wellington (1993). While they differ in some ways, each is critical of the process which has led, in their view, to the aims of education being circumscribed by, or even becoming identical to, the needs of industry. What becomes clear when their arguments are examined closely is that they are not so much against competency-based learning in particular, as against any curriculum which does not have as its basic aim the desire to broaden and empower. These arguments are largely an ideological objection to the legitimacy of economic and industrial considerations in any curriculum and are not specific to competency approaches *per se*.

It is not necessary, however, to draw a dichotomy between the needs of industry and the needs of the individual. While it is clear that some parts of a course may concentrate on the broadening of individuals, it is not necessarily the case that a course with other ends cannot be a broadening experience. It is certainly not the case that, by its nature, a competency-based approach will prevent a course from meeting the needs of both industry and individuals.

Implications of the integrated approach for teaching and work-based learning

One implication of an integrated approach to competency is that there should be an emphasis on problem-based curricula and similar approaches (Prawat 1993, Boud and Feletti 1997). That is, courses should be focused around authentic problems from work settings. This idea is congruent with psychological literature, both recent work on situated learning and that on expertise. Gonczi and Tennant (1994) suggest that, in addition to curricula based on solving problems in real situations, curricula should be based on the ways in which experts tackle problems.

It is crucial to distinguish between expertise as an outcome and the acquisition of expertise as a process, though. For example, Chi *et al.*'s (1988) summary of the generic qualities of expertise notes that experts are faster and more economical, partly because they do not conduct an extensive search of the information available. This does not imply that novices should be warned against conducting extensive searches of the data or urged to take short-cuts. Quite the contrary, extensive searches of the data are presumably important at the novice stage, and in this sense expertise is built upon the experience of being a novice. As facilitators of learning, however, we are concerned with how experience is used to become 'expert'. Should the curriculum be 'staged' from novice to expert and based upon an analysis of the levels of competence at each stage? Or should some pedagogical method, like problem-based learning, be employed which mimics the workplace learning process, and therefore contains within it the seeds for the development of competence and expertise? The latter would be the most compatible with the integrated notion of competence, but it would never be able to replicate certain aspects of the real workplace such as the workplace culture and the affective experience of being a beginning worker.

Any programme designed to facilitate the development of expertise in a particular domain should take into account the way in which experts in that domain use their experiences for learning. Teachers need to understand the conditions under which experience can lead to expertise and the teaching methods which will facilitate the development of any generic skills.

Evans and Butler (1992) constructed a model of expertise in welding and attempted to tease out the implications for curriculum and teaching. Welding is a complex skill in which 'motor, perceptual and conceptual factors [are] involved'. They concluded that their model has significant implications for curriculum and for the teaching of this skill. First, the teaching of the skill usually ignores 'task feedback clues', which their model shows are an essential part of expert welding. Second, they claim there is a need to allow in the curriculum for overall planning, for mental rehearsal, for monitoring and regulating the process, and observing and interpreting the outcome. All these things are part of their model of expert performance which they take to be synonymous with competence. Of these elements, a number, but particularly the needs for the monitoring and regulation, are underrepresented in the welding curriculum and in teaching and training more generally.

Components of skilled performance required in real-world tasks were identified by Gott (1995) in her work with the US Air Force. She ascertained what cognitive models can be used to inform training and how these can be put together in curricula to produce skill acquisition. She argued that as skills needed in the workplace become more cognitive, under the influence of advanced technology, they become more difficult to observe and separate into discrete components. Hence the need for cognitive models based on real-world expertise rather than the acquisition of individual skills as is typical in many courses. Such models, she claims, have demonstrated that experts engage in 'adaptive opportunistic reasoning that involves the co-ordination of ... procedural, device (or system) and strategic control knowledge' (p. 64). She further argues that skill acquisition requires 'successive approximations of targeted expertise'. The implications for curricula and training derived from this are that there is a need for learning which is situated, sequenced and supported. While she goes on to suggest that this can be done through the use of computer tutor systems, her analysis has implications for teaching and learning generally. Simulations, coaching with immediate feedback, and observations with explanation by experts, are methods which suggest themselves.

Implications of the integrated approach for assessment

An integrated approach to competency also has implications for assessment. In a competency-based approach, 'assessment takes on a more significant role, becoming an integral part of the learning process as well as a means of evaluating it' (Jessup 1991: 46). In the 1990s, assessment reform was seen as a vehicle to address a wide range of educational issues extending beyond the classroom. For some it had the potential to improve classroom practices. This reform included:

- reducing the power of standardised assessment to determine what is taught;
- demystifying assessment by providing students with a clear picture of what needs to be learnt; and
- breaking down the dichotomy between knowing and doing (otherwise known as propositional and procedural knowledge).

Assessment reform could also reduce the power of educational institutions generally, by recognising skills and knowledge learned informally. More conservative proponents also saw competency-based assessment as a way of ensuring that institutions produce the sorts of students that industry wants. Many industry groups, for example, have argued that to gain middle-level qualifications, students should be competent to industry standards and should be assessed on the job, undertaking real tasks.

Much of the literature used to discuss the nature of competency-based assessment is unrelated to the rise of the competency-based approach to learning, but it has much to say that is relevant to it. The emergence of a holistic, performance-based approach to assessment, however, suggests that we are moving towards assessment which:

- is standards or criterion referenced;
- is direct or authentic;
- is based on teachers' or trainers' judgement; and
- uses multiple sources of evidence.

If this is achieved, competency-based assessment should be more valid than traditional approaches to assessment.

Standards- or criterion-referenced assessment

The advantages of criterion-referenced assessment, that is judging performance against predetermined standards, are clear. If it is possible to specify learning outcomes which cover the aims of the curriculum, then these could be taught and assessed in unambiguous ways, thus overcoming problems of validity, reliability and fairness. The central problem with criterion-referenced testing, however, is its task-based approach to the conceptualisation of competence, and the consequent potential for reductionism and overemphasis on observed behaviours, from which knowledge and understanding of the appropriate constructs cannot necessarily be inferred. Griffin (1995) suggests, however, that this need not be a problem. He interprets competency in terms of a progression of tasks or stages. His work provides at least the theoretical possibility of marrying measurement with judgement and evidence-based approaches with competency assessment.

Criterion-referenced and competency-based assessments are almost always contrasted with norm-referenced assessment, though a number of writers have pointed out that it is not possible to escape from norms, since all assessors have ideas about what is reasonable performance in the domains they are familiar with. Nevertheless, there are differences between the assumptions of a measurement model and a standards-based model and these differences lead to quite different assessment practices. Taylor (1994) suggests that the main assumption of the measurement model is that of trait theory: that is, that humans differ from each other on various traits; that it is possible to measure these differences relative to others; and that we can do this reliably. The aim of such a system is to rank individuals, usually using standardised tests and usually arriving at a single score obtained through psychometric analysis and manipulation.

The assumptions of the standards model, on the other hand, are quite different from those of the measurement model. The standards model claims that:

- it is possible to set public standards;
- most learners can achieve them;
- different performances can reflect the standards;
- assessors can internalise the standards; and
- assessors can judge different performances consistently.

Such assumptions can present difficulties, but they also suggest the need for a multifaceted approach to assessment based on what an individual can do. Furthermore, what an individual needs to be able to do is anchored in publicly defined standards, criteria and targets.

Direct, authentic and performance assessment

The case for performance-based assessment is put forcibly and clearly by Wiggins (1989), Frederikson and Collins (1989), Linn (1993) and Bailey (1995). They argue that assessment that is designed to test performance standards (or competency standards) can motivate learners better than norm-referenced tests; that this kind of assessment can fulfil validity criteria and so be acceptable to the testing profession; and that it is more valid than traditional tests. The validity criteria proposed by Linn (1993) are:

- *consequences*: that is, what impact does such testing have on learner performance and motivation, on disadvantaged groups, etc., and on teachers' assessment procedures?
- *fairness*: that is, does it provide opportunities for all to learn, and will all institutions be able to deliver teaching and assessment equally well?
- *efficiency and economy*: that is, can we afford it and are we able to implement it?
- *generalisability*: that is, how transferable are performances from one task to another?

Frederickson and Collins (1989) propose directness (or authenticity), reliability and transparency, in addition to content coverage, as criteria of validity. By 'directness' they mean a test which evaluates a cognitive skill through a performance which is as close as possible to the real work situation in which the skill will be used. By 'transparency' they mean that criteria for judgement should be clear to learners. Finally, Wiggins (1989) adds to the list of criteria the need for content coverage through multiple performances.

How convincing are these special criteria for validating performance assessment? Messick (1994), a recognised leader in the measurement establishment, suggests that there is a need to meet more general validity criteria. He claims that the specialised criteria proposed for direct and authentic performance tests do not adequately address the problems of assessment. They are either too narrow or broad to achieve its purpose, or the people being assessed are asked to undertake irrelevant tasks which might prevent them from adequately demonstrating the competencies that should be the focus of the assessment.

The reason he gives for this conclusion is that there are inadequate distinctions made between, firstly, assessing performance *per se* and the constructs which the performance represents, and, secondly, assessing breadth and depth in the chosen domain. One way of clarifying these distinctions is to examine the differences between product and process (or performance) assessments. Where product is the focus of assessment, Messick claims it is not possible to infer the attributes that underlie the product. Where the focus is the construct and the performance or process is the vehicle through which the construct is assessed, issues of generalisability need to be considered. Thus according to Messick, the extent to which one can infer from an assessed performance the attributes which enable performance in other contexts is uncertain, but they are often conflated.

The response to this from those who support an integrated, holistic model of assessment is to focus assessment on constructs rather than on tasks, and to use multiple assessments where tasks serve as the vehicles for assessing the construct. In other words, there is a need to choose appropriate and sufficiently general tasks from which the possession of attributes (and hence competency) can be inferred.

The validity of such methods is enhanced by collecting a wide range of evidence on which to base an assessment judgement. An approach of this kind has been advocated by Bailey (1995). He argues that there is a need to adopt an evidence-based assessment strategy, akin to the way the legal system makes judgements in the courts. In the legal system, as much evidence is collected as is needed to make a safe judgement, either 'beyond reasonable doubt' or 'on the balance of probabilities'. Similarly, sufficient evidence is needed to make a safe judgement about occupational competence. Judgements are made, as they are in social science research, on the basis of three sets of evidence which produce triangulation.

Finally, the literature argues that the assessment of competence needs to be direct. The potential advantages of directness are obvious, but as Linn (1993) argues, there is still a need to provide empirical evidence of construct validity and particularly of consequential validity. Some of the most interesting evidence of this kind comes from recent work in the legal professions (Gonczi *et al.* 1994). For example, a recent review of the Specialist Accreditation Program for solicitors in the New South Wales Law Society (Armytage *et al.* 1996) found that the Program benefited the public and the legal professions by:

> offering the public and the professions a reliable means of identifying solicitors as having special competency in an area of practice; encouraging improvement in the quality, speed, and cost of legal services; [and] providing practitioners with an incentive and opportunity to improve their competency.
>
> (p. 129)

The Program was based on an assessment strategy which sought to determine whether solicitors met criteria specified in sets of competency-based standards. The reviewers used focus groups and a survey to assess the perceptions of clients. They concluded that there had been an increase in clients' expectations as a result of the scheme, and that there were high levels of satisfaction among clients:

> When asked whether the assessment had influenced their practices, 62 percent of all the successful candidates reported that it had. In the specialist area of wills and estates, the proportion was as high as 79 percent. The candidates identified a range of improvements, such as: better office procedures; increased awareness of precedents; heightened awareness of time limits in practice; and increased knowledge of law and legal principles.

This study provides strong evidence for the consequential validity of competency-based assessment. Similar results need to be gathered from other professions and occupations, however, before we can make generalisations about the validity of such assessment.

Further questions about competency-based assessment

There remain unanswered questions about competency-based assessment using performance assessment. These are:

- the degree to which contextualised assessment needs to be supplemented by decontextualised assessments;
- whether to assess complex as opposed to disaggregated skills.

The first question, concerning contextualised assessment, would seem to be of greater concern to general education, since assessment for occupational certification should be quite clearly specified in competency standards. Hence contextualised assessments should be able to assess the appropriate attributes. The need to use decontextualised assessment in general education is outside the scope of this argument. However, it does appear that the less clear are the constructs being assessed, the greater the need to test decontextualised knowledge.

There is no easy answer to the question of whether to assess complex or disaggregated skills. There is a relationship between the parts of a skill and the whole complex skill. Often, learners' capacity to synthesise and integrate parts of a skill depends on the learners' ability to perform the constituent parts. Perhaps it is wise, then, to attempt to assess both complex and holistic as well as disaggregated skills. This approach, however, can become behaviourist, which is exactly what holistic performance assessment seeks to redress. The extent to which one needs to assess disaggregated skills is an empirical question on which there has been little research to date.

The reliability of performance assessment

Much of the discussion of competency-based assessment has so far concentrated on validity issues. The final issue I want to discuss relates to questions of the reliability of performance assessment and competency-based assessment.

The major threats to reliability are sampling issues (how many observations of performance are sufficient?), the subjectivity of scoring, and how consistently we can generalise from the specific performance to the larger domain. There has been relatively little research done on reliability issues in competency-based or performance assessments, and clearly more needs to be undertaken. What there is comes from the professions (mostly medicine) and while it does not answer all the questions above, it does suggest that the judgement of experts is quite consistent.

Questions about sampling and generalisability have been covered to a certain extent by the previous discussion of validity. Although there are questions about the degree to which scores across contexts can be generalised (Swanson *et al.* 1995), this does not necessarily mean that performance assessment cannot be reliable. Rather it suggests that a *variety* of assessment methods need to be used in a competency-based assessment system – that performance tests are not a panacea.

Finally, the development and implementation of a competency-based assessment system depends on a sound conceptualisation of the nature of competence and an understanding of the general literature on assessment. Such knowledge and understanding are not enough, however. Issues of management, feasibility and acceptability often involve 'political' questions as well as technical ones. Designers of assessment strategies must take into account the needs of the various stakeholders – a process which involves negotiation and compromise. They will also need to consider the cost-effectiveness of their strategies.

Conclusion

The enriched version of competency-based learning outlined in this chapter – the integrated approach – has enormous potential for learning at all levels. It points to occupational preparation which is social in orientation, which centres on learning in authentic settings like workplaces, and allows for the possibility of the development of expertise at a relatively early stage. Importantly, it demonstrates the need to see practical training and theoretical learning as indivisible. For teachers in formal institutions and trainers in enterprises it means a reconceptualisation of education and training, reducing the importance of formal training sessions and elevating the role of coaching, mentoring, simulations, case studies, critical incident analyses and problem-solving in actual work settings.

This reconceptualisation of the concept of competency also has substantial implications for assessment. It requires at least a partial shift from indirect 'measurement' approaches to assessment to direct, authentic, performance-based assessment based on multiple sources of evidence and the use of professional judgement.

References

Armytage, L., Roper, C. and Vignaendra, S. (1996) *A Review of Aspects of the Specialist Accreditation Program of the Law Society of New South Wales*, Sydney: Centre for Legal Education.

Bailey, M. (1995) 'Competency assessment, evidence and the discourse of judgement', *Australian and New Zealand Journal of Vocational Education Research* 3(1): 1–13.

Boud, D. and Feletti, G. (eds) (1997) *The Challenge of Problem-Based Learning*, second edition, London: Kogan Page.

Brown, J. S., Collins, A. and Duguid, P. (1989) 'Situated cognition and the culture of learning', *Educational Researcher* 18: 32–42.

Chi, M. T. H., Glaser, R. and Farr, M. J. (eds) (1988) *The Nature of Expertise*, Hillsdale, NJ: Lawrence Erlbaum.

Dewey, J. (1958) *Experience and Nature*, New York: Dover.

Evans, G. and Butler, J. (1992) 'Thinking and enhanced performance in the workplace', Paper presented at the Fifth International Conference on Thinking, Townsville, Queensland.

Frederikson, J. R. and Collins, A. (1989) 'A systems approach to educational testing', *Educational Researcher* 18(9): 27–32.

Gonczi, A. and Hager P. (1991) 'Competency based standards: a boon for continuing professional education', *Studies in Continuing Education* 13(1): 24–40.

Gonczi, A. and Tennant, M. (1994) 'The false war: competency-based education and its critics', Proceedings of the NSW TAFE Curriculum Conference, Sydney, October.

Gonczi, A., Hager, P. and Oliver, E. (1990) *Establishing Competency Based Standards in the Professions*, Canberra: Australian Government Publishing Service.

Gonczi, A., Hager, P. and Palmer, C. (1994) 'Performance-based assessment and the NSW Law Specialist Accreditation Program', *The Journal of Professional Legal Education* 12(2): 135–49.

Gott, S. (1995) 'Rediscovering learning: acquiring expertise in real world problem solving tasks', *Australian and New Zealand Journal of Vocational Education Research* 3(1): 30–69.

Greeno, J. (1997) 'On claims that answer the wrong questions', *Educational Researcher* Jan./Feb.: 5–17.

Griffin, P. (1995) 'Competency assessment: avoiding the pitfalls of the past', *Australian and New Zealand Journal of Vocational Education Research* 3(2): 34–60.

Hager, P. and Beckett, D. (1995) 'Philosophical underpinnings of the integrated conception of competence', *Educational Philosophy and Theory* 27(1): 1–24.

Hager, P. and Gonczi, A. (1993) 'Attributes and competency', *Australian and New Zealand Journal of Vocational Education Research* 1(1): 27–44.

Hager, P. and Gonczi, A. (1996) 'Professions and competencies', in R. Edwards, A. Hanson and P. Raggat (eds) *Boundaries of Adult Learning*, London: Routledge.

Jessup, G. (1991) *Outcomes. NVQ and the Emerging Model of Education and Training*, London: Falmer.

Lave, J. (1988) *Cognition in Practice*, Cambridge: Cambridge University Press.

Linn, R. L. (1993) 'Educational assessment: expanded expectations and challenges', *Educational Evaluation and Policy Analysis* 15: 1–16.

Messick, S. (1994) 'The interplay of evidence and consequences in the validation of performance assessments', *Educational Researcher* 23(3): 13–23.

Newman, M. (1994) *Defining the Enemy*, Sydney: Victor Stuart.

Prawat, R. S. (1993) 'The value of ideas: problems versus possibilities in learning', *Educational Researcher* 20: 5–6.

Raizen, S. (1994) 'Learning and work: the research base', in S. Raizen (ed.) *Vocational Education and Training for Youth: Towards Coherent Policy and Practice*, Paris: OECD.

Raven, J. (1996) 'Researching competence', *Higher Education Review* 28: 74–89.

Stevenson, J. C. (1994) *Cognition at Work: The Development of Vocational Expertise*, Adelaide: National Centre for Vocational Education Research.

Stevenson, J. C. (1996) 'The metamorphosis of the construction of competence', *Studies in Continuing Education* 18(1): 24–42.

Swanson, D. B., Norman, G. R. and Linn, R. L. (1995) 'Performance-based assessment: lessons from the health professions', *Educational Researcher* 24: 5–11.

Taylor, C. (1994) 'Assessment for measurement or standards: the peril and promise of large scale assessment reform', *American Educational Research Journal* 31(2): 231–62.

Walker, J. (1993) 'A focus on policy', *Review of Australian Research in Education* 2: 3–15.

Wellington, J. J. (1993) *The Work Related Curriculum*, London: Kogan Page.

Wiggins, G. (1989) 'Teaching to the (authentic) test', *Educational Leadership* April: 41–7.

Wolf, A. (1993) *Assessment Issues and Problems in a Criterion-based System*, London: Further Education Unit.

Part IV

Futures

13 Envisioning new organisations for learning

Victoria J. Marsick and Karen E. Watkins

It is impossible to understand fully learning in the future workplace of the twenty-first century. The rapidly changing world in which we have been living is giving birth to a host of new ways of understanding work, jobs, organisations, technology and change. Those who design and run organisations in the future will be products of this new era and will bring mindsets to their positions that are in the process of becoming. We cannot predict the exact nature of future shifts, nor whether or when we might again enter a more stable time period. Yet, as we stand on the cusp of the year 2000, we can review some of the shifts of the last decade and highlight some of the issues that we think hold particular significance for re-evaluating the ways in which we think about learning at work.

Much of our work over the last decade has highlighted the shift away from a compartmentalised, almost assembly-line, approach to learning towards a holistic, integrated vision of a learning organisation. While the logic of the learning organisation may hold up in an ideal world, we recognise that reality is never ideal. In this chapter, we first adopt a historical perspective on this shift. We use several metaphors developed by Morgan (1997) to address the changing nature of organisations and workplace learning. We turn then to a review of current trends, with a focus on the relationship between learning and the development of intellectual capital and knowledge management. We look at the learning organisation in light of these metaphors, and then examine implications for different stakeholders – specifically, managers, employees and HRD professionals. We conclude with reflection and critique on the future of workplace learning.

Metaphors for organising and learning

Training became a field of practice about the time of the Industrial Revolution, although it did not become widespread until the First World War. Prior to the era of training, people frequently learned informally through apprenticeship-like models: 'From first-hand experience, managers at mill companies learned that improving employee skills could result in dramatic increases in productivity' (Harkins 1991: 27). Yet it was not for another fifty years or so that training became institutionalised: 'It was the introduction of management training before World War II that opened the door to systematically increasing overall productivity through employee training programs' (ibid.). Harkins points out that Peter Drucker, often considered the father of management in the USA, counted only three university continuing education programmes and two companies in the 1940s that regularly trained managers: Sears Roebuck in the USA and Marks & Spencer in England. Drucker was incorrect of course since many companies were already engaging in managerial training including those in the petroleum industry, government and other major industries (Watkins 1996). What is significant is that the model of training that was prevalent was that of on-the-job training and classroom-based training.

Training grew more formal for a number of reasons. Organisations became successful by establishing hierarchy, stability and predictability, and uniform standards and practices. Yet managers – who were frequently entrusted with the responsibility for their staff's development – were not very good at helping others learn. Managers were well situated to guide their employees and often held valuable implicit knowledge about performance and desired standards, but their skills were in getting work done rather than in helping employees learn. Trainers gained leverage for organisations by identifying needs and making standards explicit, distilling the best practices of people who successfully met these standards and combining this with external expertise on the topic, and packaging the information systematically to teach it to others.

Trainers in the past were concerned with developing basic skills and knowledge for a generation of people who were not accustomed to pursuing higher education. Today, the workforce is more educated, although demographic trends indicate a growing gap between a relatively smaller number of highly educated, well-prepared workers and a much larger proportion of less educated people who have not had access to the same opportunities, especially in terms of computer literacy. Today's workers are being trained to be proactive problem-solvers, with an emphasis on enhancing behavioural skills, sensitivity to the organisation's culture or way of doing business, and employee values and motivation. The focus is on strategic thinking, knowledge creation and management, and an ability to thrive on constant change.

There are many reasons for these changes in focus, not the least of which are the forces external to organisations which have shaped the way business is conducted, companies structured and training designed. Four metaphors help to understand the forces behind these changes: the machine, organic systems, brain, and chaos/complexity (Morgan 1997). Table 13.1 lays out these metaphors, as well as implications they hold for design of jobs and organisational structures, and for the systems of learning that flow from them. As will be seen, there is a big difference between the linear machine metaphor and the other three metaphors. The brain and chaos/complexity models incorporate basic elements of the open system model. As well, each succeeding metaphor can be seen as growing from the limitations of the prior metaphor, and either building on or replacing it as a primary organiser. However, we recognise that all of these metaphors can operate simultaneously in different parts of the same organisation for different purposes.

Machine metaphor

In the early Industrial Age, organisations functioned much like machines. Jobs were clearly defined, separated and orchestrated into a whole by a series of hierarchically arranged managers. An icon of this era is Frederick Taylor. His ideas, referred to by the shorthand of Taylorism, included five key principles (Morgan 1997: 23; Morgan's italics):

1   *Shift all responsibility for the organisation of work from the worker to the manager*. Managers should do all the thinking relating to the planning and design of work, leaving the workers with the tasks of implementation.
2   *Use scientific methods* to determine the most efficient way of doing work. Design the worker's task accordingly, specifying the *precise* way in which the work is to be done.

Table 13.1 Metaphorical lenses for understanding organising and learning

Metaphor	Nature of work	Organisation's structure	Learning design
Machine	Clearly defined, separate, coordinated	Bureaucratic and hierarchical	Instructional systems design: systematic training designed and conducted by experts
Open systems	Interactive with other work, interrelated	Networked	Andragogy: learning is negotiated, self-directed and participatory
Brains/holograph	Work is self-regulated	More autonomy for individuals; increasing boundarylessness	Informal and incidental learning: continuous learning that is single and double loop
Chaos/complexity	Work is self-initiated, subject to random shifts	High level of decentralisation; virtual and knowledge-based structures	Action-based learning; little clear guidance in weighing choices

3   *Select* the best person to perform the job thus designed.
4   *Train* the worker to do the work efficiently.
5   *Monitor* worker performance to ensure that appropriate work procedures are followed and that appropriate results are received.

Uniform training could be designed to ensure that people filled jobs in this machine. Standards were clear, and there was often one best way to solve a problem. For example, Lillian Gilbreth trained managers in her home in the Tayloristic efficiency techniques she and her husband Frank developed (Watkins 1996). It was more efficient to do most training in the classroom, and then expect that skills could be transferred to similar conditions on the job. 'Training' often implied dependency of the learner on the organisation's official representatives, including the teacher/trainer who ensured accountability. Instructional systems design (ISD) evolved to help trainers diagnose problems, locate specific deficiencies, and tailor solutions to meet these clear needs. (See Table 13.2 for more detail on ISD.) Today we would look at models of enhanced on-the-job training such as that developed by Jacobs and Jones (1995) as excellent examples of the application of instructional systems design to performance problems – Table 13.2 elaborates.

Table 13.2 Descriptions of models of training/learning

Model	Description
Instructional systems design (Rothwell and Kazanas 1994 and 1989)	Performance needs of individuals and systems are identified against clearly specified standards; objectives are set to address gaps; learning activities are designed to meet objectives, and gains evaluated against pre-set criteria
Andragogy (Knowles 1980); self-directed learning (Candy 1991)	Individuals identify own needs and learning goals in order to maximise their abilities; individual plans are developed that take account of learning-style preferences; learning methods are often participatory and experience based; evaluation is tailored to individual differences as well as organisation's needs
Informal and incidental learning (Marsick and Watkins 1990, Boud *et al.* 1993)	Individuals continually learn from their experience through reflection on action in light of prior learning and re-evaluation of prior insights and frames of reference; learning can be focused on tactics/strategies or on underlying assumptions that shape action
Action technologies (Brooks and Watkins 1994)	Peers join together to use real-life problems or challenges as laboratories for learning; learning includes cycles of problem framing, experimentation, reflection, and reframing; action often leads to individual and systems changes

Open systems metaphor

As we moved into the Information Age, scholars and practitioners began to describe the organisation as an open system that interacted with its environment. Systems are like the human body with its myriad interdependent parts. Another way of thinking about a system is a mobile: if you push one part of the mobile, it affects all the other parts. A key theorist whose work informed this metaphor was Ludwig von Bertalanffy. Morgan (1997: 40–1) summarises key principles of open systems as follows:

1   the modelling of the open system after organisms;
2   the idea of homeostasis or self-regulation towards a steady state;
3   the notion of entropy, that is the tendency to 'deteriorate and run down';
4   the essential focus on interrelationships among structure, function, differentiation and integration;
5   requisite variety, which states that 'internal regulatory mechanisms of a system must be as diverse as the environment with which it is trying to deal';
6   equifinality, that is 'in an open system there may be many different ways of arriving at a given end state';
7   system evolution, that is systems can evolve if they can 'move to more complex forms of differentiation and integration, and greater variety'.

In the open systems model, the learning of one person or work group affects that of others; they are mutually interdependent. Learning does not necessarily take place in classrooms; people frequently learn with one another as they carry out tasks. However, even though employees take more initiative for their learning in the open system, they participate in a series of explicit and implicit negotiations about the nature of their tasks and their learning with others with whom they interact, including the manager and human resource developer. These negotiations are required to maintain desired balance among relationships. The andragogical model of learning, developed by Knowles (1980), is well-suited to the systems model because andragogy emphasises a negotiated learning process around goals and outcomes for evaluation, while allowing the learner greater freedom to match pacing and choices of learning methods to individual preferences. (See Table 13.2 for more detail on andragogical model.) Andragogy is self-directed learning (Candy 1991), but in practice it also allows for joint modification of plans by learners and institutions.

Brain metaphor

In the last decade, we have moved more towards an understanding of organisations as brain centres that are self-organising, self-monitoring, self-correcting entities. The brain metaphor involves organic, neural inter-connections through which information is processed almost simultaneously. To function like a brain, people must interact more quickly and effectively to identify problems before they become catastrophes and solve them creatively. Morgan (1997: 103) identifies principles of holographic design that characterise organisations as a brain:

1   build the 'whole' into the 'parts';
2   the importance of redundancy;
3   requisite variety;
4   'minimum specs';
5   learn to learn.

The brain image thus suggests that people and organisations be more proactive in scanning their environment, taking corrective action, and learning from the new situation. Learning in a brain-like organisation is more truly a self-directed, self-monitoring, self-correcting continuous process. Not only do people learn to keep up with their own needs; they also learn to help the entire brain-like enterprise flourish. In a very simplistic sense, 'training' is a top-down, expert-centred approach, that is delivered frequently in a classroom, or with the help of technology, to the learner who uses a formal, self-learning package. Continuous learning is a bottom-up, learner-centred approach, that is coterminous with experience; that is, it calls for a model of learning from experience under conditions of very little structured design. Marsick and Watkins (1990) describe this kind of learning as informal or incidental, which is, essentially, learning from experience (Boud *et al.* 1993). (See Table 13.2 for more detail on informal and incidental learning model.) In addition, in order to self-regu-late, learning must be both single loop and double loop (Argyris and Schön 1978). Single-loop learning involves changes in tactics and strategies when things do not turn out as desired or predicted. Double-loop learning involves changes in the fundamental way in which problems are under-stood. Double-loop learning is required for self-regulation because individuals must, at times, change basic directions, which requires reframing basic lenses through which they view the world.

Chaos/complexity metaphor

Lately, scholars have been looking at organisations through the lens of chaos and complexity theory. Examples are drawn from physical phenomena in nature and the galaxy:

> Complex nonlinear systems like ecologies or organisations are charac-terized by multiple systems of interaction that are both ordered and chaotic...random disturbances can produce unpredictable events and

relationships that reverberate throughout a system, creating novel patterns of change...despite all of the unpredictability, coherent order *always* emerges out of the randomness and surface chaos.

(Morgan 1997: 262)

Wheatley (1992) is well known for her thinking on how chaos theory applies to management. Chaos theorists pay attention to the idea of 'attractors', which are pulls on a system to move in a direction. Systems are often pulled between several strong attractors, which are then responsible for the patterns that emerge. When systems move towards the edge of their equilibrium points, they may encounter alternative 'bifurcation points that are rather like "forks in a road" leading to different futures' (Morgan 1997: 265).

Chaotic change is enhanced by the simultaneous move in organisations to decentralise so that people and units can more easily respond to flux in their environment. Concomitantly, decentralisation enables people to be pulled by other attractors. People often find themselves mentally free to move from one organisation or cause to another, as well, in part because of the change in the psychological contract away from promises of lifelong employment. While on the one hand this freedom is liberating, it also comes with a lessening of links to organisations and to the social norms that have helped people to make sense of random existence. People thus find that they are increasingly being asked to look after themselves. They are told that they are responsible for their own learning, and are pushed towards self-directed learning and self-managed careers. Knowledge can be freely accessed, which provides for rich information, but at the same time, the individual can count on less help from systems in choosing and weighing the ideas that might be of greatest value to an unpredictable future. The organisation is often tied together by knowledge-based design principles rather than by the old hierarchical order; and work is frequently done virtually through the use of technology.

In chaos-based organisations, self-directed learning is still required, but overriding the self-initiation is a push away from prior planning and a pull towards simultaneous action and learning. These learning models also speak to the way in which individual action is shaped by the system's culture and structure. A family of related approaches to learning, based on action research, that fit well in this era are those that have been termed action technologies (Brooks and Watkins 1994). They include action research, action learning, action science and collaborative enquiry. (See Table 13.2 for more detail on action-based learning model.) All of these designs involve learners actively in investigating real problems, and in building their learning around these issues in real time. These learning models are inductive and organic; learners discover and meet needs in relationship to the problem they are investigating. They can apply what they learn immediately at work, and they can also take into account in their solutions the rapidly changing work environment. Action-based learning models frequently lead to changes in the system as a whole because learners question collective values, belief systems and ways of organising work in their search for solutions. The action project causes dissonance, which enables unfreezing of old ways. The apparent chaos that often ensues allows new patterns to emerge.

Learning organisations

How can we conceptualise a field that has grown so far beyond its earlier training identity as a teacher who works not in schools but in business, government and industry? It is clear that the short time perspective of short-term training courses is inadequate. The dawning acknowledgement that organisational changes of processes, culture or structure create accompanying learning demands has meant that the field must encompass more than training. The 1990s have seen the articulation of new models of workplace learning that emphasise the integration of learning into workplace practices and processes.

The concept of a learning organisation has emerged in recent years to take account of many of these changes (e.g. Field with Ford 1995, Pedler *et al.* 1991, Redding and Catalanello 1994, Senge 1990, Watkins and Marsick 1993). The learning organisation has been defined as an organisation which learns continually and has the capacity to transform itself (Pedler *et al.* 1991, Watkins and Marsick 1993). The idea of a learning organisation is based on models of organisational learning that have been in the literature for many years (e.g. Argyris and Schön 1978, 1996, Fiol and Lyles 1985, Hedberg 1981, March and Olsen 1976, Meyer 1982). It can be argued that all organisations learn, or they would not survive, but learning organisations demand proactive interventions to generate, capture, store, share and use learning at the systems level in order to create innovative products and services.

Many authors agree about what a learning organisation is, although they frequently operationalise core components differently. Most authors focus on learning of the system as a whole, as well as key changes in the way in which work is designed and the organisation is structured in order to allow for free flow of information, knowledge creation and management, and a culture that supports continuous learning (Gephart *et al.* 1997). Critics of the concept have noted its bias towards idealistic, normative outcomes, the complexity of interventions needed to implement it, and difficulties in measurement of impact (Marsick and Watkins 1997).

Knowledge management and intellectual capital

Recently, a related vein of literature has emerged on knowledge management and intellectual capital (Edvinnson and Malone 1997, Nonaka and

Takeuchi 1995, Stewart 1997). It speaks to the tangible outcomes of the learning organisation: knowledge as a product, its creation and management within the system, and its contribution to knowledge outcomes that are captured through the idea of intellectual capital. Knowledge creation is frequently looked upon in the literature as a hierarchy of increasingly complex levels of integration: data, information, knowledge and wisdom. Data are the raw material out of which people develop information. Information is then woven together to create knowledge, larger meaning chunks that signify patterns and relationships. Wisdom, at the pinnacle of the hierarchy, involves judgements about the value and use of knowledge. Learning – of individuals, and subsequently, of the entire system – is the process that makes the creation and use of knowledge meaningful (Watkins and Callahan 1998).

Management in several corporations has actively sought to incorporate knowledge creation and exchange as part of its mission to prompt employees to enhance their capacity to produce the most desirable results. Unfortunately, more efforts fail or disappoint than succeed (Lucier and Torsilieri 1997). One reason for this may be the difficulty in measuring intellectual capital. A measurement approach which is growing in popularity is that of the balanced scorecard – of adding *return on knowledge assets* to the traditional *return on financial assets* to the organisation's yearly accounting metrics.

Measures for intellectual capital grew out of dissatisfaction with conventional economic measures of value. Many of the assets brought to an organisation today reside in intangibles that are the result of knowledge resident in people or systems and products that they create. In the manufacturing age, these intangibles were often identified as 'good will'. In today's knowledge era, intellectual capital is most frequently described as having three components (Stewart 1997, Edvinnson and Malone 1997):

1 human capital, that is the people who work in a system themselves with all of their knowledge, experience and capacity to grow and innovate;
2 structural capital, that is what remains behind when people leave the premises: systems, policies, processes, tools or intellectual property that become the property of the system itself;
3 and customer capital, that is the system of relationships that an organisation has with its clients irrespective of the people who work there or the structural capital that is in place.

Strassman (Knowledge Inc. 1996) argues that the number of firms destroying knowledge capital is greater than the number of firms creating it. Re-engineering and downsizing play a critical role in destroying knowledge capital.

The people who possess the accumulated knowledge about a company are the carriers of Knowledge Capital. They are the people who leave the workplace every night and may never return. They possess something for which they have spent untold hours listening and talking while delivering nothing of tangible value to paying customers. Their brains have become the repositories of an accumulation of insights about how 'things work here'.

(p. 4)

Strassman continues, 'Anybody can cut costs by consuming capital.' He explains:

when they downsize they do not calculate what it will do to their Knowledge Capital. What they do, invariably, is slim down, reduce costs and destroy assets in the process. Five years later they wonder why the company is in worse shape than it was before.

(p. 5)

Learning organisations extend capacity to use learning as a strategic tool to generate new knowledge in the form of products, patents, processes and services, and to use technology to capture knowledge.

Applying metaphors to the learning organisation

The idea of the learning organisation can be differently understood by looking at it through the lens of different metaphors as discussed earlier in this chapter. Table 13.3 lays out some broad implications for how three sets of stakeholders might view learning, depending on the predominant lens through which they view this idea. Each lens leads to different decisions regarding what is important and what should be changed.

The machine metaphor actually does not lend itself well to a learning organisation, but it can be used to depict a training organisation in which employees are effectively and efficiently assisted to learn what the organisation wishes them to do best. Some of the better-known organisations before the knowledge era provided for this kind of learning very well. This model is still useful when operations are fairly routine, although under this metaphor, employees can be treated in a de-humanised manner for the specific skill they contribute. Managers in this model can help clearly to identify learning needs, provide incentives and resources for training, and measure success against clear standards. Employees are asked to follow the lead of managers. Therefore, when their best interests are not the same as those of the organisation, employees might join together through collective action to bargain for their rights. Learning is often compartmentalised in this model; neither managers nor employees encourage learning outside of a clearly defined job description. Hierarchy prevails, so that employees are

Table 13.3 Metaphorical lenses: implications for the learning organisation

Lens of learning	Implications for managers	Implications for employees	Implications for HRD
Machine	Provide incentives and resources for training; direct employees to perform to organisation's standards	Improve effectiveness and efficiency as specified; challenge managers through industrial relations	Hire or train employees to fill skill needs; provide instruction to meet defined needs and standards
Open systems	Assist employees in identifying needs and resources; act as coach and mentor; monitor against mutually negotiated goals	Negotiate learning with managers; adjust goals based on feedback; collaborate across boundaries to build knowledge and skills	Identify needed competencies and set up systems for self-directed learning; partner to ensure that needs are met
Brain/holograph	Model learning; integrate work and learning; provide for job enrichment and rotation; encourage cross-functional teams	Diagnose system's needs; challenge assumptions; initiate/monitor learning to meet own and system's needs	Design work to integrate learning across functions; provide for variety and continuous learning; build capacity to cross boundaries
Chaos/complexity	Provide structure and incentives to share knowledge; empower; align vision; act as resource for learning	Build portability of skills and job mobility; experiment and take risks; challenge restrictions and norms	Provide simultaneously for autonomy and for sharing across boundaries; unfreeze status quo

not given more information than deemed necessary for efficient operation of routine procedures. Curiosity and risk-taking are not encouraged or rewarded. The human resource developer in this model needs to hire the right people, and ensure that they gain the knowledge and skills identified to meet the challenges of their jobs. HRD staff are often engaged in contracting for, designing, delivering and evaluating training oriented to transferring expert knowledge and best practices that have been shown to lead to performance according to a desired standard.

The learning organisation concept begins to operate when, minimally, the open systems metaphor prevails. The networked structure common to this model provides incentives for a balanced, negotiated system of learning in which individuals take more initiative for their own learning, and can also get feedback regarding the way in which their actions impact on others in the organisation. In this model, there is more incentive to collaborate across boundaries and to negotiate towards win–win relationships with peers and managers. Arrangements can be developed that provide opportunities for learning, and that allow for mutual building and sharing of knowledge. While individuals take more initiative for learning in the open systems model, those who are designated as having more authority (be they managers or union representatives) are often accorded more responsibility for ensuring that learning goals are set, provided for, resourced and met. While managers are directors under the machine model, they often find themselves playing the role of a facilitator in the open systems model. HRD staff collaborate with managers, employees and collective bargaining units. They create systems that enable everyone more easily to determine knowledge and skill requirements for various roles and functions so that individuals can take the initiative in planning for their learning. Technology often aids in this process through computer-based skill assessments and self-managed learning systems. Technology also allows for the design of effective knowledge creation and management systems.

Under the brain metaphor, the learning organisation concept takes a leap forward. This is the intelligent enterprise that prizes knowledge creation and innovation. In order to be self-monitoring and self-regulating as a system, employees and managers alike seek to ensure that everyone takes an active role in scanning the environment and using this knowledge to improve products and services. Individuals seek out experience in the system as a whole, and are empowered in this model to act more frequently on behalf of the system when decisions fall close to their area of responsibility. Employees are as active as are managers in identifying and meeting learning needs for themselves and the organisational systems. Managers often take on a modelling role. Rather than direct operations, they clear blockages that get in the way of the free flow of information, and seek to involve employees actively in problem framing and reframing. Managers and employees alike are more active to challenge current thinking and assumptions that interfere with a flexible response to the shifting environment. Barriers break down between levels of the hierarchy, and between managers and bargaining units, because interests are more greatly aligned around a common vision. HRD staff actively help managers and employees alike to design work so that learning can also take place, and so that everyone knows as much as possible about the relevant work of others in the system. HRD staff seek to build the capacity of individuals and groups for continuous learning.

The chaos/complexity model may be best suited to the level of experimentation and risk-taking that is demanded for the building of intellectual capital in society. However, this model also holds the greatest risks for specific companies and enterprises which may fall short of what is needed to survive in an increasingly competitive environment. New patterns emerge from chaos, but it is hard to predict where they will emerge or who will have developed the skills, knowledge and capacity to take advantage of these new opportunities. This model of learning requires the simultaneous and almost paradoxical nurturing of both autonomy for individuals and concern for linkages across individuals so that the larger system can benefit from what individuals have learned. Managers in this learning model need to provide incentives and opportunities to learn rapidly for both individuals and systems. Empowerment in this model is even stronger than in the brain model, but so too is the need to adjust continually and align the vision to take advantage of what is being learned. Individuals cannot count on the organisation to provide compensation for what they know over time, and, hence, must build portability of knowledge assets. Sacred cows need to be continually challenged if individuals and systems as a whole are to evolve into new forms that can flourish in the future. HRD staff in this model must create structures and advocate for resources so that individuals can meet rapidly changing needs for knowledge and skills. They must also find ways to involve actively representatives of the entire system in learning, decision-making and in building a collective knowledge base. HRD staff can serve managers and employees better when they help to unfreeze reliance on the status quo so that space is opened up to experiment and to use learning to change structures, cultures and systems. In this approach, training and education are part of the larger research and development role of the organisation, working to build knowledge capital of a different kind.

The above analysis, of course, assumes that any given organisation falls fairly clearly under the sphere of influence of one or other of these metaphors. In real life, this could well not be the case. Organisations need to develop the capacity to diagnose their learning orientations, and, when necessary, to add to their repertoire of learning responses or to change them. This becomes more complex if we return to our assumption that all of these metaphors can operate simultaneously in different parts of the same organisation for different purposes. In addition, it seems likely that different individuals could hold a viewpoint on learning that might not be shared by the dominant culture. In these cases, the perspectives of different individuals and groups will come into conflict. Schein (1996) points out that in many organisations there are actually three cultures which function in any organisation at any time – that of operators, of engineers and of executives. These differences are not typically recognised, or adequately taken into account, in analysing or addressing issues around the organisation's culture. And, as Field and Ford (1995) point out, in some organisations the conflict of perspectives is suppressed, with a resultant loss of learning. In a learning organisation, with a minimum of an open systems perspective, it should be possible to surface, identify and address conflict constructively and, optimally, to view difference as a catalyst for more effective learning. Nevertheless, it is critical to remember that the lens through which either the organisational culture or the training function views learning is a coherent, but also a limiting, perspective. Diagnosing the prevailing metaphor is one step towards moving beyond its limitations.

Critique of the learning organisation concept

Some take a pessimistic view of the power relations in organisations, and the feasibility of changing these to empower workers to the extent required in a learning organisation. Darrah (1995), for example, analyses workplace training at 'Kramden Computers' to see how the production floor can be viewed as an arena for learning and how training may reify extant social relationships in the workplace. He argues that the function of training may be to 'obscure organisational schisms that can only be addressed through deeper changes in the workplace' (p. 31). He suggests that workplace training and workplace learning are linked and neither is a simple matter of efficient pedagogy. Rather, the organisation of work and the allocation of power deeply influence what is learned. While few would argue with Darrah's assertions, one could counterargue that he is again blaming the victim since trainers are seldom positioned to address these fundamental changes and they, too, are aware of the dilemmas he notes. It is precisely because workplace learning is more than a simple pedagogical interaction that we have seen the emergence of conceptualisations of workplace learning that combine knowledge of pedagogy with knowledge of organisational behaviour and culture.

A broader critique comes from Korten (1995) whose powerfully well-documented critique of corporate greed and power raises the question of individual versus organisational rights. Noting the hold that industrial interests gained over government following the chaos of the Civil War, President Lincoln said that corporations had become enthroned and corruption and greed would follow that would destroy the Republic. Later, the courts continued to take away the controls citizens had imposed until the case of *Santa Clara County v. Southern Pacific Railroad* in 1886 which ruled that a corporation was a natural person under the US Constitution which thereby afforded corporations the protection of the Bill of Rights. Korten notes that this was a dramatic victory for corporations since they received the rights of citizens without the responsibility of citizenship. With globalisation, corporations are citizens of no country and responsible only to themselves. Korten suggests that there has been an increasing 'sanctification of greed' and with it less and less concern for the individual and the communities in which corporations reside. Democratic pluralism is lost as is the balance of civic, individual and corporate interests.

Korten argues for corporate social responsibility within corporations. Moreover, he asks human resource developers and managers to use their considerable organisational and group facilitation skills to work with communities to take back their power. Korten argues that the way to transform organisations is to change the balance of power between the vested interests of managers and stockholders which now makes it unnecessary for them to change at all. Korten's idea of human resource developers and managers is that they are a citizen first and a corporate employee second. Zorro or the Scarlet Pimpernel by night and the weak professional class by day is an interesting image and reflects Korten's belief that the powers invested in corporations in 1997 are virtually unstoppable from within. His is an arresting and compelling case and also disturbing for professions which have always seen themselves as those who help organisations transform themselves from within.

The idea of the learning organisation has also been questioned as a tool of management which again holds employees responsible for transforming and changing their reluctant organisations (Schied *et al.* 1997, Welton 1991). Some labour leaders are envisioning new roles for unions that emphasise partnership, collaboration and consensus building, and they see learning as central to their new focus (Field with Ford 1995, Scully 1994). Nonetheless, more organisations have invested in learning organisation experiments focused on the learning and changing of employees than have invested in changing the underlying structures of power and knowledge creation in the organisation.

Other critics have asked: learning for what? If we create organisations which learn faster, better and deeper, and the outcome is to feed corporate profits at the expense of people, societies and the environment, is this not similar to making a more effective gas for the Nazi gas chambers? Again, this is a dramatic form of the question, but the issue is important. Korten quotes Goldsmith who notes, 'What an astounding thing it is to watch a civilisation destroy itself because it is unable to re-examine the validity under totally new circumstances of an economic ideology' (Korten 1995: 87). Those who raise this question are sensibly asking us to question the validity of a vision of the learning organisation that is only process oriented. What is learned is also significant.

Conclusion

We might well ask where this critique and analysis leads us. How do we reconcile the metaphors of organisation with the learning responses, without falling into the traps the critics identify? One approach implied in this discussion is that organisations must evolve developmentally, starting with the metaphor that now prevails and moving towards one which permits higher-level learning and a more complex learning approach. Another thought is to imagine that the society as a whole is moved by a dominant metaphor. If this were the case, it might be most imperative to align the learning system with the prevailing metaphor. Yet, this seems either too prescriptive or alarmist. An approach more in keeping with our thinking is to seek to create a learning system which incorporates selected elements of each metaphor, tailored to the needs of the industry, the organisation, the division and the individuals who work in this organisational culture.

References

Argyris, C. and Schön, D. (1978) *Organizational Learning: A Theory of Action Perspective*, San Francisco: Jossey-Bass.

Argyris, C. and Schön, D. (1996) *Organizational Learning II: Theory, Method, and Practice*, Reading, MA: Addison-Wesley.

Boud, D., Cohen, R. and Walker, D. (eds) (1993) *Using Experience for Learning*, Buckingham, UK, and Bristol, PA: The Society for Research into Higher Education, and Open University Press.

Brooks, A. and Watkins, K. E. (eds) (1994) *The Emerging Power of Action Inquiry Technologies*, New Directions in Adult and Continuing Education, San Francisco: Jossey-Bass.

Candy, P. C. (1991) *Self-direction for Lifelong Learning: A Comprehensive Guide to Theory and Practice*, San Francisco: Jossey-Bass.

Darrah, C. (1995) 'Workplace training, workplace learning: a case study', *Human Organization* 54(1): 31–41.

Edvinnson, L. and Malone, M. (1997) *Intellectual Capital: Realizing Your Company's True Value by Finding its Hidden Roots*, New York: Harper Collins.

Field, L. with Ford, B. (1995) *Managing Organisational Learning: From Rhetoric to Reality*, Melbourne: Longman.

Fiol, M. C. and Lyles, M. A. (1985) 'Organizational learning', *Academy of Management Review* 10(4): 803–13.

Gephart, M. A., Marsick, V. J. and Van Buren, M. E. (1997) 'Finding common and uncommon ground among learning organization models', in R. Torraco (ed.) *Proceedings of the Fourth Annual Academy of HRD Conference*, Baton Rouge, LA: Academy of Human Resource Development, 547–54.

Harkins, P. J. (1991) 'The changing role of corporate training and development', *Corporate Development in the 90s*, Supplement to *Training*, Minneapolis, MN: Lakewood, 26–9.

Hedberg, B. (1981) 'How organizations learn and unlearn', in P. C. Nystrom and W. H. Starbuck (eds) *Handbook of Organizational Design*, Vol. 1, London: Oxford University Press, 3–27.

Jacobs, R. and Jones, M. J. (1995) *Structured On-the-Job Training: Unleashing Employee Expertise in the Workplace*, San Francisco: Berrett-Koehler.

Knowledge Inc. (1996) 'Leading lights: knowledge strategist Paul Strassmann, Interview', *Knowledge Inc. Executive Report*.

Knowles, M. (1980) *The Modern Practice of Adult Education: From Pedagogy to Andragogy*, second edn, New York: Cambridge Books.

Korten, D. (1995) *When Corporations Rule the World*, San Francisco: Berrett-Koehler.

Lucier, C. E. and Torsilieri, J. D. (1997) 'Why knowledge programs fail: a C.E.O.'s guide to managing learning', *Strategy and Business* No. 9: 14–28.

March, J. G. and Olsen, J. P. (1976) *Ambiguity and Choice in Organizations*, Norway: Universitetsforlaget.

Marsick, V. J. and Watkins, K. (1990) *Informal and Incidental Learning in the Workplace*, London: Routledge.

Marsick, V. J. and Watkins, K. E. (1997) 'Organizational learning: review of research', in L. J. Bassi and D. Russ-Eft (eds) *What Works and What Doesn't: Assessment, Development, and Measurement*, Alexandria, VA: American Society for Training & Development. 65–86.

Meyer, A. (1982) 'Adapting to environmental jolts', *Administrative Science Quarterly* 27(4): 515–37.

Morgan, G. (1997) *Images of Organization*, Thousand Oaks, CA: Sage.

Nonaka, I. and Takeuchi, H. (1995) *The Knowledge Creating Company*, New York: Oxford.

Pedler, M., Burgoyne, J. and Boydell, T. (1991) *The Learning Company*, London: McGraw-Hill.

Redding, J. and Catalanello, R. (1994) *Strategic Readiness: The Making of a Learning Organization*, San Francisco: Jossey-Bass.

Rothwell, W. and Kazanas, H. (1994 and 1989) *Human Resource Development – A Strategic Approach*, Amherst, MA: HRD Press.

Schein, E. H. (1996) 'Culture: the missing concept in organization studies', *Administrative Science Quarterly* 41(June): 229–40.

Schied, F. M., Carter, V. K., Preston, J. A. and Howell, S. L. (1997) 'The HRD factory: an historical inquiry into the production of control in the workplace', in P. Armstrong, N. Miller and M. Zukas (eds) *Crossing Borders, Breaking Boundaries: Research in the Education of Adults*, Proceedings of the 27th Annual SCUTREA Conference, Birkbeck College, University of London, 404–8.

Scully, E. (1994) 'The role of labor unions in the learning organization', Unpublished manuscript.

Senge, P. (1990) *The Fifth Discipline: The Art and Practice of the Learning Organization*, New York: Random House.

Stewart, T. (1997) *Intellectual Capital: The New Wealth of Organizations*, New York: Double Day Currency.

Watkins, K. E. (1996) 'Workplace learning: changing times, changing practices', in F. Spikes (ed.) *Workplace Learning*, New Directions in Adult and Continuing Education Series, San Francisco: Jossey-Bass.

Watkins, K. E. and Callahan, M. W. (1998) 'Return on knowledge assets: investments in educational technology', *Educational Technology* XXXVI(4): 33–40.

Watkins, K. E. and Marsick, V. J. (1993) *Sculpting the Learning Organization*, San Francisco: Jossey-Bass.

Welton, M. (1991) *Toward Development Work: The Workplace as a Learning Environment*, Geelong, Victoria: Deakin University Press.

Wheatley, M. (1992) *Leadership and the New Science*, San Francisco: Berrett-Koehler.

14 The dominant discourses of learning at work

John Garrick

Many perspectives are presented in this book. Some support each other, others do not. Indeed there are ambiguities and internal contradictions in theories about 'learning' and 'work'. Yet each makes important contributions to our understanding. To draw conclusions about possible futures for workplace learning this chapter identifies four of the most influential discourses on learning at work. These are reflected in this book and throughout the literature more generally. They are: human capital theory; experience-based learning; cognition and expertise; and generic skills, capabilities and competence. These discourses are themselves subject to the broader influences of contemporary economic views of the world. They contribute to new *operational* knowledge about learning. In this chapter a case is made for learning based in the workplace to be viewed as containing far more possibilities than the prevalent narrow interpretations of competence, and the economic or utilitarian outcomes sought in many locations.

In addition to the multiple perspectives emerging in workplace learning discourses, at least two common themes can be identified. The first is that which suggests that the provision of a supportive learning environment is critical to the success of learning and training endeavours. Within this theme is a view that people learn best by moving from the concrete to the abstract and that suitable guidance is needed within the workplace. As learning is embedded in the realities of workplace processes, systems and technologies, one's *experience* becomes vital. This leads to the second theme: the dominant *policy view* of workplace learning which holds that workplace learning is a planned and structured process drawing on frameworks which extend beyond a given enterprise. Competency-based training and assessment is an example of this policy view of learning.

In this chapter I argue that public policy will eventually need to shift away from a centralised, 'one best-way' approach – towards more decentralised, innovative learning, training and assessment processes. Indeed, Casey (Chapter 2), Beckett (Chapter 6), Probert (Chapter 7), Solomon (Chapter 8) and Butler (Chapter 9) all variously argue that workplace learning is an interdisciplinary 'field'. Indeed, as Barnett puts it in Chapter

3, learning at work exists in conditions of 'supercomplexity'. Barnett and Casey both stress the powerful influences that are exerted on an individual's learning that emanate from the extraordinary changes taking place in the nature and purposes of work – its structures, organisation and the effects of new digital communication technologies. In reflecting on the contributions of these main theories of workplace learning, I offer some ideas about future directions.

Dominant discourses on workplace learning

This section examines the dominant discourses of work-based learning. It seeks to clarify key issues associated with each of these discourses, examining their effects on how learning and 'new knowledge' are constructed at work. These discourses are not mutually exclusive; each relates to the other in a variety of ways. In some ways they are all sub-discourses of contemporary market economics which exert powerful influences on our understanding of learning at work. Market economics permeates, in some way, all contemporary theorisations of learning in work contexts. Although it is obvious that people acquire knowledge and skills at work, it is not always obvious that this is a product of deliberate investment – a hallmark of western economic systems. We are getting close to a situation in which what it is *to know* in the modern world appears to have no secure base beyond markets, and these are currently *the* sites of power.

Human capital theory

Human capital theory refers to the productive capabilities of human beings. Human capabilities are acquired at a cost and, in turn, command a price in the labour market – depending on how useful they are in producing goods and services. Theodore Shultz (1977: 313) in his famous treatise on 'investment in human capital' said that

> much of what we call consumption constitutes investment in human capital, but nowhere do [intangibles including key aspects of education] enter into our national accounts...[yet] the quality of human effort can be greatly improved and its productivity enhanced through investing in human capital.

The idea of investing in human beings as a form of capital has, since then, fuelled a very powerful discourse of workplace learning. This discourse involves thinking in terms of human value (and performance) as a return on investment in a cost-to-benefit ratio. Human capital theory is thus a way of viewing the preparation of workers to meet the labour requirements of a market economy.

Human capital theory provides 'the most compelling arguments related to increasing the net worth of workers' skills and abilities', argue Marsick and Watkins (1990: 20). They suggest in Chapter 13 that there are enormous human, intellectual and cultural capital benefits of promoting workplace learning opportunities for employees. Other theorists such as Hart (1993) assert that this representational framework has been deployed in workplaces with some unintended outcomes. For instance, Hart claims that a human capital approach to learning has the affect of making employees economically active but politically passive. The mobilisation of workplace learning is a form of collusion between management and big unions that ultimately serves capital interests. This claim is based on the premise that:

> Production is, above all, production for profit; that nature is dead, malleable matter entirely at our disposal; and that the immense social and environmental costs of our way of production can therefore be externalised, and [therefore] do not figure in our calculations of growth and development.
>
> (Hart 1993: 26)

Marsick and Watkins (1990) reject Hart's critique on the grounds that the USA in particular needs to increase greatly the flexibility of its human capital base or face turbulent, even violent, upheaval in order to become more economically productive. Their theory, which advocates a 'holistic' approach to learning at work, has influenced much that has been written within the field of HRD on learning in the workplace. Their approach involves changes to work structures and patterns to include learning organisations, team approaches, quality circles, TQM and so on. However, these may not necessarily result in 'improved learning'. The current focus on restructuring or 'remodelling' workplaces and making workers more empowered – to effect ever greater efficiencies – rests on taken-for-granted notions about work such as its relationship to 'progress' and 'development', and these can hide the many tensions that exist between 'learning for work' and 'work for learning'.

The 'informalisation' of learning at work is a concept, derived in part from human capital theory, that is gathering momentum in many workplaces. It is thus worth briefly examining what is implied by the terms 'incidental' and 'informal'. According to Marsick and Watkins (1990: 8), informal and incidental learning, although interconnected, are not necessarily the same. They define incidental learning as a by-product of some other activity such as sensing the organisational culture, or trial and error experimentation. As such, incidental learning is not planned or intentional, as it may be with self-directed learning, or where help is consciously sought from advisers, coaches or mentors. A key distinguishing feature in Marsick and Watkins' definition is that informal learning is intentional, incidental learning is not. Such a distinction may, however, be dubious as they themselves point out in subsequent works. It is unwarranted to separate 'self-directed' learning from the beliefs and values that influence 'incidental' learning. The 'incidental' is thus incorporated within the term 'informal'.

Another way of thinking of learning at work is not in terms of the informal or incidental but as 'accidental' – a spontaneous, contingent form of learning where something fruitful or transformative happens without deliberation. The totally unexpected and playful still (thankfully) happens from time to time and one does not realise its significance until after the event. Such serendipity can occur as spontaneous experience – like a jolt or surprise that shapes one's learning. This suggests that learning at work can be obtained 'unconsciously, existentially; through the mere experience of living in a particular "environment" or "context"' (Bagnall 1990: 1).

A critical point here is that in workplaces, individuals' activities tend to be 'formalised' by factors such as cost considerations, production, time frames, industrial relations, managerial requirements and work organisation. Activities reflect the requirements of work contexts, but from a human capital standpoint, learning is inextricably linked to economic analyses. In making distinctions between informal and formal learning it is thus important to think about how learning is being framed theoretically and contextually: what factors may be shaping one's learning at work?

In Chapter 13, Marsick and Watkins offer some metaphors, such as 'machine', 'open systems', 'holographic' and 'chaos' to describe key factors influencing work-based learning environments. The metaphors provide useful tools for identifying different types of learning environments and have one thing in common: certain work conditions can enhance (or reduce) the effectiveness of workplace learning. Here again, the importance of specific contextual factors is critical. Marsick and Watkins expand on the factors they believe underpin the defining characteristics and key conditions which, they claim, promote effective learning in organisations, highlighting the growing importance in business and academic worlds of 'intellectual capital'. This notion emphasises the 'intangibles' associated with people's knowledge and learning.

The notion of intellectual capital draws on key elements of informal learning and human capital theory. The management of intellectual (and cultural) capital, even when well intentioned, is most likely to be driven by political imperatives, production demands, efficiency requirements and cost-effectiveness issues in market economies. In spite of this likely scenario, the increased emphasis on 'managing' intellectual (and cultural) capital further illustrates the complexity and diversity of the ways learning can be configured within organisations.

At work, what one learns will also touch on ethical issues. These are often neglected in literature on learning organisations, workplace learning and informal learning. Yet as Probert (Chapter 7), Solomon (Chapter 8) and Butler (Chapter 9) each assert, significant problems exist within human capital theorisations of workplace learning including the gender, political, social, cultural and situated ethical issues that accompany it. These writers argue forcefully that it is not so much the relationship of workplace learning to formal learning, or how learning can be enhanced, or how it is defined, that is most critical. Rather, it is the social, cultural and discursive effects on people (including relationships between people at various levels of work) that warrant careful consideration. Indeed the relationship between *the applications* of a human capital approach to workplace learning and the lived experience of individuals at work requires far greater attention than it is given in contemporary research.

Experience-based learning

Learning from experience is based on a set of assumptions identified by Boud *et al.* (1993: 8–14) as:

- experience is the foundation of, and the stimulus for, learning;
- learners actively construct their own experience;
- learning is a holistic experience;
- learning is socially and culturally constructed; and
- learning is influenced by the socioemotional context in which it occurs.

Powerful tensions exist within and between these assumptions – for example, that learners 'actively construct their own experience' whilst, at the same time, 'learning is socially and culturally constructed'. On the surface, these assumptions represent a dichotomy. Such a dichotomy warrants exploration as important differences exist between adult education as practised within an individualistic discourse of personal empowerment, and pedagogy of critical social theory. That both are assumed to underpin learning from experience is intriguing as they carry such different implications for practice and for the cultural politics of work.

Adult learning theory – within the discourse of 'personal empowerment' – holds that learning can be most effective if one's emotions are engaged in the learning process. Indeed, there has been an upsurge in interest in emotion in learning at work. The interest in the role of emotion in learning has been taken up by many adult educators, workplace trainers, facilitators and mentors who operate within the 'humanistic' tradition and 'human resource developers' interested in 'emotional intelligence' (Gardner 1993). The humanistic tradition holds that the individual may be most productive when he or she feels that work is personally meaningful, not simply an instrumental means to another end. What is 'personally meaningful', and how one 'feels' about work, are thus critical to both learning and performance. But these connections can also reflect how difficult it can be to reconcile the differences in the above assumptions.

An attempt to construct a framework for making sense of experiential learning that addresses this problem is Weil and McGill's (1989) 'villages'. They view experiential learning (1989: 3) as 'a spectrum of meanings, practices and ideologies which emerge out of the work and commitments of people'. In this spectrum, they discern four emphases on experiential learning. Each emphasis is the basis for a cluster of interrelated ideas, concerns and values which they refer to as 'villages'. The villages include:

1 the assessment and accreditation of prior experiential learning experiences;
2 experiential learning and change in higher and continuing education;
3 experiential learning and social change;
4 personal growth and development.

Weil and McGill hold that a person or organisation which knows only their own village will not understand it. It is through dialogue across villages that we are enabled to consider what we intend and what we do from new perspectives. Boud (1989: 38) supports the need for dialogue across villages, but adds (p. 40) that 'at the heart of the main traditions is *the role of autonomy*, and the variety of approaches which might promote the individual's autonomy'. He goes on to point out that these approaches can be located within the main traditions in adult learning which include:

• training and efficiency in learning;
• self-directed learning and the andragogy school;
• learner-centred education and the humanistic educations; and
• critical pedagogy and social action.

The traditions, which highlight the main conceptions of experiential learning, share a central notion, autonomy, even though they interpret this notion in quite different ways (Boud 1987). Irrespective of the approach adopted, the subject's autonomy is of central importance to all modernist notions of education. However, as Usher (1992: 201) puts it:

> adult education works with an ethics of personal empowerment and autonomy. In this sense, adult education is part of the educational project of the Enlightenment and because of this is cast in and expresses itself through a discourse of individual agency.

It is worth asking: how good an account of reality does the theory of experiential learning, most common in adult education and workplace learning practices, provide? Experiential learning theory presupposes a great deal about individual 'agency'. It also places reflection as 'the bridge between experience and learning' (Usher 1992: 206). It is precisely this presupposition that is being adopted in many workplace learning programmes, training activities and staff development plans (including performance review systems). Indeed, experience is being 'managed' and 'turned into' learning in ways that are in contrast with the old style of didactic transmission of disciplinary knowledge in which learners are cast as the passive recipients of someone else's wisdom. As Beckett has aptly put it in Chapter 6, things have moved 'past the gurus' and into new forms of learning. But new forms of learning from experience should not be read unproblematically. For, as Usher and Solomon (1998: 8) argue, 'the educational discourse of experiential learning intersects happily with the managerial discourse of workplace reform...since both [discourses] shape subjectivity in ways appropriate to the needs of the contemporary workplace'. The point here is that there are complex relationships between workers/learners and their managers (or supervisors) who often double as learning advisers, coaches and mentors. The intersection of the experiential learning discourse and contemporary managerial discourse means that performance and learning outcomes, power and surveillance are more aligned. The activities (formal or informal) of employees are being made more accountabie than ever before.

Cognition and expertise at work

Understanding how the mind works is central to discourses of cognition and expertise. However, uncertainties about the relationship between cognitive and social contributions to thinking and acting have led to an erroneous view that *the mind* can be conceived as being isolated from *the social* world (for instance, see Bredo 1994). The false separation of self, identify and the social prompts questions about how theories of cognition and expertise are being used to interpret and understand how, and in what ways, workplaces influence the construction of knowledge. Cognitive psychology provides an account of the construction of individuals' representations of knowledge in memory (Billett, Chapter 10). *Representations*, says Billett, are usually referred to as forms of conceptual and procedural knowledge (cognitive structures). It is these representations which are acquired, organised in memory and deployed (re-presented) in routine and non-routine cognitive activities such as problem-solving, transfer and learning.

Problem-solving is viewed as a process which transforms existing knowledge, thereby assisting the construction of cognitive structures and cognitive development (Anderson 1993). Therefore, constructing new knowledge is analogous to problem-solving – the transformation of knowledge is to apply it to other similar or not-so-similar situations. The ability to deploy effectively cognitive structures in non-routine situations (e.g. complex problem-solving and transfer) within a domain of knowledge distinguishes experts from novices (Glaser 1989, Gott 1989, Wagner and Sternberg 1986). An example here is a motor mechanic in a particular garage who has to respond to the demands of a 'road-service' breakdown. The ability to transfer knowledge from one situation to another is critical here. Within cognitive psychology, this simple example serves to illustrate the principle that knowledge and skill required for workplace performance, although associated with a particular discipline or subject matter, need to be generic. This principle has fuelled the notion of 'generic competencies' (which I examine in the following section).

Chi *et al.* (1981) and Glaser (1984) point out that the categorisation of problems by the means of their solution, another hallmark of expertise, is dependent upon how individuals represent the problem and construct problem spaces, or the solver's representation of the problem, from which to secure a solution. Within cognitive psychology, knowledge acquisition and cognitive development occur through problem-solving (both routine and non-routine) which is cognitive activity similar to learning and transfer (Billett 1995). This perspective views thinking as *a skill determined internally* by the extent and organisation of cognitive structures.

Billett's work makes the point that much of the cognitive literature, with some notable exceptions such as Gott (1989, 1995) and Greeno (1989), offers an explanation of thinking and learning which is disembedded, and which fails to account adequately for the lived-in world such as workplaces. Consequently, within cognitive psychology, expertise has become conceptualised as essentially a cognitive phenomenon in which thinking is a skill and the utility of internal attributes are emphasised at the expense of social and cultural contributions to thinking and acting. Therefore, this account of representations of knowledge in memory remains incomplete. It fails to identify the sources of these representations of knowledge and how these sources influence representations. Neither does it advance a sufficient account of how knowledge is constructed.

A broader view of knowledge construction is the constructivist perspective which views the sociohistorical origins of knowledge and its appropriation through social mediation (Vygotsky 1978, 1987). This involves the appropriation of knowledge as the outcome of an interpretative construction – mediated by individuals' personal histories interacting with socially sourced knowledge (see Billett 1995). This view of knowledge construction emphasises the mutuality between individuals and the social and cultural circumstances in which they act. This constructivist perspective is, however, yet to provide a comprehensive account of the different types of knowledge which are constructed or how these may be deployed in goal-directed activities of workplaces.

Expertise too can be conceptualised in different ways across different communities, even when an activity, apparently similar at the sociocultural level, is being undertaken. Proposed characteristics of expertise, as outlined from a sociocultural view, reveal its relational, embedded, competent, reciprocal and pertinent nature. Billett (1998) claims that *expertise*:

(i)   is *relational* in terms of requirements of a particular community of practice (workplace);
(ii) is *embedded*, being the product of extensive social practice, with meaning about practice derived by becoming a full participant, over time, and with understanding shaped by participation in the activities and norms of that work practice;
(iii) requires *competence* in the workplace's discourses, in the routine and non-routine activities of practice, mastery of new understanding, and the ability to perform and adapt existing skills;
(iv) is *reciprocal*, shaping as well as being shaped, by the workplace practices which include setting and maintaining standards of *the culture of practice*;
(v)   requires *pertinence* in the appropriateness of problem solutions, such as knowing what behaviours are 'acceptable' and in what circumstances.

In this theory of expertise, it is important to note that the above qualities reflect the embedded values of particular workplaces and include the 'culture of practice' which Solomon, in Chapter 8, points out can be quite problematic terrain. Any understanding of expertise therefore needs to take account of the particular circumstances in which that 'knowledge' has its origins and is then 'transformed' by participants.

Generic skills, capabilities and competence

Berryman (1993) offers an account of the skill requirements of contemporary and future workplaces that she argues are a responsibility of education. Thus Berryman is concerned with learning *for* the workplace rather than learning *in* the workplace. However, according to Hager (1998), the skills that she claims schools should develop can be read as requirements for effective workplace learning to occur. Berryman's generic skills list for schools includes reading and quantitative skills, higher-order cognitive thinking skills and various interpersonal skills. Berryman's list also supports work by Carnevale *et al.* (1993) that indicates the types of skills employers are seeking for today's workforce.

Hager (1998) and Gonczi (Chapter 12) claim that once serious attention is directed to workplace skills and competence, the more generic skills and attributes tend to be viewed as learning outcomes that are just as important as the learning of specific skills or the capabilities to perform particular tasks. However, simplistic assumptions about the transferability of such generic skills are misplaced. Even within the same occupation, job demands vary so much between different companies and contexts that the notion of generic competencies provides a stronger conceptual framework for skill recognition as it makes little sense to try to specify exact competencies for particular occupations. For instance, recent research in the USA by Stasz *et al.* (1996: 102) found that

> whereas generic skills and dispositions are identifiable in all jobs, their specific characteristics and importance vary among jobs. The characteristics of problem solving, teamwork, communication, and disposition are related to job demands, which in turn depend on the purpose of the work, the tasks that constitute the job, the organisation of the work, and other aspects of the work context.

Similar findings resulted from Australian research on 'key competencies' (Gonczi *et al.* 1995, Hager *et al.* 1996). Hager *et al.* argue that common ground must be found between the disparate approaches to teaching generic competencies to provide a significant and productive link between trainees' performance in both education and the workplace. These researchers are pointing to an unprecedented degree of convergence between workplace learning and formal education. In such a convergence, the importance of context-specific learning (at work) will, in all likelihood, require of university courses and vocational training providers the delivery of a strong emphasis on operational know-how. In many industries and government agencies, policy understandings of such instrumental knowledge currently rest upon competency-based education and training frameworks, which, as Gonczi points out in Chapter 12, are indebted to theories of cognitive psychology. With operational knowledge being privileged through this theoretical lens what we see is a version of learning, largely about preparing people for the marketplace, that resonates powerfully with the human capital theory described earlier in this chapter.

Some directions for future knowledge and learning at work

Each of the theories covered in this book has something to offer. However, none has established an overarching claim on workplace learning, although advocates of each of the influential discourses discussed earlier may dispute this. The argument here is that the most useful ways of theorising workplace learning tolerate and recognise the productive potential of diversity and ambiguity, while at the same time enabling skill development *and* the creation of new knowledge. How this is to be done is one of the main challenges facing the future of learning at work. This is, of course, contested terrain. There is no precise or measurable conception of workplace learning that adequately accounts for the range of influences upon it. This is, in part, why Matthews and Candy in Chapter 4 stress the importance of promoting 'learning environments' as being central to the potential for learning at work – especially given work contexts of continual and rapid change.

As I have argued, many contemporary views of learning at work are influenced by human capital theory. Some are squarely indebted to this theory for their justification. Human capital theory is primarily interested in how to make learning effective in order to enhance performance. This perspective has major implications for the roles of managers, HRD practitioners, staff development facilitators, organisational developers and line supervisors. For instance, employees are now frequently expected (by managers and peers) to learn continuously, and they want to have their learning 'recognised'. In some instances such recognition can translate to extra remuneration. Recognition of prior learning can also lead to credit in formal award courses such as university degrees.

A variety of implementation strategies to promote learning at work is prevalent in many industries. The strategies, including the development of on-site mentors, coaches and supervisors with educational skills, are already requiring new approaches to performance reviews, staff development, infrastructure support and clearer 'educative' roles/links between workplace supervisors and staff. Leadership roles are becoming more 'educative' and supervisory/managerial functions more 'developmental' to enhance staff performance and clarify career pathways.

A key assumption about learning at work here is that it has something to do with individuals (subjects) apprehending experience, reasoning, or logically thinking through their work experience and giving that experience 'meaning'. Unfortunately, much of the research on work-based learning fails to acknowledge the representational effects of its own theorising, 'authorising' particular types of experience. The 'truth' about learning at work is that it is framed by the assumptions of the particular way it is viewed. Proof of an individual's on-the-job learning currently relies heavily on the observable and measurable. This perspective assumes an objective reality, which in part accounts for why observable competencies have become so popular in vocational education and training discourse. Subjective experience is not, however, an incontrovertible starting (or concluding) point in any analysis or theory of what has been learnt from one's experience at work.

Indeed, the notions of 'reflection', 'experience', 'experience-based learning', 'competence' and 'cognition' at work are all widely used. They reflect prominent discourses about learning at work. They also contain significant tensions, ambiguities and internal contradictions and, furthermore, counterpoint each other. The different discourses hold different meanings of workplace learning illustrating the sheer complexity and diversity of factors that directly (and indirectly) shape one's learning including *what counts* in the workplace. Confronted with this, some theorists have placed their emphasis on particular factors that they believe are especially influential in professional learning processes. For instance,

Hager in Chapter 5 cites Argyris and Schön (1978) to highlight the importance of non-routine circumstances for stimulating significant experiential learning, suggesting that it is *the non-routine* that forces professionals into the kind of reflective thinking that changes beliefs, values and assumptions. Billet (Chapter 10), Tennant (Chapter 11) and Gonczi (Chapter 12) variously argue that the conceptual underpinning of this approach stems from a sociocultural theory of cognition. This theory holds that *the social setting* in which cognitive activity takes place is integral to that activity, not just the surrounding context for it. This perspective is sometimes referred to as 'situated learning' (Lave and Wenger 1991) and offers a powerful theorisation of workplace-based learning – enough to have captured the attention of a wide variety of US and European enterprises.

Organisations – large and small – are now looking for ways of developing appropriate cultures of learning in workplaces. Even small subcontractors are being encouraged through mechanisms such as government tendering policies to have training plans for employees. For large business organisations, universities are now beginning to enter the market of providing work-based courses. Such courses can be designed for enterprises that can afford to pay for designer programmes that will enhance learning and credential employees. That such a market exists is testimony to the growing phenomena of formalised workplace learning. Garrick and Solomon (1997) argue, however, that some dangers for employees do exist for their *incorporation* into workplace culture through seductive organisational reward systems, including formalised workplace learning. Further, Usher and Solomon (1998: 6) point out that

> with the replacement of what constitutes legitimate knowledge (as constituted by disciplines and therefore outside the organisation) to that constituted by performance agreements (and therefore within its control), the organisation can also ensure that the 'right' performative things are learnt.

When work *is* learning there is clearly a range of critical issues and tensions arising. With the growth of interest in and demand for learning at work, future directions appear to include the need for workplaces to be active in supporting workers/learners as well as deconstructing the limiting conceptual differences between 'workers', 'managers', 'supervisors' and 'educators'. This deconstruction could involve, for example, a surfacing of the effects of the related power imbalances that such distinctions construct. In the competitive world of business it is, nonetheless, reasonable to expect that organisations will want universities that will give credence to the learning that it (i.e. the organisation) sees as valuable. One of the futures of learning at work thus holds a notion of workplace-based qualifications – located in organisations – suggesting more contextually specific learning than delivered through conventional formal (institutionally based) courses.

The varying characteristics of workplaces as learning environments therefore become very important in the new production of knowledge. As Matthews and Candy (Chapter 4) and Marsick and Watkins (Chapter 13) variously argue, workplaces as learning environments are usually defined as arenas of activity in which socioculturally determined practices occur, with practices being shaped by the requirements of the particular workplace. Billett elaborates on this in Chapter 10, pointing out that individuals construct knowledge through guided engagement in the goal-directed activities of the practice. The significance of this is that learning is held to occur through engagement in routine and non-routine problem-solving activities influenced by a particular community of practice. He adds that

> as the exigencies of the particular workplace provide goals (what is or is not expert performance) and activities (shaped by the activity system), these socially determined contributions have cognitive consequences. As expertise is something undertaken and acknowledged in particular practice, it is held to be related to activity at the community level, rather than being something which is disembedded from practice. However, this expertise will be more or less transferable to other communities which engage in similar activities (eg. occupations) at the socio-cultural level.
>
> (1998: 48)

From Billett's perspective, workplace learning is an ongoing process influenced by the circumstances in which activities are engaged. Everyday participation in work tasks provides opportunities for learners to generate tentative solutions to vocational tasks and then attempt to secure those solutions. Therefore, as these procedures are tested and modified it is likely that concepts associated with goals and subgoals will become deepened through rich associations, linkages and purposeful organisation. Over time, this theory holds that work activities result in the development of a repertoire of goal-securing schemata which are associated with expert performance. This results in knowledge being constructed, indexed and organised in ways that are purposeful in terms of workplace goals, and enhancing the prospect of transfer to other situations and circumstances – particularly those in which similar outcomes occur. Further, Billett proposes that the knowledge secured through workplace learning will be more or less transferable across settings in which the same sociocultural practice is conducted. But clearly there are limitations to conceiving of workplaces as 'learning environments'. Billett (1998) identifies five specific problems:

1 construction of 'inappropriate' knowledge;
2 access to 'authentic' activities;
3 possible reluctance of experts;

4 limits on access to expertise; and
5 the opaqueness of some forms of conceptual knowledge.

These are not the only types of problems associated with workplace learning as various philosophical, political, gender and ethical considerations about the nature and purposes of 'learning' are not included in this list. Some of these concerns, as I have already mentioned, suggest that workplace learning and training reforms are moving toward focusing *on people as resources* as distinct from the processes and networks to which they are connected.

One thing has become perfectly clear through this book: there are no simple formulae or solutions to follow. The glossy 'empowerment' promises that accompany many high-tech solutions for organisations to be learning enterprises tend to be like politicians' promises – unlikely ever to be delivered in full, if at all. Future learning and future work are more likely to be characterised by complexity, diversity, consumer choice (now aptly illustrated by the proliferation of Internet 'info-cation' products) and attention to the situated ethics that help us to understand better the many meanings that accompany learning at work. There is now an opportunity for the divide between individualistic, enterprise-focused and socially focused conceptions to begin to dissolve. The misapprehensions of industry bodies, employers, trade unions, formal education institutions and academics – on whether workplace learning should or should not be considered as 'valid' knowledge – are now being dramatically tested. Workplace learning is firmly on their agendas and there is no returning from here.

References

Anderson, J. R. (1993) 'Problem solving and learning', *American Psychologist* 48(1): 35–44.

Argyris, C. and Schön, D. A. (1978) *Organizational Learning: A Theory of Action Perspective*, Reading, MA: Addison-Wesley.

Bagnall, R. (1990) 'Lifelong education: the institutionalisation of an illiberal and regressive ideology?', *Educational Philosophy and Theory* 22(1): 1–7.

Berryman, S. E. (1993) 'Learning from the workplace', *Review of Research in Education* 19: 343–401.

Billett, S. (1995) 'Workplace learning: its potential and limitations', *Education and Training* 37(4): 20–7.

Billett, S. (1998) 'Understanding workplace learning: cognitive and sociocultural perspectives', in D. Boud (ed.) *Current Issues and New Agendas in Workplace Learning*, Adelaide: National Centre for Vocational Education Research, 47–68.

Boud, D. (1987) 'A facilitator's view of adult learning', in D. Boud and V. R. Griffin (eds) *Appreciating Adults Learning: From the Learner's Perspective*, London: Kogan Page, 222–39.

Boud, D. (1989) 'Some common traditions in experiential learning', in S. W. Weil and I. McGill (eds) *Making Sense of Experiential Learning: Diversity in Theory and Practice*, Buckingham: SRHE and the Open University Press, 38–49.

Boud, D., Cohen, R. and Walker, D. (1993) 'Understanding learning from experience', in D. Boud, R. Cohen and D. Walker (eds) *Using Experience for Learning*, Buckingham: SRHE and The Open University Press, 1–17.

Bredo, E. (1994) 'Reconstructing educational psychology: situated cognition and Deweyian pragmatism', *Educational Psychologist* 29(1): 23–35.

Carnevale, A. *et al.* (1993) 'Workplace basics: the skills employers want', *Community, Technical, and Junior College Journal* 59(4): 28–33.

Chi, M. T. H., Feltovich, P. J. and Glaser, R. (1981) 'Categorisation and representation of physics problems by experts and novices', *Cognitive Science* 5: 121–52.

Gardner, H. (1993) *Multiple Intelligences: The Theory in Practice*, Cambridge, MA: Harvard University Press.

Garrick, J. and Solomon, N. (1997) 'Technologies of compliance in training', *Studies in Continuing Education* 19(1): 71–81.

Glaser, R. (1984) 'Education and thinking – the role of knowledge', *American Psychologist* 39(2): 93–104.

Glaser, R. (1989) 'Expertise and learning: how do we think about instructional processes that we have discovered knowledge structures?', in D. Klahr and K. Kotovsky (eds) *Complex Information Processing: The Impact of Herbert A. Simon*, Hillsdale, NJ: Lawrence Erlbaum.

Gonczi, A., Curtain, R., Hager, P., Hallard, A. and Harrison, J. (1995) *Key Competencies in On-the-Job Training*, Sydney: UTS. A report commissioned by the NSW Dept. of Industrial Relations, Employment, Training and Further Education.

Gott, S. (1989) 'Apprenticeship instruction for real-world tasks: the coordination of procedures, mental models, and strategies', in E. Z. Rothhopf (ed.) *Review of Research in Education*, Washington, DC: American Educational Research Association.

Gott, S. P. (1995) 'Rediscovering learning: acquiring expertise in real world problem tasks', *Australian and New Zealand Journal of Vocational Education Research* 3(1): 30–68.

Greeno, J. G. (1989) 'A perspective on thinking', *American Psychologist* 44(2): 134–41.

Hager, P. (1996) 'Relational realism and professional performance', *Educational Philosophy and Theory* 28(1): 98–116.

Hager, P. (1998) 'Understanding workplace learning: general perspectives', in D. Boud (ed.) *Current Issues and New Agendas in Workplace Learning*, Adelaide: National Centre for Vocational Education Research, 31–46.

Hager, P., McIntyre, J., Moy, J., Comyn, P., Stone, J., Schwenke, C. and Gonczi, A. (1996) *Workplace Keys: Piloting the Key Competencies in Workplace Training*, Sydney: UTS. A report commissioned by the NSW Dept. of Training and Education Co-ordination.

Hart, M. (1993) 'Educative or miseducative work: a critique of the current debate on work and education', *The Canadian Journal for the Study of Adult Education* 7(1): 19–36.

Lave, J. and Wenger, E. (1991) *Situated Learning – Legitimate Peripheral Participation*, Cambridge, Cambridge University Press.

Marsick, V. J. and Watkins, K. E. (1990) *Informal and Incidental Learning in the Workplace*, London: Routledge.

Schultz, T. W. (1977) 'Investment in human capital', in J. Karabel and A. H. Halsey (eds) *Power and Ideology in Education*, Oxford: Oxford University Press, 313–24.

Stasz, C., Ramsey, K., Eden, R., Melamid, E. and Kaganoff, T. (1996) *Workplace Skills in Practice*, Santa Monica, CA: Rand/National Center for Research in Vocational Education.

Usher, R. S. (1992) 'Experience in adult education: a post-modern critique', *Journal of Philosophy of Education* 26(2): 201–14.

Usher, R. S. and Solomon, N. (1998) 'Experiential learning and the shaping of subjectivity in the workplace', Paper presented to the 6th International Conference on Experiential Learning (ICEL), 'Experiential Learning in the Context of Lifelong Learning', Tampere University, Finland, 2–5 July.

Vygotsky, L. S. (1978) *Mind in Society – The Development of Higher Psychological Processes*, Cambridge, MA: Harvard University Press.

Vygotsky, L. S. (1987) *Thought and Language*, ed. A. Kouzulin, Cambridge, MA: The MIT Press.

Wagner, R. K. and Sternberg, R. J. (1986) 'Tacit knowledge and intelligence in the everyday world', in R. J. Sternberg and R. K. Wagner (eds) *Practical Intelligence – Nature and Origins of Competence in the Everyday World*, Cambridge: Cambridge University Press, 51–83.

Weil, S. W. and McGill, I. (1989) *Making Sense of Experiential Learning: Diversity in Theory and Practice*, Buckingham: SRHE and the Open University Press.

Index

Printed in the United Kingdom
by Lightning Source UK Ltd.
109198UKS00001BA/9